RUDOLPH
VALENTINO
THE MAN BEHIND THE MYTH

by ROBERT OBERFIRST

A BERKLEY MEDALLION BOOK
published by
BERKLEY PUBLISHING CORPORATION

Citadel Press
222 Park Avenue South
New York, N.Y. 10003

Library of Congress Catalog Card Number 62-21008

SBN 425-03458-5

BERKLEY MEDALLION BOOKS are published by
Berkley Publishing Corporation
200 Madison Avenue
New York, N.Y. 10016

BERKLEY MEDALLION BOOK ® TM 757,375

Printed in the United States of America

Berkley Medallion Edition, APRIL, 1977

PROLOGUE

RUDOLPH VALENTINO died a lonely, love-starved man, although millions of love-starved women were in love with him. He was the symbol and personification of romance and sex when the Charleston and Black Bottom were the national dance crazes. Valentino's name on a theater marquee spelled romance because he was the King of Sex—The Screen's Greatest Lover. Valentino's final motion picture, *Son of the Sheik*, was regarded as a sensation by the millions of women who flocked to see the greatest lover of them all.

This was the jazz age, the "Roaring Twenties," a giddy era of escape and nonsense, remembered both for its high old times and its ludicrous experiment with Prohibition.

There were Valentino fan clubs in all parts of the globe. Valentino was an international institution making modern-day Presleys or Fabians look like immature local boys with limited, short-range appeal. Women of all ages and in all countries worshipped Valentino as though he were a god. Men were jealous of him.

The legend of Valentino is stronger today than ever, and tends to obscure the man behind the legend—the lonely immigrant boy who came to America from Italy before World War I; who struggled to obtain a job in his chosen field of agriculture; who became penniless and was forced into a dancing job which he didn't like, but who perversely became the world's greatest tango dancer; who retained his youthful dreams of becoming a farmer and purchasing farm land in sunny California, but who backed into an acting career instead and attained a success unparalleled in motion-picture history. His unhappy marriages and his desperate hope of reconciliation; his cherished but vain hope of having a family and children of his own; and the clash of his worlds—the world of the great star and that of a basically simple and naïve Italian youth—also went into the molding of Valentino the man.

This is the story of that man—a story that for too long has gone untold.

CHAPTER ONE

NINETEEN TWENTY-SIX! The heart of the "Roaring Twenties!"

The year President Coolidge was trying on Indian head-dresses and smoking peace pipes; the year of the Charleston and the Black Bottom; of swallowing live goldfish for kicks and sitting atop flagpoles for a lift; of marathon dances and bike races. The Sesquicentennial Exposition was being held in Philadelphia; Dempsey was to fight Tunney for the championship; a dozen swimmers would again attempt to conquer the English Channel.

Prohibition reigned and the "speaks" were doing a land-office business. Everybody's neighbor was a bootlegger, every college boy had his hip flask under his raccoon coat and every gangster had his tommy gun. Or at least that's the way it seems now.

It was a year of big songs: "May Time," "All Alone," "Memory Lane," "California, Here I Come," "Pretty Baby," "June Night," "After I Say I'm Sorry," "Always," "Remember" and "In A Little Spanish Town."

It was the last year the silent screen would reign supreme. Next year would come talkies and a whole new era in the movies, and eventually the brightest stars of 1926 would be almost forgotten names.

But this was 1926 and the silent stars shone bright: Mary Pickford, Douglas Fairbanks, Charles Chaplin, Lillian and Dorothy Gish, Richard Barthelmess, Clara Bow, John Barrymore, Marion Davies, Colleen Moore, Billie Dove, Norma Talmadge, Gloria Swanson, Pola Negri, Mae Murray, Joan Crawford, Esther Ralston, William Farnum, Tom Mix, Thomas Meighan, Adolphe Menjou, Lupe Velez, Gilbert Roland, Buck Jones, Monte Blue, Rod La Roque, George Jessel, Richard Dix, William Haines, Conrad Nagel, Ramon Navarro, Dolores Costello, Norman Kerry, Will Rogers and the great screen lover, Rudolph Valentino.

Valentino! Beautiful Valentino, Handsome Valentino. His name was on the lips of women throughout the world. They packed theaters to see his face and just for a minute imagine they were the girl his arms encircled.

Valentino. His name was mentioned everywhere. In the newspapers . . . the newspapers. He was headline news the morning of Sunday, August 15.

VALENTINO COLLAPSES

SCREEN STAR GOES UNDER KNIFE

New York, Aug. 15—Rudolph Valentino, screen star, collapsed suddenly today in his apartment at the Hotel Ambassador. Several hours later he underwent an operation for gastric ulcers and appendicitis at the Polyclinic Hospital. The actor is reported to be in serious condition . . . .

"Serious condition. . . ." The words struck fear into the hearts of the world's women. By the hundreds of thousands they streamed to church to pray. The man who made silent but oh such passionate love to them in the quiet of the movie theaters was in serious condition. How serious?

The newspapers didn't know. They depended on daily reports issued by the hospital. The world waited. Thousands of people massed outside Polyclinic Hospital waiting for news. Young women wept silently; older women prayed. All were tense; all were hopeful.

How serious?

The surgeon knew.

"Scalpel." He made the incision. A deft stroke and the abdomen was open.

"Increase anesthetic."

The sound of the patient's labored breathing reverberated off the walls of the operating room.

The surgeon probed. An inflamed appendix and a colony of gastric ulcers. The incision was lengthened. The surgeon shook his head. He pointed to the lining of the abdomen—the peritoneum. It was inflamed, eaten away.

"Peritonitis. Advanced stage."

The other doctors nodded in agreement.

The appendix and the ulcers were removed. The peritoneum was medicated to neutralize the inflammation.

"Suture."

The wound was sewed up.

"Bandages."

The wound was bandaged.

"Intravenous."

A nurse prepared the intravenous injection. It was administered.

The patient was wheeled to his room. All through the corridors nurses stared, their eyes misty.

In conferences, doctors wondered: "Why did he evade medical treatment? His condition indicates a long history . . . too long."

His condition was serious. And then, the news. The patient was convalescing. Rudolph Valentino was recovering. The world sighed with relief.

Outside the hospital people turned to each other. "He'll be all right." "Rudy is too tough to stay sick." "Thank God, he feels better."

He regained his strength with each passing day . . . Tuesday . . . Wednesday . . . Thursday. He slept most of the day.

Friday, August 20. The newspaper headlines broadcast the news:

VALENTINO TAKES TURN FOR THE WORSE

The doctors shook their heads. "Peritonitis, uncontrolled. Pleurisy and septic poisoning throughout the entire system. Resistance feeble."

Throughout the week end news bulletins blared:

VALENTINO CONDITION GRAVE

The world waited . . . and prayed . . . and waited. . . .

Monday, August 23rd, 1926. Rudolph opened his eyes. The nurse stepped to his bedside.

"Please raise the shade," he asked. "I want to see the sunlight."

But the shade was up and the room was flooded with sunlight.

Moments later, at 12:10 P.M., Rudolph Valentino died.

1926! The heart of the "Roaring Twenties!"

Death claimed the body of the screen's greatest lover. Immortality claimed his name. Rodolpho Alfonzo Rafaelo Pierre Filibert Guglielmi di Valentina d'Antonguolla— Rudolph Valentino—became legend at the age of thirty-one years, three months, seventeen days. . . .

Valentino's life in America is a case history in misunderstanding. Because he became an American screen idol most people tend to forget he was foreign to the ways of America.

His outlook on life was that of a better-than-middle-class Italian brought up in a home filled with sentimentality and close family ties. Honor was a principle to die for; love of family and ancestry was a principle to live for.

Valentino's taste in clothes annoyed many who forgot his was a European taste; Valentino's personal habits offended many who forgot his European upbringing; his way of expressing himself, his temperament, his treatment of friend and foe, his dreams, his very way of life were foreign to the American way, and were, therefore, misunderstood.

To understand, to know Valentino you must start at the beginning. . . .

CHAPTER TWO

"TELL me again, Mama," the child pleaded as he snuggled in her lap.

And she told him again of her life in Paris, of the great siege of the city during the Franco-Prussian War and how she had endured it and had come through it alive.

"And now the fight, Mama."

She smiled and held him close as she retold the story of his ancestors. If she left anything out, he was sure to remind her.

"One of your ancestors, named Guglielmi, quarreled with a member of the House of Calonna, one of the three oldest and most influential families in Rome. The quarrel was to be settled by duel, as all disputes of that time were settled. . . ."

"You forgot to say that the fight was over a woman's honor."

"That's right, my little one. The member of the House of Calonna had behaved dishonorably toward a woman and your ancestor came to her aid." The child relaxed again. "The duel resulted in Guglielmi killing the Calonna, and in order to save their lives, your ancestor and his aides fled to southern Italy where they settled among the peasants at Martina Franca, in the Province of Lecce."

"I, too, defend the honor of a woman," the child said. He hopped off her lap and fought off unseen adversaries with his sword. "That will teach them to dishonor a woman," he said. His mother planted a kiss upon his cheek and the child crawled back into her lap.

5

"Oh, tell me about the massacre, Mama."

"It was because of the massacre by a wild band of brigands at Martina Franca in 1850 that we now make our home here in Castellaneta," she began. The story was of death and torture and ended with, "Those who survived the massacre fled to this village and made a new and good life for themselves."

The boy was fascinated by these tales. He never grew tired of hearing them or reliving them.

His mother, Beatrice Barbin Guglielmi, was a slight French woman with hair so shining and glowing it seemed to have trapped a sunbeam. A devoutly religious woman, she kept the symbols of her faith around the house. She was compassionate, understanding and imaginative. The daughter of a Paris surgeon, Pierre Filibert Barbin, she was swept off her feet by a captain in the Italian Cavalry. She married Giovanni Guglielmi and went with him to live in the village of his ancestors, a drowsy sun-drenched place called Castellaneta, in southern Italy.

Her husband was a farmer and veterinarian. He was a handsome man who worked hard and loved nature passionately.

Life on the farm for the newlyweds was an idyll. The farm consisted of a white, thick-walled house, with spacious rooms, a huge courtyard with many trees, and servants' quarters in the back. It was peaceful and serene, and the couple was very happy.

On May 6, 1895, Beatrice gave birth to a boy, their second son, whom they christened Rodolpho Alfonzo Rafaelo Pierre Filibert Guglielmi di Valentina d'Antonguolla. The baby had olive skin and strange, slightly slanted eyes.

The couple's elder son, Alberto, was a settled, dependable, practical boy who favored his father. But Rodolpho had inherited his mother's vivid imagination. Although he respected and admired his father, Rodolpho was devoted to his mother. His father, he knew, was disappointed with him because instead of following orders he wandered off, and—coming upon the ghost of Calonna, fought a duel. He was gone for hours—and returned empty-handed. Alberto always

6

did as he was told. There were no duels to be fought or ladies to be won.

When he was eleven, Rodolpho fell in love with a ten-year-old village girl named Teodolinda—a "lady" for whom he fought in all of his daydreams. Although he loved her, he sometimes found himself exasperated. One day, he pushed her and she fell. She went home crying. Rodolpho was called into his father's study.

"A girl is like a flower, Rodolpho. Both must be handled gently and tenderly for both can easily be crushed." The child remembered the lecture. He had expected to be physically punished; instead his father had spoken to him man to man. The thought kept Rodolpho in line for several days, but eventually he slipped back into his dreams of romance and adventure.

Warm day followed warm day. Rodolpho ate well, slept well, dreamed well. One happy day preceded the next happy day.

Then—suddenly—everything changed. . . .

Rodolpho was late in coming home—again. He knew his parents would be angry with him and he wanted to keep his promise not to do it again, but there was always another duel to be fought, and time would escape him. He hated to face his family, but he was hungry and would have to go home eventually, so why not now. As he approached his house, he realized with a quickened pulse that there were visitors. With people around, his father wouldn't be too harsh. He skipped into the house, ready to fling himself into his mother's arms.

Many people gathered outside his father's door. Among them were the village doctor and the priest. The boy stopped. He searched for his mother, a sinking feeling coming upon him. His mother came to him. Her big brown eyes were red-rimmed, her cheeks tear-stained. Alberto and his sister Maria were standing off to the side, their faces a reflection of their mother's. She beckoned to Rodolpho and led him to his father's room.

Lying on a bed, which had suddenly enlarged in Rodolpho's eyes, was a man who resembled the father he had so often disobeyed. No dashing cavalry officer this, but a thin, sickly man. Giovanni was dying from overwork and a collapsed heart. His mother pushed Rodolpho closer to the bed and the shrunken figure upon it.

"My son, remember your duty to your mother and your country," his father said. He patted the boy's head with his hand. Then his father's eyes closed and there was silence. His father was dead.

The thought of all the things he could have done to make his father's life easier brought a lump into the boy's throat. He wanted to cry. But not here, not before his mother and all those people. He whirled around and ran through the house. He hid behind the barn, threw himself upon the ground and cried.

For all the men he had killed in imaginary duels, this was the first man he had ever seen die, and it wasn't the glorious thing he had imagined.

After his father's funeral, Rodolpho was sent to the Dante Alighieri College, the equivalent of a grammer school, where he remained until he was thirteen. Then he was sent to a military academy. Rodolpho's adventurous spirit was glad to be away from home, but he missed his family. Between thoughts of home and his vivid imagination, he was too busy to pay much attention to his studies. He read books of romance and adventure; he transported himself to the world of knights and dueling musketeers. He was far happier in the realm of his imagination than in the real world.

Technical books bored him. His imagination removed him from the domain of disciplinary rules and regulations. He, therefore, was not a model student. He did only what interested him, and what interested him had nothing to do with the curriculum. He was punished time and again.

On one occasion the school officials devised a supreme punishment for the boy. It happened the day King Vittorio Emmanuele and his Queen were to visit the village. Knowing his love of royalty and dress-up occasions, the school officials locked up Rodolpho's clothes. He was to stay behind while the rest of the academy went to see the King. The boy just *had* to get out. He stole a uniform many sizes too large for him, sneaked out of the dormitory, and went to the stable to acquire a mount. No horse. No matter. There was a donkey, perhaps a little sagging, perhaps a little weary, perhaps a little aged. No matter. This would be his white charger.

With his head held high, he rode to town. Once there, he found an advantageous spot from which to see the procession. Hoots of laughter greeted him. The school officials, their faces red, ignored the ridiculous figure in his too-big military outfit upon the ancient donkey.

Afterwards, Rodolpho returned to the academy where the officials were waiting for him. He was expelled.

His mother said she was disappointed in him, but it was hard for her to remain angry. After all, his love of ceremony had been instilled in him through her stories. How can a mother berate a child for living the things she herself loves?

A family council was held. His mother was tempted to keep the boy at home, but his uncle—who had taken over the management of the farm—would not have it. The Guglielmis were always well-educated.

The College della Sapienze, in the quaint and ancient town of Perugia, was Rodolpho's next school. There he learned Spanish and French along with other subjects. He tried hard to please his mother, but he still could not concentrate on his studies, although he enjoyed reading poetry. Tasso and Ariosto were his favorites. But he managed to master his subjects and still live in his imaginary world. On his fifteenth birthday, he left the school.

While in Perugia, Rodolpho had done a lot of thinking. To please his family and himself he decided to enter the Royal Naval Academy. The dullness of the studies would be offset by the thoughts of the glamor of being a Naval officer. But his chest expansion was short an inch, and he was not accepted for the Academy. He returned home, depressed.

After a few weeks, his mother suggested he take up scientific farming. His fathers and grandfathers had been farmers and the country was always in need of them. Rodolpho thought about it, saw it as a way somehow to make up to his father for his disobedience, and enrolled at the Royal

Academy of Agriculture in Genoa. Here, the boy applied himself. He loved to watch things grow.

The people at home were amazed—all except his mother. Rodolpho was an excellent student. He graduated from the Academy with the highest honors, at the head of his class. This time his homecoming was sweet. His mother was happy, his family pleased.

Rodolpho was ready to take his place in the world. He would work for the land, taking up where his father had left off. But he found it hard to concentrate, to settle down, and his mother suggested he take a vacation.

"Paris, Mama?" he asked.

No. He was too young to visit such a sophisticated city by himself.

"Please, Mama. Please."

She consented.

His things were packed and he was off on his first real adventure.

As he sat in the train moving through Italy toward Paris, over plains, across rivers, through mountain tunnels, past cities and towns, he realized that the world was a tremendous place, overflowing with its bounties.

He was puzzled. Where in this gigantic scheme did he fit? Where? The train wheels click-clacked the question over and over: What place is mine? What place is mine?

Finally Paris! In song and story he had heard that magical name. His mother had trembled when she had talked of Paris—the beautiful, romantic, frolicking, devilish city. Paris—the city of dreams! City of wishes fulfilled! City of love and champagne!

He walked out of the station onto the streets, satchel in hand. He walked from street to street—some narrow, some wide, some straight, some winding, some so suddenly and mysteriously cut off that he had to find his way out as best he could.

The people fascinated him. They seemed so preoccupied, so busy with their individual affairs. And yet there was a warmth, a friendliness that somehow reached him, and soon he felt more at ease.

10

He stood on the paved walk of the Champs-Élysées and watched the summer sun descending behind the countless spires and chimney pots in a blaze of orange, gold and amber, a royal backdrop for this city of cities. He stood there, transfixed, spellbound by the galaxy of gas and electric lights beginning to glow as the twilight purpled into dusk and the dusk darkened into night. He heard the pulse beat of the city—the honking of the automobiles, the clop-clop of cab horses trotting on the ancient cobbles, the sound of music from some dance place hidden in the mass of brick and stone, the carefree laugh of a young girl, the whistle of a distant train.

This was the world he had read about in books and heard about from the lips of his mother. This was Paris.

He picked up his satchel and looked for lodgings.

That night, Rodolpho went to the Café Pierre. On the following night he dined at the Café L'Anglaise. On the next night, he visited the Folies-Bergère and stared in wonder at the almost naked gyrating ladies on the spotlighted stage. Then another cabaret, the Fen de Joie, where he dined and had champagne.

In two weeks his money dwindled to a dangerously low figure, but Rodolpho did not stop spending and did not think of returning home. Eventually, he told himself, he would begin his career as a scientific farmer.

Rodolpho met Paul Duval, a native Parisian, who took him to more places where he could drink champagne and see girls undress.

And the money dwindled, on the best of food . . . on the best of wine . . . and on the many girls who were quite willing to share their evenings with the two young men. It was gay . . . it was exciting . . . it was expensive . . . until, one day, Rodolpho discovered his money had just about disappeared.

He could not face the disgrace of writing to his mother for more money, at least not just yet. Duval suggested a way to recoup his funds. Go to Monte Carlo; win it back!

So he went to Monte Carlo and lost the rest of his money. He was compelled to write his mother asking for enough money to return home. By return came a one-way ticket home.

A reception committee awaited him, for Rodolpho had no way of knowing that a report of his Paris escapades had been relayed to his family. His mother, his brother and sister, and his relatives were gathered to mete out punishment.

"Rodolpho, you have disgraced our name—so your uncle says," his mother said. "We must punish you. You must be taught a lesson, your uncle has advised me."

She stood there trying to look stern, but every once in a while their eyes would meet and Rodolpho saw no anger, only love and understanding.

"The decision has been reached," she said, "that you must leave our village until you can bear our name with pride."

And then her voice grew even sterner and her eyes twinkled even brighter.

"My son, I have decided that the punishment should fit the crime. You will be sent to America, where if you are massacred by Indians, at least you can perhaps fight honorably and not disgrace our good name. If you must carry on like your disgraceful, duel-fighting ancestors, your escapades will not cause the tongues of our village to wag."

Her eyes shone bright. She kissed his cheek and whispered, "May God go with you, my little one."

On December 9, 1913, Rodolpho set sail on the S.S. *Cleveland* bound for New York. He was eighteen years old.

CHAPTER THREE

AN unnatural silence hovered over the S.S. *Cleveland* on December 23, 1913. The ship was entering the approach into New York harbor. The passengers lined the ship's railing.

Suddenly: "There she is . . . there . . . over there. See!"

"Where? Where? . . . I see her. I see her!"

A deafening cheer swept throughout the ship. The passengers, most of them immigrants, had sighted the shores of America. Off in the distance was the skyline of New York, a mass of steel and concrete angles—all purplish and gray—reaching past the horizon into the clouds.

The sight sent a chill down the spine of Rodolpho Guglielmi. In the midst of the laughing, cheering passengers he stood with a smile on his face. His hands clenched the railing, his knuckles straining as though they would burst through his skin.

Before him was the promise of his greatest adventure, excitement that would exceed his escapades in Paris. Yet, inside him, fear gnawed. He was alone, on his own, no mother to turn to for comfort, for advice, for understanding. He was an ocean away from the familiar in a country with strange customs, whose people spoke a language unknown to him.

The ship pulled into its mooring. Down went the gangplank and on it filed the streams of disembarking passengers, through Customs and into the great city whose streets were deep canyons walled off by immense buildings.

Aboard ship he had felt he was properly armed—in a Manhattan bank he had four thousand dollars to his credit; in his pocket he had a diploma and a letter written by his brother Alberto to the Commissioner of Immigration, saying that Rodolpho was an honor graduate of the agricultural academy and qualified as a gardener or farmer.

In his suitcases he had fine clothing and accessories purchased in Paris and in his heart he had the strength of a great dream—to become a great scientific farmer. America had big farms, acres and acres of good soil. He would produce better fruit, better cattle, better vegetables. He would bring his mother to him, and she would be proud of her son.

But on the streets of New York where there were more people than he had ever seen in one place at one time, he felt like a speck of dust, a speck of dust in a land of concrete and steel mountains. And how does dust conquer mountains?

He headed toward West Forty-ninth Street and Giolotti's, an apartment house for Italians about which he had learned from some passengers on the ship. The question now plaguing him was: How do I find my way? There was no one he could ask. He couldn't speak the language. After hours of walking in what seemed to be all directions, he reached his destination.

Once there, he rented an expensive suite of rooms. That night he put on his best suit of clothes, pomaded his dark hair to a patent-leather finish and went out to eat.

He dined at an expensive French restaurant, the Continental, where he was to spend many nights communicating in French. Other nights he ate at Bustonaby's, where he talked of Italy with the waiters and enjoyed the fine Italian food.

It was at Bustonaby's that he made his first friends in America—Count Alex Salm, his brother, Count Otto, and George Ragni, three young men who spoke French and enjoyed living luxuriously.

They had noticed Rodolpho eating alone and asked him to join them. It was at their insistence, and with a girl to whom they introduced him, that Rodolpho took his first dance steps in this country. He admitted to being a poor dancer, but he had an ear for music and an almost animal grace.

Charmed with his friends, and envious of their dancing ability, Rodolpho urged the Count to teach him to dance. He learned quickly and at every opportunity he implored his friends for further lessons.

One Sunday, when the four were visiting the monkey cages at the zoo, Rodolpho asked Alex about a dance he had seen done the night before. With the monkey as an audience, Alex taught Rodolpho the steps of a dance called the "tango"—the dance that ultimately became the trademark of Rudolph Valentino.

Throughout the winter of 1914, the four friends visited the swank nightspots—Maxim's, Delmonico's, Bustonaby's, and other cafés—dancing till dawn. Rodolpho was sought after by ladies anxious to tango with the dark-skinned youth who danced with the ease of a leaf fluttering from a tree.

During the day, the four roamed through the city's stores, rode around on the subways, visited sites such as the Brooklyn Bridge, toured the museums, and searched for adventure on the East Side and at burlesque shows.

When on his own, Rodolpho visited the library to learn English by studying Italian-English dictionaries, and to read up on agriculture, dairy farming, and flowers indigenous to American soil and especially to California, where he had decided to purchase land.

Much of his time was spent at the movies watching the greats: John Barrymore, Lillian Gish, "Little Mary" Pickford, Florence Turner and Maurice Costello.

Rodolpho broadened his world. He moved from Giolotti's to an apartment building where only English was spoken. He drifted from his three friends to seek the company of Americans.

Winter melted away and spring bloomed into summer. Rodolpho's finances neared depletion. A decision was made. The gay cabaret life had to end; the struggles for subsistence and survival must begin.

He moved to less expensive quarters. He went to the Commissioner of Immigration, showed his letter, and was directed to the New York Labor Bureau, where a job was found for him at an estate in Jericho, Long Island. His employer, Cornelius Bliss, Jr., intended to have an authentic Italian landscape.

Rodolpho, for a while, worked enthusiastically with the flowers and lived in quarters on the estate. His dream was of owning a California farm and bringing his mother to live with him—for a while. But he was restless for excitement. He felt stifled tending the flowers and mowing the lawn and pulling the weeds and spraying the insecticide.

He was feeling especially bored the day he discovered a motorcycle belonging to a workman. There were some pretty girls on a road near the estate, pretty enough to show off for. He took the bike, sped to the top of the hill, bent low over the handlebars, and hurtled toward the girls. The air roared by his ears, his hair waved in the breeze. As he passed the girls, he turned to wave, lost control, and went off the road into a ditch. He wasn't injured, but the bike was a wreck.

He offered to pay for repairs, which satisfied the owner, but Mr. Bliss found the incident inexcusable. Rodolpho was fired.

Back he went to the Labor Bureau, and then off to another job on an estate in New Jersey. After two weeks of picking bugs off roses, he left. Bug-picking was no job for a graduate of the Royal Academy of Agriculture.

Fully repentant, he went back to Mr. Bliss for help and, through him, obtained a job as a caretaker in Central Park. He picked more bugs. About the middle of August, his foreman suggested he ask the Park Commissioner for a more responsible job, something more fitting a graduate. The Commissioner was impressed. He told the boy to take the Civil Service test.

But Rodolpho wasn't a citizen; therefore, he could not work for the Park Department. Out of work again, he returned to Mr. Bliss.

An offer of money to help tide him over was made, but Rodolpho felt he could not take charity. Penniless and despondent, he went back to New York City. He raised some money by pawning possessions. He moved into a two-dollar-

16

a-week tenement room on Columbia Street near the Williamsburg Bridge. All he owned was pawned for trolley and subway fare to seek a job. Finally, he was forced to move from his room into a dollar-a-week flophouse on the Bowery. He was destitute.

Wearing shabby clothes, run-down shoes, his face cut up from shaving too often with the same blade, he discovered he wasn't equipped for work other than gardening. Worse, when he looked for employment, prospective bosses couldn't pronounce his name and grew impatient trying to.

To solve the one problem, he Americanized his name, shortening it to Rudolph and—for the sake of euphony—using his ancestral name, Valentino.

To raise enough money for food, Valentino swept out stores, earning twenty-five and fifty cents at a time. He slept on a bench in Central Park and had no idea how to improve his situation.

Everything seemed to be going against him. Added to his personal money problems were the letters from his mother, which he picked up once a week at the post office. War had broken out in Central Europe. Although Italy was not as yet involved, his mother wrote that money was scarce and food was scarcer. Could her son help out by sending some money?

Destitute, lonely, trapped, he couldn't fall any farther and he didn't know how to pick himself up. Hunger burned in his belly. His armor was shattered and the barbs of the Fates were ripping him apart.

He sat on a park bench—he was too hungry to do much else—his head low, his spirit lower. A tramp sat down beside him. Valentino was never to learn the man's name. All he knew was that the man prided himself on being a professional hobo. He told Valentino to seek out his friends, ask for their help. "If they are true friends, they will be happy to assist. Don't starve on pride; no one will think of you as a hero for it."

Rudolph walked to the apartment where his friends the Salms lived. They had moved to a different building, the superintendent said. He gave Valentino their new address, a tenement building. There, Valentino found his once dapper friends as seedy and despondent as he was. The war, Count Alex told Valentino, had cut off his funds from Europe. They lived with assistance from friends and Valentino was welcome to share what little they had.

Valentino refused the offer, thanked him, and left. He was not too proud to go to Maxim's or some of his other old haunts and ask for a job as a waiter or kitchen helper. There were no jobs, but at Maxim's the head waiter recalled that Valentino was a good dancer and an offer was made. Would he be interested in serving as a dance partner for the wealthy women who dined at the restaurant unescorted? There would be tips, a room above the restaurant, and free meals.

The idea of being a dancing man—a gigolo—repelled Valentino. He loved to dance, but to dance for a living? It wasn't work for a man of breeding, he felt. But the hunger gnawed. There was nothing else for him. He accepted the offer, borrowed money for clothing, and was ready for the music.

He experienced a frightening moment that night as he stepped into the softly lighted interior of the café. But he couldn't deny the feeling of excitement caused by the glamour and romance.

He danced with them all—the thin, the clumsy, the self-important—complimenting each, accepting tips awkwardly. The word passed throughout the city . . . "There is a divine Latin dancer at Maxim's whose tango is like no other this side of heaven." The ladies flocked to the café to dance with the dancing man and gladly tipped him five or ten dollars.

Valentino earned twenty to thirty dollars a night. He had clothes and money again. More important, he became more assured, more confident of his dancing ability. The necessity of dancing so many different styles polished the rough edges, giving him finesse.

In time Maxim's provided Valentino with professional partners, and the dancing man staged exhibitions. Business was booming. Valentino's dancing ability was recognized by the café set.

The next change in Valentino's life occurred when a young chorus girl came to Maxim's to dance with him. The girl,

Bess Dudley, became an admirer and friend. It was she who offered him an opportunity to leave Maxim's.

Renowned dancer Bonnie Glass and her partner, Clifton Webb, were breaking up their act. Bonnie, a good friend of Bess's, needed a new partner. Valentino hesitated when Bess said the job could be his—it was beyond his ability, he said—but she insisted and an appointment with Bonnie Glass was arranged.

Bonnie had heard of Valentino. She hired him at fifty dollars a week. No more would he have to dance with just any woman who waved money at him. He was a professional now, dancing for a living. He had a steady income providing him with enough money so he could send some home and save some. Except he just couldn't seem to save. A friend needed a loan, a stranger needed some help, Valentino needed new shoes, a shirt, another suit. He held on to none of his money.

Bonnie Glass and Rudolph Valentino were a successful dancing act. They toured the vaudeville circuit and made repeat appearances at the Palace. With their success, Bonnie opened her own café, the Montmartre, and later another, the Chez Fisher. Overflow crowds flocked to see them.

The men marveled at the beauty of Bonnie; the women made Valentino the object of their adulation. He, however, kept to himself, his youth a barrier to understanding his appeal, his shyness a barrier against having romantic interludes.

The barriers, however, melted away under the influence of a radiant, dark-haired South American beauty who approached him one night and urged him to dance the tango with her.

Her name, she told him, was Mrs. Jack de Saulles, and she talked to him of Paris and Spain and Italy. They shared memories of places each had visited.

She returned to the café night after night. With her in his arms, Valentino's loneliness left him. He felt happy for himself and sympathetic toward her as she unfolded her story of an unhappy marriage.

The daughter of a cultured South American family, she

had married Jack de Saulles, a Yale athlete, after an impulsive courtship. Before marriage her husband had had a reputation as a playboy. Marriage hadn't limited him. His escapades in various boudoirs made spicy items for newspaper gossip columns.

Her only escape was dancing. After watching Valentino dance, she told him, she knew she would have to have at least one dance with him. So they danced each night, and talked, and her warmth and sensuous beauty spread fire through his body. He passionately wanted this woman, yet couldn't seem to forget that she was married.

Undoubtedly it was respect for his mother, his religion, and his family's strict moral code that prevented him from telling this woman of his love. Valentino himself never fully understood what made him decide to stop seeing her.

Years later, in reminiscing about this woman, he was to say, "I suddenly felt that I should stop seeing her. It was an impossible dream."

Their relationship ended on an abrupt note. He walked her to her apartment one night and stopped in front of her door. His arms slipped about her waist and his lips met hers. He kissed her passionately. He then quickly left her and never saw her again. But he was to read about her in the newspaper accounts of how, in a fit of rage over her husband's latest escapade, and driven by the torment of the battle over custody of their child, she had shot and killed her husband, and was acquitted after a long, drawn-out trial.

Valentino kept busy dancing. His fame by now had spread along the east coast. The act played to standing-room-only audiences. One of the more vivid recollections Valentino had of his professional dancing days was an appearance in Washington, D.C., with President Woodrow Wilson in the audience.

Valentino sent as much money as he could manage to his mother. Italy was in the war now, and, according to his mother's letters, the situation was desperate.

He felt he had to do something more dramatic than send home money and he decided to join the Italian Air Force. He went to Roosevelt Air Field on Long Island to take flying lessons, but was rejected as a student because of defective eyesight.

At the airfield he met another student, one of many friends who would reappear at a vital point in Valentino's life and become motivating forces in Valentino's rise to fame. The student was Norman Kerry, who also became a Hollywood star. But Kerry's story comes later.

Meanwhile, Bonnie Glass married a wealthy businessman and decided to retire. This ended her dancing act with Rudolph Valentino.

A tour of the booking agents led Valentino to Joan Sawyer, another well-known dancer. He danced with her for six months.

However, the war in Italy and the urgent desire to bring his mother to the safety of the States forced Valentino to make his move. He had learned of an Italian Agricultural Society in San Francisco, headed by the president of the city's Italian-American Bank, that helped settle Italian immigrants on farms.

To get himself to San Francisco he took a seventy-five-dollar-a-week job with a traveling one-night stand revue, a show called *The Masked Model*. This time each glide of his foot seemed to take him closer to California and to his farm.

He worked hard in the show, which got as far as Ogden, Utah, and folded. He had, however, managed to save enough money to buy a train ticket to San Francisco.

It was a year and half after he first stepped foot on American soil, a time within which he experienced luxury and destitution, learned to dance and make his way on his own, but he was finally to fulfill his dream, he thought.

Rudolph Valentino was still a dreamer.

Valentino developed while in New York, winning friends and engendering affection. In time to come what was sown would be reaped.

His character was also beginning to take shape; not cement-solid but free as a leaf in the breeze. No honest cares had he; none did he want.

With all the hardship he experienced, it in no way pre-

pared him for the responsibilities of the future. He was naïve. He accepted life in its minute-by-minute motion, pausing only to dream of the past or the future.

He was a man of physical beauty, but a boy at heart. Without the strong, wise guidance of his mother he was lost, as would be any boy in a playland.

CHAPTER 4

THE words were uttered by the chairman of the Italian Agricultural Society.

"I'm sorry we cannot help you. You must have a thousand-dollar down payment before we can help you acquire farm land."

The words jolted Valentino. He had come all the way to San Francisco with a dream that sustained him. He left the office of the Society disillusioned. He needed time to think, time to formulate a plan of action, time to find work to raise money for a farm.

Valentino rented a room on California Street near Kearny Street, not far from San Francisco Bay. From his window he could see across the blue waters to the Oakland shoreline and the fertile farm land for which he longed.

This was California. An American replica of Italy, he thought—the same blue waters as in the Bay of Naples filled San Francisco Bay; the hills in and around San Francisco, the thick foliage of trees, the lush green of the tall grass—all were as it was in Italy.

It was a beautiful day in July of 1915. Valentino walked the city streets and boulevards. He walked for miles along the shoreline of the Bay, and finally sat down for a few moments on the concrete steps of a building on Market Street.

There, while the automobiles and horse-drawn wagons vied for space, Valentino planned and thought. He needed money; therefore, he needed a job. He could work either as a dancer or a gardener. He had to raise at least a thousand dollars and the quickest way toward that goal was dancing.

So he got up and started walking again, not aimlessly this time, but on a tour of booking agents. He got results toward the end of the day, a referral to a show called *Nobody Home*, featuring Richard Carl. There was a spot open for a dancer. He got the job.

He tried, tried hard, for three weeks. If his thought of the farm had not been uppermost in his mind, he never would have stayed with the show a week. His heart was not in it. Even though he was earning money for his dream, he felt he was prostituting himself and his dancing by remaining with the show. Finally he could no longer bear to betray himself and his dancing. He quit.

He turned to selling bonds on the installment plan. After a two-week training course, he was out on his own. He was pleasantly surprised when he actually landed some sales. At once his imagination went to work. He envisioned himself as a master bond salesman, selling thousands of bonds, getting rich and acquiring one of the largest vineyards in California.

But because of the war in Europe, and America building its defenses, the Government issued Liberty Loan Bonds. His sales fell off, thus ending his career in selling.

It was during this time, while trying to determine what to do next, that he found himself before the local British recruiting office. The Liberty Bonds having forced him out of selling now seemed like an omen. He walked in and offered his service and, if necessary, his life, to the Royal Flying Corps. He was rejected because of faulty vision in his left eye. The doctor told him his eye was "on the brink." Valentino was once again frustrated and disappointed.

"But I can see as well as anyone," he protested.

"Sorry," the recruiting officer said.

"Then I'll cross the border into Canada and enlist there."

The recruiting officer's voice softened. "You'll be rejected there, too, boy—and you'll have to pay your way back again . . . Cheer up; this isn't the worst thing that could happen to you."

Valentino was in a dilemma: the Service didn't want him;

bond selling was now out of the question; the thought of dancing for a living again made him miserable. What was he to do? He couldn't decide. Should he try selling some other line? Say lingerie or cosmetics, or automobiles or—or what? He knew he couldn't work in an office because of a language barrier, but surely there was something—short of ditch-digging.

What was he to do? He couldn't decide and he didn't have to. Fate made the decision for him by reuniting him with two former New York friends.

One was Norman Kerry, who by this time had become a Hollywood star. Kerry, in San Francisco, shooting a picture with Mary Pickford, urged Valentino to go to Hollywood, where he could get work as an extra. It would mean only five dollars a day to start, but it was the gateway to the future as an actor.

Valentino thanked his friend for the offer and told him he would let him know, after he had thought it over.

Going to Hollywood, Valentino felt, would not solve his problem of raising money to get his farm. He could earn more money through his dancing. Also, who was he to think that he would be given a part as an extra once he got to Hollywood? True, Norman had had no experience and had managed to make a go of it, but Norman was not like Valentino. And Norman had no hopes of becoming the best scientific farmer in America.

So he continued to search for work in San Francisco but could find none—not even dancing. His commission money from bonds was almost depleted, and thoughts of his days of destitution in New York began to plague him.

What was he to do? He finally decided. Better Hollywood than starvation. His decision made, he faced another problem. How was he to get there?

A chance meeting with another friend solved this problem. The friend, Frank Carter, husband of musical comedy star Marilyn Miller, was appearing in a one-night stand in Al Jolson's *Passing Show*. Jolson's show was to play Los Angeles and Carter arranged free passage for Valentino.

Delighted, Valentino sent a telegram to Norman Kerry

saying he was coming to Hollywood. The next day he climbed aboard the train with the Jolson troupe and was on his way.

Carter lost no time in introducing his friend to the members of the Jolson cast. A few of them had seen him dance with Bonnie Glass in New York and "were delighted to have a fellow showman aboard."

They began to coax him to dance for them—just once—a brief exhibition of the tango. He looked at Carter helplessly, but Carter could only shrug his shoulders.

One of the men produced a violin, another an accordion, and tango music filled the coach. One of the show girls—dark-eyed, lithe of figure—stepped into his arms. She smiled as she moved closer.

"Let's dance for them, Rudy, and give them what they want. Otherwise they're not going to let you alone."

"Well, I suppose one little dance will not hurt." he said stiffly. He felt it was the least he could do to pay for their kindness.

He put his arm about the girl's waist. She was slender and graceful as a butterfly. In a moment they were gliding up the train aisle. All eyes were focused upon them, including Al Jolson's. The applause which greeted the final chord of music was long and loud.

"Some day the world is going to want this boy," Jolson said. He rolled his eyes in familiar Jolson style. "Imagine his looks and my voice! *Mama mia!* What a combination."

The train sped on. Valentino stared out of the window, missing nothing. The California countryside rolled by . . . the mountains, the lakes, the boundless vineyards, the orange groves. His reverie was disturbed by a soft, feminine voice:

"You sure can dance. Where did you learn?"

It was the girl he had danced the tango with. She sat down next to him, leaned close and offered him a cigarette.

"It always sounds silly to say, but a friend taught me—in front of a monkey cage."

"I don't care if you learned in front of the laughing hyenas. You certainly can dance." She inhaled deeply. "How come

26

you're headed for L.A.? Why don't you stick with Jolson? He liked your dancing, and I'm sure he could find a spot for you in the show."

"I was thinking of trying my luck in Hollywood," Valentino said.

"Movie-struck, huh, kid? It's an awful tough grind, but if that's what you want, I hope you make it." She snuggled closer and her voice became soft. "But if you want to succeed in show business, you have to stop being shy. Being good-looking isn't enough. When you danced with me, you made me feel like the loveliest woman in the world. Now you act as if you're thinking of a way to make me disappear."

"Oh, I'm sorry," said Valentino. "Of course I don't want you to go away. Please stay."

As the train sped on, he found more to talk to her about. He told her about his home in Castellaneta and his life in New York. Her replies, her expressions, reminded him of someone he had known. He could not think who until she unloosed her hair. The raven-black tresses touching her shoulders were like those of his first ladylove—Teodolinda. So that was what Valentino called her. She accepted it as a term of endearment.

Calling her Teodolinda swept Valentino's shyness away completely. That night, in an empty compartment, Valentino was repaid for all the dragons he had killed for his ladylove.

When the train pulled into Los Angeles, the girl clung to him as he rose to leave the coach.

"Good-by, Rudy." Her dark eyes pleaded with him. He shook his head, smiled and kissed her.

"Thank you for everything, my little Teodolinda. Perhaps we will meet again."

Her eyes closed and he walked quickly down the aisle. He could feel her tears upon his cheek.

Frank Carter intercepted him and gripped his hand. "Best luck, Rudy. I hope what you are looking for is waiting for you."

"Thanks, Frank. And please thank Mr. Jolson for me."

Carrying his suitcase, Valentino swung onto the station platform.

"Rudy, you son of an old dog!"

"Norman, my friend."

The two friends embraced briefly before getting in Kerry's car. They drove up Broadway.

"I've already made reservations for you at the Alexandria Hotel," Norman told his friend. "It's one of our finest hotels. Wait until you see the room and the view."

Valentino was a little embarrassed. "Couldn't I stay at a hotel with less of a room and a view? My funds are rather low, I'm afraid."

"Nonsense. Don't worry about the money. I'll take care of that. Rule Number One, Rudy, and you had better learn it, is to put on a good show. People will remember you if you say that you can be reached at the Alexandria. If you say you can be reached at Mother Dowdy's Slum, well, they'll remember you then, too, but not kindly. No, we're shooting for big game for you. You have to have the fancy equipment. There's a lot at stake."

"I believe you, it's just the money . . ."

"Phooey on the money. If things work out the way I think they will, you'll be able to pay me back soon and live like a king besides. Now just put your faith in me, *amigo*."

They deposited Valentino's suitcase with a bellboy to whom Kerry gave a large tip, climbed back into the car and drove to Hollywood, up Highland Avenue to the intersection at Sunset Boulevard. Hollywood seemed nondescript. There were only a few small-town streets, a few houses, a few stores, and a few automobiles.

"It doesn't look like much," Valentino commented.

"Ah, not yet. But then, this is just the outside, the clothes, so to speak. Wait until you see its heart. That's where I'm taking you, now, to the studio section. We'll start with Metro."

At the Metro Studio gate, the car was stopped by a uniformed guard. The guard peered into the car, greeted Kerry by name, and passed them through. They also visited the Famous Players-Lasky and Fox Film Studios.

Norman pointed out the various sets and stages. There

were Indians roaming about in large numbers, dressed in full war headdress and battle paint. There were cowboys by the score in complete Western regalia, from broad-brimmed hats to spurs. Horses stood idly, waiting. African natives carrying deadly-looking spears of papier-mâché stood around with Civil War soldiers in the uniforms of the Blue and Gray; Minutemen from the American Revolution lounged near German, French, and Italian soldiers in battle dress.

Valentino stared wide-eyed at the era's screen stars roaming around the studios: Lillian and Dorothy Gish, Mae Murray, Earle Williams, Alla Nazimova, Gloria Swanson, William Farnum, William S. Hart, Henry B. Walthall, Theda Bara.

Kerry pointed out the directors: Emmett Flynn, James Young, Douglas Gerrard, Robert Z. Leonard, Fred Niblo, Rex Ingram and the great D. W. Griffith.

Valentino was entranced by the scenes being photographed. The area was congested with electric cables and klieg lights.

On one set a man was making ardent love to a cow-eyed "vamp." On another, a villain was exchanging blows with the hero. He watched the actors going through their paces— opening, rolling, and narrowing their eyes; contorting their faces to express love, hate and fear; moving their hands excessively; mouthing words in an exaggerated way—all for the silent camera. He watched comedians throwing pies at each other, and practicing pratfalls.

Everything was overdone and exaggerated. If an actor had to say, "It's a nice morning," it was done in a two-minute sequence with wild oration and gestures to match.

Valentino deplored the methods used. The over-intense, ham acting disturbed his sense of timing and grace. He felt the actors looked ugly. In some cases he thought they defeated themselves; a tragic episode emerged as a grotesquely comic one. There should be more naturalness, he thought. Movies should depict real life.

When he confided his feelings to Norman, Kerry said, "The industry is in its infancy. It has a long way to go, of course. The public can't get enough of the pictures. When you're a star, maybe they'll listen to you.

"We're entering the movie industry at an ideal time. Not only can we grow with it, but we can perhaps help the industry to grow."

Valentino agreed to the possibilities.

"I'll introduce you to some of the people—the people who count—directors, actors, scenario writers. You'll get to know them and they'll get to know you. In this business pushing yourself forward and making a good impression is very important. When I introduce you, make sure you show your teeth in a smile."

Norman took him up to a few directors and a few stars. Valentino smiled stiffly, acknowledged the introduction and stood listening to the others talk. He felt out of place. They gave him cursory glances as though to say, "Here's another stage-struck kid, another hopeful to clutter up the sets and the casting offices."

"No more, Norman," he said as they left one group. Norman looked at him quizzically and Valentino hurried on to say, "My head is already swimming with the immensity. So much going on. So many faces. If you introduce me to any more people, I'll never be able to remember their names or faces."

Norman laughed heartily and slapped him on the back.

Back in his nice room with the nice view, Valentino had difficulty in sleeping. His thoughts were a-whirl. This, then, was Hollywood. A ramshackle cluster of studio buildings, construction going on at a crazy pace, a strange assemblage of people embarked upon the undertaking of supplying diversion for the masses. Entertainment—the product of little Hollywood—was packed into cans and shipped to all corners of the world like canned salmon or sardines.

Hollywood. It was like a booming camp of a new gold strike, but a different sort of gold strike. This time the gold was laughter, tears, passion.

Despite his feelings about the artificiality of the acting performances he had seen, Valentino was excited about the motion pictures. The industry was like a newborn pony waiting to be taken through its paces. He couldn't shake the feeling that perhaps he could teach it something to make it great. Hollywood was almost like a giant farm—and it didn't require a thousand-dollar down payment.

CHAPTER FIVE

TAKE physical beauty, mix with an image that is as distinct as a trademark, add personality and imagination, sprinkle freely with the intangible of appeal and you have . . . a Rudolph Valentino.

Valentino had all that is needed to be a movie star. Physically, he was handsome. He didn't have the grotesque muscles of a weightlifter, but a finely proportioned muscular body, well coordinated for grace. He moved with the delicacy of a flower swaying in the breeze.

He was slightly over five feet eleven inches tall and weighed 167 pounds. He was dark-complexioned and smooth-skinned. His face had the classic lines of a Greek statue—a finely chiseled nose, deep-set dark eyes which slanted slightly, giving him an unusual mark of identification. His smile was warm; his teeth were straight and gleaming white.

He had an imagination and was blessed with an intelligence which enabled him to translate imagination into creativity.

He had all that was needed to be a movie star and a little more—a fine baritone speaking voice, a fair singing voice and the bonus of being foreign-born and bilingual. All surefire dividends—in the nineteen-sixties.

But in the teen years of the century, having a good voice meant nothing to the men behind the scenes. Being a foreigner was a disadvantage; it meant no work except for an occasional role as a villain. Producers wanted "American types" only.

In 1915, Valentino wasn't wanted in the film industry. But he had no way—yet—of knowing this.

Twenty years old and excited about the movies, Valentino was soon to learn about the Hollywood treadmill. His lessons started the morning after he arrived.

His first stop was at the casting office at Metro. There, a pretty blond girl—a Miss Gleason—consulted a sheet of paper, smiled at him and said, "Sorry, nothing today. Why don't you try tomorrow?"

Dressed meticulously, he presented himself at each of the studios' casting offices. Each receptionist had a list of the parts for which her director was casting. She would check the list as each actor appeared before her and, if she felt that perhaps the person might fit a role, she would either have him wait to see the boss, or else take his address and other information about him.

After visiting all the casting offices on his own, Valentino went to visit the few people he had been introduced to. Here he was greeted much more warmly, but the answer was still the same: Nothing today. A few people told him they thought they knew of something. They took his address and promised to get in touch with him when there was something definite.

The next day, he started all over again. Again, everywhere he went, he was told, "Sorry, nothing today." "Maybe tomorrow." "Try again next week." "You just aren't the type." "You're the wrong type."

"The wrong type."

"The wrong type."

"The wrong type."

He was discouraged.

If even his looks were against him, how could he ever hope to get his foot on the ladder to stardom? Norman Kerry had led him to believe that with his looks he would have an easy time of it. He discovered that what Norman felt and what the casting directors felt were poles apart, and, as Norman himself had said, the casting directors were the people who counted.

He moved from the Alexandria Hotel to cheaper quarters on Fifth and Grand Streets and continued on the treadmill. The answer had not changed. "Not the type." Valentino could almost sense the words before they were spoken.

After two weeks of searching for the elusive "break," Valentino reached the point where he had to stop and take stock. He had already borrowed too much money from Norman. He missed meals and subsisted on snacks to save the little money he had left. He made his decision. He would leave Hollywood and find a job.

Norman wouldn't hear of it. He reached into his pocket and handed Valentino more money. "My God, Rudy, you're impatient. Don't you know how long it took me to get my first job?"

Valentino shook his head. He had envisioned Norman walking into a casting office, smiling at the receptionist and being offered a starring role. "How long?" he asked.

"Months," his friend answered. "Months. And then the job lasted for only a day. But I didn't give up . . . and you aren't going to either. Now, get out of here and let me get back to work. Next time you come back, I'm sure you'll have something."

Valentino had no way of knowing if Norman was lying to him about his own plight when he first arrived in Hollywood, but the little talk—truth or lie—proved enough to send him back on the rounds. Another week passed and nothing happened. But this time Valentino had not allowed himself to become discouraged. Now when a clerk told him he wasn't the type he smiled at her in his most winning way. He almost sensed the change in the girl seated behind the desk. If she could, she'd have changed her casting schedule for him.

For a time Valentino remained cheerful. Even after another two weeks of no hope had passed and money was running low again, he continued the rounds. He felt he owed it to Norman. Norman had as much as said that the money loans were an investment in his future. Backing down now and leaving Hollywood would be a betrayal of his friend's trust.

But the day arrived when he had just enough money for

34

another two days' rent. He decided he would make one final round. If nothing happened, he'd return to his room, pack up, and leave. When he could, he'd return Norman's money and write Norman a letter explaining why he had gone.

At Metro, the blond Miss Gleason was busily typing when Valentino walked into the office.

"Sit down a minute, please," she said to him.

He sat down next to a blond girl. His feet were tired and he appreciated the rest. Had Miss Gleason not been so busy, he might have attached importance to the fact that she had asked him to sit. He rested his eyes and waited. He was pretty sure the answer would be No. Miss Gleason was the nicest to him of all the receptionists, but then she appeared to be that kind of person—always nice to everyone.

As the thought ran through his head, he smiled. He wondered what luck a Miss Gleason would have if she were job-hunting. She was a type. Was there much call for her type? He smiled again. The blond girl sitting next to him smiled back. He lowered his eyes.

"Good morning, Mr. Flynn. The boss is expecting you," Miss Gleason said cheerily.

Valentino looked up. A keen-eyed, brisk-walking young man in knickers and Norfolk jacket walked by. Valentino recognized him as one of the directors Norman had pointed out to him. The director nodded toward the waiting hopefuls as he went through the door marked *Private*.

Valentino wondered if he should wait until Flynn left the office, introduce himself and ask for a job. Norman said people had to push in Hollywood. Should he?

"I couldn't," Valentino thought. "I couldn't. Even if I built up enough courage to go up to him, I'd probably become tongue-tied or forget how to speak English. Pushing is not for me. I'll probably never get anyplace."

The buzzer on Miss Gleason's desk sounded, and Miss Gleason went through the door. In a few seconds, she came out. She was smiling happily as she approached Valentino.

"Congratulations," she said. "Emmett Flynn has agreed to give you a bit as an extra. Five dollars a day." She waited for him to say something. When he remained silent, she went on. "I've been plugging for you, you know. In the few weeks you've been coming in here, you've made me feel very feminine. Anyone who reminds a woman that she is a woman deserves a break. How do you feel?"

A sputter of words broke loose. "I don't know how to thank you," he said. "You're an angel. It's wonderful. Thank you so much, so many times." He was thinking of the five dollars a day. He could pay his own rent, buy his own food. He could stay on in Hollywood. "When do I start? Where do I go? What do I do?"

Miss Gleason laughed. "One thing at a time."

He followed her to the desk where she filled out a pass for him.

"As I said, you'll be working with Mr. Flynn. His picture is *Alimony*, starring Josephine Whittel, the wife of Robert Warwick, the actor. One of our best writers, Hayden Talbot, did the script. It's a fairly good picture. That piece of paper I just gave you will get you into the wardrobe department. They'll take care of your costume. From there, go to Stage Four. You're on your way."

Valentino impulsively seized her hand and held it to his lips. She blushed a bright scarlet.

"Don't forget to visit us again, when you're a big star," she stammered.

Valentino turned in a big hurry. He was on his way! He bumped into the blond girl who had sat next to him. He caught her and steadied her.

"I'm glad you finally got something," she said, to overcome his embarrassment at almost knocking her off her feet. "My name is Alice Taffe; perhaps we'll meet around here. Isn't it wonderful to get your first part?"

"How do you know it is my first?"

She giggled. "We're all the same, so starry-eyed our faces almost blind people. I was the same way. Good luck to you." She leaned closer to him. "That's the casting director with Mr. Flynn."

Valentino got a fleeting glimpse of the boss. Mr. Flynn came toward them.

"I think I have a part for you in *Alimony*," he said to

Alice. She smiled graciously. He turned to Valentino. "So you're the young man who makes Miss Gleason feel feminine. What's your name?" Valentino told him. "Italian, eh? Well, you look it. Italians are great artists, generally. Caruso's my favorite. . . . Well, let's go to work." He exited briskly.

Alice Taffe took Valentino's hand. "Come on," she said. "I'll show you the way."

She led him to Wardrobe, wished him luck again and walked away. He didn't see her until after their part in the picture that day was over with. Both had walk-on bits. Afterward, they stood by the cameras watching the director shout instructions through his megaphone.

"You were wonderful," Alice said.

"So were you, Alice. Isn't it exciting?"

She nodded.

"I'm free for the rest of the afternoon. Would you like to walk?" Valentino asked.

"Let's get out of our costumes first. I'll meet you back here."

They walked out to the farm area along the road that skirted the edge of Hollywood. Valentino pointed to the oranges and the lush melon vines. "See how dark green those vines are? That isn't just an accident. Nitrate and irrigation is the secret. A farm like this has many secrets. I want one like this or even bigger."

He told her about his dreams of his own farm. She couldn't imagine how he could be interested in being a farmer when the screen beckoned with so much to offer.

"A means to an end," Valentino said. "I don't see where I can make a steady living out of this kind of work. One day, I work. The next day, no one knows me."

"That's because we're just starting out. Look, even if you did own this farm, you would have to start from someplace. You couldn't just expect to sell your melons to everyone. You would have to seek them out and convince them that your melons are worth tasting. With acting, it's the same thing. The only difference is that you are the product. You have to have confidence in yourself. That's the main thing, really. When people start to know you and want to see you, that's when you become a star and famous. Don't you think it's worth starving for?''

"I guess so, but how do you know that you will ever become a star?''

"I've had a few parts, not good ones, but I have been seen. The big one could be around the corner. I don't know. You never know when something will kill a crop, right? Well, how do you know that tomorrow isn't the day for stardom? I wouldn't leave because I might leave the day before the big happening. Then I would be to blame for not allowing the big break to come my way. The same goes for you.''

"I wish I had your faith.''

"I'll have faith for both of us. All right?''

"All right,'' he answered, taking her hand. She was a sweet, outgoing girl and he was attracted to her because she somehow seemed older than her eighteen years. He decided he would like to see more of her.

Near a grove of redwoods she suggested they rest. They sat on moss and she leaned her head against his shoulder. He put his arm around her shoulders. Daylight had faded. Twilight came, and a few stars appeared in the sky. She snuggled closer to him. She touched her hand to his cheek and stroked it gently. He leaned over to kiss her. Her arms went around his neck. She pulled him closer to her. Their bodies molded together as they kissed, each kiss longer, deeper, more fulfilling.

Alice, for all her self-assurance, was much like Valentino. She suffered times of depression and deep loneliness. She was love-starved and affectionate. Each found a need in the other, and the need poured out in kisses . . . in caresses . . . and finally, in sleep.

Valentino awoke to find Alice leaning on one elbow and looking down at him.

"Hello,'' she whispered. She kissed him again.

"You must be starved,'' he said. "Look at all the stars. And the moon! You should have made me get up.''

"I was sleeping, too. When I woke, I didn't have the heart to disturb you. You looked so peaceful.''

"We had better go. We have to be back on the set at seven." He stood and helped her to her feet. "I know of a place—Tony's—where the spaghetti is excellent."

They walked back arm in arm.

At Tony's, Valentino told her about his struggles in New York, his brief career as a dancer with Bonnie Glass and then Joan Sawyer. This impressed Alice.

"Why don't you follow it up, Rudy?"

"I don't want to make dancing my career. I love dancing. And the tango—it is part of me. I dance to relax."

They discussed California, San Francisco, Los Angeles, Hollywood. They talked about farms again, and Valentino's face lit up. They talked about flowers, especially roses. Roses were everywhere in this section, on the lawns, in the parks, on the meadows, all varieties and colors, in overwhelming profusion. And then he told her, "There is a little rose with only four petals—and it grows wild. I saw one in Central Park, New York. I also saw a few along the edge of a wood in New Jersey. Such perfume! Such beauty . . ."

"You know, Rudy, sometimes you speak like a farmer. And sometimes like a poet."

"I like to read poetry and I have a secret ambition to write poems. Maybe I will make up one about you."

"Why, Mr. Valentino—"

"I mean it."

They laughed. Tony, the proprietor, came forward. "Well, how you like the spaghetti?"

"Tony, I could not cook it better. It is superb," said Valentino.

"Next time you come with this pretty girl I make maybe some of my extra-special ravioli. All right?"

"All right, my countryman." Valentino gave him a playful tap on the shoulder.

It was time to go. They rose and bade Tony good night.

In the shadow of the boarding house where Alice lived he held her as though he would never let her go and his lips found hers.

"See you tomorrow, Rudy?"

"Tomorrow."

He left her standing there, and as he headed to his apartment he recalled another moment like this of someone else, dark-eyed and tempestuous, left standing at an apartment door.

He walked to his rooms and thought of tomorrow. Now at least he had something to look forward to. The strangest of things—he would be an actor, though fleetingly, in front of the camera.

Valentino did not go right to bed. He sat at the tiny table and wrote:

"Alice, not only beautiful but oh so wise—"

He chewed on the pencil as he began to search his mind for a word to rhyme with wise. Realize? Rise? Compromise?

He tried to complete the second line of the couplet. The pencil dropped from his fingers and his tired eyes closed. He fell fast asleep in the chair. And he dreamed of a girl with blond hair that smelled like fresh-mown hay.

For the next two days while the two were working in *Alimony* life was like a dream. They spent their days on the set and at night they walked, talked, and were happy. Things were going well . . . too well.

One night, Norman Kerry came to visit Valentino.

"Rudy, I've brought a friend," he said. In walked Hayden Talbot.

Talbot had an idea for a movie centered around a character. "Valentino," he said, "you are the man I want to play the character."

The words struck Valentino with the force of a battering ram. Had it come? Was success here? So suddenly?

"It will take time to write the script, but I want to promise you you will get the part," Talbot said.

So all Valentino had to do was wait. Work and wait, until the script was finished.

The next day, and the next, and the next, he visited casting offices. Days dragged into weeks, and the weeks into a month. He saw Alice less frequently because he had little money and would not take money from her.

Money. It was getting scarcer and scarcer with each day's tour of the casting offices. And each day at the casting offices he constantly heard the words that reminded him he had no money:

"I'm sorry, you're not the type . . . you're not the type . . . you're not . . ."

Valentino had to look around for another way to earn an income. There was nothing he did as well as dancing. He turned to it once again. Although he had vowed not to follow it as a career, he would use it temporarily, and perhaps Fate would bring him good fortune, so that he could leave it. He had to admit to himself that as a dancer he was good. People noticed him and accepted him. So long as they accepted his dancing as an art, he could tolerate it.

He began to search for a dancing engagement, and when he wasn't haunting the various night spots, he visited the Metro lot and spent time talking to some of his acquaintances. It was there he met Alice and told her of his revised plans.

She approved. "You are a wonderful dancer, Rudy, and important people—maybe directors and producers—will catch your act. That may be just the thing you need. It will take you away from the lot for a while. I'm sure something good will come of it."

She changed her clothes and they walked out to the cluster of redwoods and, there, with the sun flickering through the restless leaves, they lost themselves in each other.

The girl in his arms stirred Valentino's thoughts. He couldn't keep from reflecting that if he had followed farming he would now have achieved something and more than likely would have had a wife, a family, as his father had done.

Alice suddenly moved. She turned his face toward her and said, "Rudy, I want you to promise me something."

"Anything. Do you want me to acquire the moon for you?"

"No, nothing so exerting. I just want you to promise that no matter where you are or what you do, you won't forget me. If we were just two ordinary people, we might have met, fallen in love, and married. Being what we are, we couldn't. We would probably devour each other. Sometimes it makes me sad. . . . But then I think of our names in lights, and I know it's all right."

"You silly little girl. How could I ever forget you? Haven't we been part of each other in the brief time we've known each other? Aren't you the one with the faith for both of us? I could not forget you—even if I wanted to." He kissed her again.

Eventually they walked to Tony's for a ravioli dinner, and afterwards, he walked her home, promising to meet her the next day. As he walked home, he remembered what she had said about their not being ordinary people. Maybe not, he thought, maybe not. He didn't know what to feel. Marriage to Alice had not entered his mind in so many words, but now that she had said it was impossible, he felt a sense of loss. Valentino liked the thought of long relationships. With a girl, the longest of relationships was eventual marriage. And yet, he wasn't ready to marry. Neither was Alice. She was right, so why was he making so much of it?

The next day, Alice ran up to him between shootings.

"I heard that a new tavern called the Watts just opened on the outskirts of Los Angeles. It's run by someone named Baron Long. Why don't you go see him? There's a rumor that he's looking for a dance act." She kissed his cheek. "Good luck."

He made the trip. There were others there with the same idea. Valentino waited his turn and sat across from the businessman. He told him of his previous dancing experience and his previous partners. Long rubbed his chin and said nothing. The boy had a look about him. Long was pretty sure the ladies would notice it, too.

"All right," he said finally. "You have yourself a job. You can start tonight."

"And the pay?" the youth asked.

"Thirty-five dollars a week with meals."

Valentino hesitated. "I earned over a hundred with Miss Glass."

"This isn't New York, boy. That's the offer. Take it or leave it."

"I'll take it." I have to, he thought, the barrel is empty.

That night he gave his performance of the tango. His partner, attractive Marjorie Tain who later starred in Christie

Comedies, followed easily and gracefully. When Valentino wasn't resenting the fact that he was back doing something for a living that he had vowed he wouldn't do, he had to admit that they were pretty good. The applause which greeted their final steps was well deserved.

Besides the satisfaction of earning a steady income—which meant freedom from borrowing from his friends, which meant being able to send money to Italy, which gave him a feeling of well-being because he was working—Valentino knew he was being seen by the Hollywood set. The patrons were from Hollywood and Pasadena, and Valentino recognized many of them from various studios. Perhaps Alice's faith would pay off and some night a big producer would come to him and beg him to take a leading role in an epic movie.

He bought some new clothes, which always made him feel better. He bought Alice little gifts and took her to movies—on a busman's holiday—and to concerts. The two young people were very happy with each other; they shared their joys and their fears and knew that they were understood.

After his performance one night, one of the guests sent Valentino a note. It read: "Try the Hotel Maryland. I think they'll want you."

Valentino went to the manager of the Hotel Maryland the next day. The hotel was a popular gathering place for the elite of the motion picture industry. It was more exclusive than the Watts. He was booked for Thanksgiving Day.

With his new partner, Kathryn Phelps, he was acclaimed and applauded enthusiastically. As they took their last bows, Valentino saw the faces of leading stars sitting at the tables. Again, he felt hope leap within him.

The proprietor of the Maryland, a Mr. Linnard, had been on a business trip in November. When he returned, he was met on all sides with the news of the sensational dance team who had appeared at his club. Valentino was immediately sent for and offered a year's contract.

To say that he wasn't tempted would be a lie. But there were other considerations. The offered salary, for one thing, was low; for another, a year seemed like an eternity. If his

43

chance should come while he was tied down to the contract at the Maryland, he could never forgive himself. He refused. He tried to talk Mr. Linnard into hiring him on a weekly or a monthly basis. Mr. Linnard refused.

With the money he had accumulated at Watts and the Maryland, Valentino went back to visiting the casting offices. By this time he was a familiar figure and not an unpleasant one. Many a casting clerk cast him seductive glances and put more meaning than job-hunting into, ''Try tomorrow.'' But the next day didn't hold a job for him.

His money ran out. He was hungry, but he refused to call upon Norman for more money. He had never actually asked Norman for money; he wasn't going to start. It was bad enough that he accepted the money Norman forced upon him.

He sought comfort where it would be most comfortable, with a fellow countryman. He went to Tony's meaning to ask Tony to trust him for a meal. He arrived before most patrons arrived, so he was surprised to see Alice at one of the tables. She smiled broadly and waved him over.

''You're a bad boy, Rudy. I haven't seen you in ages. Sit down and tell me what's happened.''

He sat across from her.

''I have reached the end of my patience and endurance,'' he said. ''I've tried hard, very hard. I go to the casting offices every morning. I ask everybody I see, everybody I know, for work. There is nothing for me. I came here tonight to ask Tony for a free meal. How low can I fall?''

Alice patted his hand. ''Let me buy you a meal, Rudy.''

''I could never allow a woman to buy me a meal.''

''Is that all I am?'' she demanded, flushing. ''I thought we were friends. If I were starving, would you watch and laugh?''

''I didn't say that,'' he protested.

''All right, then, what do you want? Ravioli?''

He gave in. After he had eaten the meal, he felt better. Over coffee, Alice made him promise not to pack up and leave—just yet. ''Meet me for lunch at the studio tomorrow. Maybe I'll hear of something.''

He walked her home and promised to meet her at Metro the next day.

Out of habit and to kill some time, he began the next day by making the usual rounds. This time he saved Metro for the last stop since that was where he and Alice were to have lunch. The answer at the various studios was the same as the day before. Dejected, he met Alice. He hated her paying for his food, but he couldn't insult her by refusing.

She hadn't heard of anything for him, but there were all sorts of rumors. She made him promise to stay the rest of the week.

"If nothing comes up for you by then, Rudy, I promise to stop interfering with your life and let you go. But please give it another week. For me."

He was leaving the lot when Emmett Flynn spotted him and beckoned him over.

"I've been looking for you, Valentino," the director said. "Hayden Talbot informed me that his latest story was written with you in mind as one of the characters. Are you free to take the part?"

"Yes. Of course," Valentino said. He was pleasantly shocked. And relieved.

"See Maxwell, in charge of production. He'll talk salary and such. We begin shooting tomorrow morning."

Valentino thanked Flynn and fairly flew to Maxwell's office in the administrative department. He found Maxwell seated behind a big desk, a heavy black cigar clenched between his teeth. Through a screen of curling smoke, he surveyed the slick-haired man before him.

"Fifty a week all right?" he asked, cigar still in mouth.

"F-fine."

"Sign the dotted line." He waited while Valentino signed. "Report to Wardrobe before you leave the studio. Be here tomorrow morning at seven-thirty sharp. Tardiness costs the studio money, so we don't like people who are late. Actual filming begins at eight. Emmett Flynn will direct. Here's the script.—I expect you to study it thoroughly." The man paused. "You play an Italian count. Looks like Talbot made it to order. Or else you were made to order. Anyway, that's it.'' The man blew a cloud of smoke at Valentino and then turned his back on him.

Taking the script, Valentino left the office, dazed, happy.

"He's quite a bear, isn't he?" the girl outside Maxwell's office said. "Don't let him scare you."

"He didn't," Valentino answered. "In fact, I would say I love the man. Absolutely love him."

He floated out of the building and went searching for Alice and Norman. Only a half-hour ago he had been on the brink of absolute despondency. And now—he had a role in a Hollywood production.

The next morning he hurried to the studio at six-thirty to make sure he missed nothing.

When it came time to do his scenes, he performed adequately. The tenseness and excitement unnerved him at first, causing him to miss many cues, but he improved as the day wore on. He obeyed implicitly every order Flynn gave him, although he privately disagreed with Flynn's interpretation of his character. And he would have preferred to see the kind of camera work that was practiced by Griffith. Flynn worked on straight and middle focus and made little or no use of angle shots, the iris, the fade, the giant close-ups of the actor's face or of an object pertinent to the action. Griffith or Ince would have gotten much more out of each scene. At times, Valentino was tempted to say something, but he was afraid of offending the director and losing his job, so he remained silent.

The initial plan was to release the picture as soon as it was completed, but this was prevented by a legal snarl. The cameramen complained that they had not been paid in full and warned they would file suit unless the matter was settled. Their warning was disregarded, but they went to court and got an injunction which prevented the film from being exhibited. Valentino felt crushed. He had pinned great hopes on the prestige and publicity this picture would bring him. While it was locked in the can, he remained as unknown to the public as before.

The picture was finally released many weeks later. It was a dismal flop. With his money used up and no offers coming in for work, it seemed to Valentino that he now had to leave Hollywood forever. He began to look about the studio in a sort of farewell inspection. He would remember, as one phase of his life, the scene of his failure. Those rambling wooden buildings housing the sets and stages, the fake Oriental temples, the simulated Indian village, the replicas of a western town and a gold mining camp—these he would remember, perhaps with scorn, when he would be living on his own farm.

With these thoughts he started to walk out of the Metro lot and out of the mad celluloid beehive. Feeling as he did, he hoped never to set foot on the lot again.

He had just about passed the front gate and had waved farewell to the guard, when he heard a voice calling him. He turned and saw Emmett Flynn.

"Mr. Flynn—"

"Rudy, wait a minute. I want to talk to you. Are you at liberty? I mean, are you free? You're not under contract to anyone else?"

"No. I haven't worked since *The Married Virgin*."

"I don't want to pull you down from your rating as a leading man, but I do have an extra bit. I think it's just for you."

"What is it?" His spirits were rising again.

"You play the part of an Italian tough guy. It's just a bone but it will pay you seven dollars and fifty cents per day. How about it?"

"Yes, and thank you. I was about to kiss Hollywood good-by."

"Report to the wardrobe department with this note, and come back to Stage Six. That's where I'm shooting the picture."

The director hadn't lied. The part was small; it lasted only a matter of minutes. But Flynn assured him, "Rudy, I don't want you to leave. You're on the payroll until this picture is finished. Who knows? I might need you in another scene."

"Mr. Flynn, you are a kind man. I'd just be in the way."

"You are not in anybody's way. Hang around, Rudy. I may want you unexpectedly."

So Valentino reported on the set on Stage Six each day and received his seven dollars and fifty cents. He took the time and the opportunity to watch everything and to learn. He studied the actors as they went through their scenes and caught their mistakes and made mental notes. He watched the camerawork and he thought about how it could be done better.

He became a fairly well-known figure on the sets and on Hollywood Boulevard and Vine Street. Directors, producers and executives began to look at him.

One director did more than look at him. He accosted Valentino one afternoon near Stage Six:

"A word with you, Valentino."

"Yes?"

"My name is Henry Otto, director for Fox Films. I like the way you comport yourself. You have a certain something that I'd like to capture. If I did, I think your personality would hit the public fancy."

"I don't know what to say."

"I'm going to have a talk with the Fox production bigwigs and see what can be done. I'll let you know."

In two days Valentino heard from Henry Otto. The reaction of the studio moguls was negative. They did not believe that an unknown like Valentino would carry enough weight to warrant giving him a lead in a production. Perhaps later, when he was more firmly established.

Valentino shrugged it off. He was now inured to Hollywood and its fantastic promises and illusionary build-ups. He had to stick to Emmett Flynn and try to earn his bread and butter as an extra.

He felt guilty, however, as time passed. The picture was nearing completion and he was not called upon to do anything else in it.

He spent some of his time visiting other sets. One visit brought him luck. Mae Murray was doing a scene and when she finished, she passed very close to him, stopped, and stared.

"Are you in the picture?" she asked. "Did they send you from casting?"

"No. But allow me to introduce myself. Rudolph Valentino. I'm working with Mr. Flynn. I was admiring your acting, Miss Murray.''

"Thank you. And may I introduce you to my husband and director, Robert Z. Leonard—Bob Leonard to his friends.''

"It is an honor, Mr. Leonard.''

Leonard smiled as he extended his hand.

"Hello, Valentino. I enjoyed watching you tango at Watts.''

Mae was all interest. She was quite a dancer herself. "Oh, yes, I remember now. So you are the one. I had a feeling I had seen you somewhere. You were divine on that floor—simply wonderful.''

A brief silence, and Mae's eyes never left Valentino's face.

"I've been thinking, Bob—my next picture, *The Big Little Person*—I'm sure Mr. Valentino would be perfect as my leading man.''

"But, Mae—'' Bob began.

"I know. He doesn't have much experience. But he's a natural for the role and he's sure to learn fast. Dashing, graceful, charming. Just what the girls all over the world are waiting for. Look at those features—those eyes, dark, flashing. And when he dances the tango—say yes, darling.''

Bob Leonard could refuse his wife little. He saw the feasibility of her suggestion and he nodded.

Just a slight, almost imperceptible nod, and Valentino, standing there, realized—though it was difficult to do so—that the gates had suddenly swung open. He could now walk into that exclusive paradise where the lights are brightest and the music is sweetest.

Mae Murray told him to be in the executive offices promptly at eight the next morning, when arrangements would be made for the signing of a contract.

He did not go back to the Emmett Flynn set, Stage Six. Instead he kept on walking. The studio buildings, the various sets, and indeed the entire film community took on a new, iridescent glow for him. Wherever he looked, he saw the world in roseate colors. The California sun seemed especially warm and intoxicating. The sky was a clean white-blue, and as he walked down Hollywood Boulevard to the outskirts of the town, he felt as if he were riding a float. He had an impulse to stop people and shout at them, "Do you know that I'm going to be leading man to Mae Murray, one of the world's most famous stars? Do you realize that I'm not going to be an extra anymore . . . that I'm going to be protected with a contract?"

He restrained the impulse. The idea of talking to strange people or shouting out good news to an impersonal street was, after all, out of character for Rudolph Valentino. He decided to find Norman Kerry and Alice as quickly as he could. They would be overjoyed to learn that their faith in him had not been misplaced. And with them, he could act like a bubbly schoolboy without being chastised for losing his dignity.

When he caught up with his two friends and gave them the news they were so delighted they decided a celebration was in order. The three of them, along with Norman's girl friend, had dinner at Tony's, then hurried to Watts. This time, Valentino was there as a guest, not an employee, and it added to his mood of exuberance. He and Alice danced until the place closed. And before he went to sleep he scribbled a letter to his mother, telling her that good fortune was coming to him. Soon, he promised, he would be sending her some real money and perhaps would arrange to bring her and sister Maria to America.

CHAPTER SIX

THE picture *The Big Little Person* dealt with an era close to Valentino's heart—an era of dashing knights and fair maidens in distress. The atmosphere on the set reawakened his old boyhood dreams of medieval splendor and chivalry. There were times during lulls in the shooting when his mind would go scooting off to the exploits of jousting knights. On occasion, Mae Murray would catch him in the middle of a reverie and tell him laughingly, "You're the first man I've ever seen who goes to sleep with his eyes open." When she pressed him to tell her what he was thinking about, he reacted like a boy whose hand had been caught in the cookie jar. He was ashamed to confess that he had never lost the traits of the adolescent dreamer. His fellow performers regarded these knights-and-maidens pictures as drivel fit only for unformed minds, and would greet him with contemptuous laughter if he ever confessed to them that he had a deep feeling for the part he was playing and that the scenes of the picture held real fascination for him.

In one scene, Valentino was told he would wear a suit of armor and ride a white horse. When the property department brought his suit, however, he recognized it as a cheap imitation and indignantly refused to wear it. It offended the illusion of reality he had built up in his mind about this picture. Leonard was startled by this display of vehemence and Valentino hastily explained that audiences would be as quick as he was to notice that the armor was tin-plate imitation. The director asked the property department to find a better suit for him, but they had nothing in stock. Valentino still balked at the imitation and finally went out himself to find a genuine suit of armor. He located one in an antique shop and rented it for the one day it was needed, even though it was much too big for him.

In order to get into the suit, Valentino needed help from some of the workers on the set. He needed more help to climb on the horse. When he was finally mounted and ready, the sun slipped behind a dark cloud and the shooting had to be held up.

Valentino, encased in that mass of metal, resolved to wait patiently upon the bony white mare. Perspiration dripped from every pore in his body, but he kept sitting there, motionless, as the sun almost spitefully continued to hide behind the clouds. For more than an hour he waited until the maddening sun reappeared. The scene was shot in eight minutes.

When they extricated Valentino from the iron strait jacket, he looked like the victim of the torture chamber in the Inquisition—bruised, lacerated, choked. But he smiled happily, for he was sure he had made the scene somewhat more realistic.

For this work Valentino received a hundred dollars a week. He found himself once again in a fairly solvent financial position. He was able to pay some debts and to send money to his mother with promises of better things to come. It was at these times—when he wrote to his family—that thoughts of his homeland, caught in the great war, came back to him. He felt an uneasiness, an inward torment.

He prayed that the war end and his family be spared.

The Big Little Person was completed, and he was grateful to Mr. Leonard when the latter informed him that he could use him as leading man again in Mae Murray's next picture, *The Delicious Little Devil*.

Valentino grew more adroit in his delineations of character. He trained himself to act in accord with the tone of the story. His movements became easy and graceful; his own personality flavored each scene, lending it the breath of life.

There was always that wistful longing in his eyes, a sense

of seeking after something, that struck a note of understanding and sympathy in the hearts of the audience. His natural good looks, his courtly manner, his suggestion of menace one moment and tenderness the next, gained for him the admiration of the feminine element, and a trickle of fan letters began.

But when *The Delicious Little Devil* was finished, Valentino was again out of work. Mae's next picture required a different sort of personality and would not suit his particular "type"—so Mr. Leonard thought. This time, however, Valentino did not have to make the rounds of the casting offices. He now had the foundation of a reputation, and a letter of introduction from Mr. Leonard to a fellow director, Paul Powell, eliminated needless foot work. Powell was beginning a picture called *A Society Sensation*, starring Carmel Myers. He took one look at Valentino and gave him a supporting role at a salary of a hundred and twenty-five dollars a week, which was the highest amount earned by Valentino in Hollywood thus far. After the completion of this picture, Mr. Powell gave him a leading part in *All Night* at a hundred and fifty dollars a week.

Valentino felt now that he had climbed two or three steps upward; he had been given a series of roles in succession without any appreciable layoff. His reputation as a villain or heavy in Hollywood was being fairly well established through those formative years of 1917 and 1918.

America was now in the war and Valentino tried once again to enlist but, as before, he was rejected because of his eye defect. In September of 1918 the dread Spanish influenza invaded the West Coast and Hollywood was struck hard, as was every other place in the land. The studios shut down completely, and actors, prop men and other employees succumbed in wholesale numbers to the scourge.

Valentino, as did many others, went to San Francisco to escape the raging epidemic, and while there he remained untouched. But he felt that he could not stay away too long. His career was just beginning to take hold and he did not want to jeopardize it. So he came back to the studio, but the disease was still rampant, and it sought him out.

He lay in bed for six weeks, battling against the spectre that hovered over him—a shadow, dark and ominous. It was a life and death struggle. There were times when it looked dangerously critical and he did not know how he was going to pull through. He fought the malady alone, for he did not believe in doctors.

But he won.

He got out of bed. He walked along Hollywood Boulevard again. He had lost much weight; he had grown thin, gaunt. He felt weak and wondered whether the studios would ever accept him again, and he worried about it.

On his first day out in the street, he was overcome with dizziness and weakness and nearly collapsed. The next day, however, he was able to take a short walk along Hollywood Boulevard. He found and spoke to Alice Taffe again. She had been lucky—the influenza had touched her only lightly. Norman, she said, had been away on location and had escaped the epidemic completely.

The two spent long hours together over the next two weeks. They ate at Tony's, sat in the park, and walked in the sunshine. At times they kissed and hugged, but mostly they maintained a relationship of warm, but platonic, friendship. Though Valentino was regaining his strength, he was afraid the time he had lost in sickness had taken the momentum out of his burgeoning career and dealt him a stinging setback. Alice tried to scotch his fears. He had made a mark in his last pictures, she said, and there was no reason why he could not pick up where he left off.

When Valentino set out to find work, however, he found Alice had been overoptimistic. The crippling effects of the epidemic still lingered on in Hollywood. Few pictures were being made. The only thing Valentino was offered was a minor supporting role in a picture called *A Rogue's Romance*, starring Earle Williams and directed by James Young. He would again be a heavy and he debated the wisdom of accepting the offer. Finally, his precarious financial condition settled the question for him. He felt he was too poor to act independent. He was unhappy with both the part and the picture, but Young did allow him to do an apache dance in one sequence and even permitted him to stage it and choose the camera angles himself.

Soon afterwards, he was introduced to the director whose work he had long admired—D. W. Griffith. Griffith was casting for his production of *Out of Luck*, which would star Dorothy Gish. Valentino was, of course, eager for the leading-man role, but Griffith told him he wouldn't fit it. Instead, he offered him another heavy role, something similar to the one he had just finished for Young. With film production still at a low ebb, Valentino felt he could not afford to be choosy. He took the role. It would be a fill-in, he decided, until production returned to normal and the demand for leading-man roles accelerated.

But even as production increased, Valentino found to his dismay that producers and directors were still not considering him for the important, romantic parts. Even the fact that America was now in the war and that some actors had gone into service (Valentino's eye defect had prevented his own earlier attempt to enlist) was of no help to him. He was the "foreign bad man" again; this type of performer was only in modest demand and was considered small shakes in the motion picture scheme of things.

Ruefully, Valentino realized that his failure to capitalize on his performances in the Mae Murray and John Powell pictures had cost him dearly. The unlucky influenza epidemic and his own incapacitation had sidelined him at the worst possible time. Furthermore, he had not used—and probably had not known how to use—publicity methods to sell himself in his new guise of leading man. By accepting minor heavy roles again to earn his keep in the aftermath of the influenza crisis, he had as much as told type-conscious Hollywood that he was back in the "foreign villain" business again and should not be considered for other roles.

When D. W. Griffith called him one day and told him he had something "different" in mind for him, his heart leaped to his throat. Perhaps now he was going to be given his chance to try his leading-man wings. But his enthusiasm was quickly short-circuited. Griffith had heard he could dance as well as play heavies and he wanted to hire him to dance on the stage of a Los Angeles theater for one week. He would form a dance act for that week with a partner named Carol Dempster and their performance would be a special prologue to the screening of Griffith's new picture, *The Greatest Thing in Life*.

Valentino took the job. He needed money and he was anxious to continue his association with Griffith. The audience received the Valentino-Dempster act so enthusiastically that Griffith extended his engagement from one week to three months. His salary during this period was a hundred dollars a week. Shortly afterwards, another Griffith picture, *Scarlet Days*, was shown at the Grauman Theater, and he was engaged to dance in a prologue to that, too.

After this, there were odd jobs—more heavy roles, and occasional dance engagements. It wasn't what Valentino wanted, but he felt he had to be practical. He had accepted the fact that his livelihood was in Hollywood. For better or for worse, he had picked a career. He was resigned to sticking it out until things got better, until he could put enough money aside for some really fertile acreage.

Though Valentino had interested himself enough in a Hollywood career to learn a good deal of the motion picture craft, he still showed little interest in cultivating motion picture people. He regarded them as overly crass, cynical, and devoid of real sentiment. They were spoiled children with too many artificial toys. He still saw Norman Kerry from time to time and had occasional lunches and dinners with Alice Taffe, but he made no other friends. He was alone most of the time. When he accepted a rare invitation to a Hollywood party, he came away from it more than ever convinced that his confreres in the entertainment business were too grasping and shallow for his tastes.

He was filled with deep emotions of love and beauty which he wanted to bring to people. He thought he could do this through motion pictures, but since he was not being given the opportunity, he tended to encase himself in a shell and simply keep these emotions wrapped around him. He felt Hollywood people would laugh if he tried to pour out his pent-up feelings to them and so he kept them at arm's length. His polite and

56

gracious manner kept them from suspecting that he held them in abysmally low regard, but his "loner" habits were becoming well-known. They were habits Hollywood people could not fathom and so when they talked of Valentino, they described him as a "queer duck," a "mystic," and an "oddball." To many people, he was a man who had had some kind of strange tragedy early in life and had not learned how to come back from it. What was the tragedy? Here the gossips were stumped again, and, if pressed, they would shrug their shoulders and say, "Who knows? He's such a strange fellow he may even have invented the tragedy!"

Most Hollywood people copied one another in dress as well as in attitude and living habits, so that they all lost their individuality. Valentino at least, had his. He had not only his "lone wolf" aura, but also his penchant for unusual clothes. He wore Basque caps, Italian-cut suits, brightly colored sweaters, and emblazoned shirts. His attitude toward individuality in dress must be explained in the light of his background. As a European of that period, he dressed with a fine disregard for what anyone might think of his tastes. It was only American men who were sensitive to the public's opinion of their raiment. Anyone who traveled extensively would have become aware of the sublime confidence that the Britishers and the continentals had that their clothing was at all times suitable. If their clothing tastes were questioned, they shrugged it off as a rude intrusion on the part of busybodies. Why was it an outsider's business what they wore?

Since Hollywood people considered everything their business, however, Valentino's dress helped make him an object of sly ridicule. It was also expensive to him. Byron Foy, one of the thirteen children of famed Eddie Foy, became acquainted with Valentino at this time and later said of him, "That fellow would go without meals in order to buy a new suit which struck his fancy!"

Though Valentino made a fair salary when he worked, he was unable to save anything. In addition to his costly clothes, he was an easy touch for struggling actors or stagehands with tales of woe. Once people learned that he was very generous

57

with his loans, they made a habit of putting the "bite"on him. When he had money, he gave it away freely. Sometimes his debtors paid him back; more often they did not. He would also spend freely to entertain people he thought might help him in his career. He wasted a good deal of money on a foreign car, a used Mercedes. He had bought it at a bargain down payment, but had to spend so much money fixing it when it broke down that he could not keep up with the payments. The car was repossessed one day on Hollywood Boulevard, where it had stalled in traffic. It had to be towed away by the repossessors and Valentino was charged for the towing.

This gave Hollywood something else about Valentino they could talk and laugh about. And while they talked, Valentino became even more introverted in his personal habits and turned to poetry to give substance to his emotional feelings and his mystical dreams of beauty and love. He began to scribble poems by the hundreds. Sometimes, he would read them to himself over and over again, then tear them up. Alone in his room, he would lie on his bed, look at the ceiling, and dream of his boyhood life in Castellaneta. He realized now that those days had been the happiest in his life, and that there had not been many happy ones since then. He thought of his mother and wondered if he would really be able to bring her to America, if indeed he would ever see her again.

CHAPTER SEVEN

THERE'S a story about a soldier alone in his trench. The enemy is all around him. He just stays in his trench, waiting. He's not sure what he is waiting for, but he waits, surviving the best he can, marking time until something happens. Suddenly a bomb goes off near him, catching him unawares. Unconsciously, he reacts. He leaps from his trench and races across the battlefield, doing everything he was trained not to do. He makes all the wrong moves, yet manages to get through the lines alive. His maneuvers aid his troops in spotting the enemy and wiping them out. The soldier earns a medal.

For Valentino, the trench was his misery and frustration. The enemy, compromise. The bomb. . . .

His mother's letters had always been an inspiration to Valentino. Even when he was at his lowest, a letter from the little Frenchwoman brought his spirits high. Her handwriting upon the page transported him across the ocean and across time. He was, no matter how depressed, happy with his mother's thoughts before him. He read each word carefully and pondered over each thought expressed. He anxiously looked forward to word from home. Words from home made him feel less insignificant, less a failure. His mother's letters were as important to Valentino as bread itself.

At first it didn't bother him that his mother's letters, instead of coming each week, or at least every second week, had dwindled to one in several weeks. There was a war going on; nothing was normal.

Then, no letters came at all.

Valentino was fearful that his mother was ill. He decided to bring her to America immediately, no matter the cost or the red tape. If she were with him he could take care of her and she, in turn, could give his life some meaning. As for the money needed, he decided to ask for a loan from the bank and use his next film part as collateral.

The next day he went to the bank where he kept his savings. He was delighted when the bank approved the loan. He planned to go to San Francisco the next day to arrange transportation with a steamship agency. His heart jumped whenever he thought of his mother's first view of America.

The next morning he awoke early, dressed carefully, and gathered everything necessary for his trip to Frisco. There was a knock at the door and he opened it with a hearty good morning. He was handed a letter. It was from Italy—in his brother's handwriting. His heart seemed to stop beating.

Don't be foolish, he told himself. Open it. Maybe Mama saved the money for the trip herself; maybe this letter tells you when and where to meet her.

With trembling fingers, he opened the envelope. He read the first line and could read no more. Tears welled in his eyes. The letter dropped from his hand and floated to the floor.

His mind's eye reread the line: "Mama is dead."

(The bomb went off.)

Valentino kept to his room for three days, trying to make some sense out of life. He had cried till the tears would come no more. Lying on his bed, staring at the ceiling, he kept going over his life with his mother. Those were happy days. There could have been more of them. Why had it had to end so suddenly? There were so many things he had stored in his heart to tell her, things he could not write in letters, but things she would have understood and explained to him.

During his period of mourning he ran into one of his friends, Douglas Gerrard, one of the directors of the Los Angeles Athletic Club. Gerrard liked the olive-skinned young man and felt that all work and no play was bad for a man. He often pleaded with Valentino to join in on some of the fun.

"You always say no," Gerrard said. "This time I'm not asking you, I'm telling you. There's a shindig at the club tomorrow night and there will be people worth meeting there. You're coming, if I have to call for you and. drag you."

"I couldn't. I don't feel very festive. T-there has been a death in the family."

"I'm sorry. But look, that's all the more reason to get out and rub elbows with people. Staying alone doesn't bring a person back. Life goes on, you know."

Valentino agreed. Gerrard had a point. Perhaps he could forget his pain for a few hours.

At the party, Valentino was introduced to Pauline Frederick, a reigning screen star, who was impressed by Valentino's polite Continental manner.

"This is the first time I've ever talked to you or even seen you in person," she said. "Douglas tells me you have been here since 1915. I don't know where you have been hiding, but now that I've met you, I expect to see more of you. I'm having a party that you *must* come to."

Valentino consented. This party hadn't been so bad; for a few minutes he had forgotten that his mother was dead . . . and worse, that he would never see her again.

At the Frederick party, Valentino noticed that almost every Hollywood celebrity was present. Upon entering the finely-furnished, gaily-lit interior of the house, he felt out of place. He had never seen so many low neck lines and bare backs; he had never seen so many jewels outside a jewelry store.

He walked up to several of the small groups which had formed all over the room. Listening to the conversations, he shook his head in bewilderment. It all seemed like such senseless, wasted talk. He quickly found a corner where he could be by himself.

Pauline Frederick moved among the crowd, seeing that everyone was provided for and that glasses remained filled. She approached him and asked what he drank, went off, found him a bottle of wine and a glass, and told him to circulate. Her attention was diverted by a group across the room.

Valentino sipped at his wine and tried to figure out a method of escaping without attracting attention from any of the groups or his hostess. He didn't want the lovely star to think he was ungrateful, but he just could not remain. Rather than to be alone among all these strangers, he preferred the quiet of his own room and his own thoughts.

He had figured out the route to take when Pauline returned to his side.

"I want you to meet someone," she said. She steered him to another corner of the room. "I think you will like her."

Valentino followed her gaze to a couch upon which was sitting one of the loveliest creatures in the room. The girl was all alone, a drink in her hand, her eyes gazing off into space. Valentino's first impression was that here was another like himself—a person lonely in a crowded room.

"This is Jean Acker, one of our rising screen stars," Pauline said. "Jean, this is Rudy Valentino, a comparative newcomer upon the scene, with a great future. Instead of each of you occupying a corner of the room alone, share this one." She left them.

"Sit down," Jean Acker said. She moved over and made room for him.

"Thank you," he said.

There was silence. She continued to gaze over the heads of the other guests. He looked at her every once in a while, trying to fathom her thoughts.

"I gather you don't care much for the party or the partygoers," she said.

"They're all right. The party is gay enough. It is just that I do not speak their language. Why are you here by yourself? Do you dislike them?"

"No, I don't dislike them." She studied his face. "Right now, Rudy, present company excluded, of course, people irritate me. Especially the male element. I came to please Pauline, no other reason."

"I, too," he said solemnly. "I have seen you many times

on the screen. I think you are wonderful.''

She thanked him and asked about his career.

He told her and then said, ''Why are you here alone? You needn't answer that if you prefer not to. It is just that you are so lovely, it is impossible to imagine you as being lonely. For me, it is different. I don't speak the language of these people because I started out speaking a different language. Besides that, I am a newcomer, a comparative nobody. You are somebody.''

''Even someone who is somebody has feelings,'' she said. ''These people either forget that or have never learned it. I . . .'' She stopped and studied his face again. ''I feel outside of it, that's all. I'm lonely and it is no joke. These people expect me to take it lightly. They think that because we earn our living by turning love off and on, we should do it when we aren't working. I'm not built that way.''

''Would you like to dance?'' he asked. He could see that whatever lay behind her statements cut into her deeply. Her eyes were almost swimming in tears.

The intimacy of the dance broke down further barriers. By the time they returned to their seats on the couch, Rudy was telling her all about himself, his dancing, his career, his heartbreaks, his loneliness.

She told him about herself. There had been a man, a wonderful, good-looking and lovable man. They were almost engaged to be married, but something had gone wrong. Now he was gone and she was alone. She couldn't help feeling there would never be another man for her. It was this which made her so unhappy.

''I have had a great loss, too,'' he confided. ''My mother just died.'' He went on to tell her how he felt about his mother's death.

She sat there, listening intently, nodding her head, expressing sympathy, helping. When the party was almost over, he offered to take her home and arranged to see her again. During their conversation, he had felt less alone. He hoped he had made her feel the same way.

They spent many hours together, dining, dancing, talking. She represented a princess out of a storybook to him. He began to think of marriage. Now, with his mother gone, he felt he should have another woman by his side. It was his birthright to have a wife and family. He considered proposing to her, but he remembered her heartache and kept quiet.

Jean looked upon Valentino as a friend, a companion who eased her loneliness and asked nothing in return. He was still a boy, but she enjoyed their hours together.

But one night when he took her home, he kissed her long and hard, and asked her to marry him. She hesitated only a second and said yes.

Both now looked forward to an end of loneliness. Together they would find the bright spots on earth; together they would be happy.

(The soldier races across the battlefield doing what he was trained not to do.)

Everyone loves a lover. Hollywood was no exception. When news of the engagement reached the ears of the movie colony, everyone built fantastic daydreams around the couple. Friends of Jean Acker's got other friends together and arranged for a small but warm reception after the ceremony. Gifts arrived and everyone sent along congratulations.

The wedding took place on November 5, 1919, at the Hollywood Hotel. The bride was flushed and pretty; the groom was flushed and handsome. After the ceremony, the merrymaking began. Norman Kerry was there and wished them all the best. When he could arrange it, he took Rudy aside and tried to discover the place of the honeymoon. Although he didn't succeed, he was happy for his friend.

"To find the right woman at the age of twenty-four is pretty good, Rudy. I hope all your sons look like you and all your daughters look like Jean."

Valentino beamed happily. He had a wife now. The family would follow. Now he would have someone to encourage him and help him, someone to lie by his side and touch him.

The party was gay. Valentino had never enjoyed a party so much. He wanted it to go on and on, everyone enjoying themselves and celebrating the happy union. Jean and he would always go out dancing and having good times. Neither of them would ever again be lonely. They would become one of the happy Hollywood couples that the gossip columnists so loved to write about. Their future was bright. Laughter would fill their lives and their hearts.

Most of the guests had early morning appointments, so the party broke up early. Jean and Rudy said good night to everyone and went to their hotel room. As Jean sat brushing her hair, Valentino went into the dressing room and changed into a robe. He came out, kissed her neck and murmured to her.

"I'll only be a moment," she said. She walked into the dressing room and was gone for a while. When she returned, she was wearing a negligee and was a vision to see.

"You look lovely," he said.

She said nothing. She sat down before the dressing table, picked up her brush and continued to brush her hair. Rudy sat watching, entranced by the movement of her hand and hairbrush along her hair.

Suddenly she put her head down on the table and burst into tears. In a moment, he was beside her, on his knees, trying to discover the reason for her sudden unhappiness.

"I'm sorry," she murmured over and over again. "I didn't mean for this to happen. I thought it might work; I really did. I've been such a fool—at your expense."

"I don't understand, little one. What is it? What have I done?"

"You haven't done anything!" she cried. "It's me, just me. Rudy, I should not have married you. I don't love you. Right now, on our wedding night, all I can think of is him, of his arms, of his lips, of his voice. I tried to force him out of my mind. It didn't work."

"These things take time, Jean. We are both young. We have lots of it. We'll make a good life together."

"No, Rudy, no! It just wouldn't work. I don't know if I will ever get over him. I couldn't be so unfair to you. I could never love you."

Valentino went back to the edge of the bed and sat there. She continued to cry. He could not, he knew, console her. His dream had shattered into a million tiny pieces.

The clock on the bureau ticked away the seconds, tiny

hammer blows in the stillness. He had looked forward to this moment when he would hold her in his arms, tell her of his love for her, and make her feel his love. This was to be the beginning of something wonderful.

He rose, gathered clothes from the closet and went into the dressing room. Fully dressed, without looking in her direction, he headed for the door.

"Good night, Jean. We'll discuss this further in the morning."

A month later, on December 6, the official announcement of their separation appeared in the papers. The gossip columnists speculated about the cause. Most of them made reference to another woman in Valentino's life.

(The soldier makes all the wrong moves.)

As Julio in *The Four Horsemen of the Apocalypse*

RUDOLPH VALENTINO

Valentino (third from the right) with the road show company of *The Masked Model*. He took a part in this show as a means of getting to California.

Jean Acker, his first wife

A great sports enthusiast, Valentino kept in
fine physical shape.

With director Fred Niblo, who gave him his first screen
test and also his big chance in *The Four Horsemen of
the Apocalypse*, which made him a star.

Natacha Rambova, his second wife

Valentino and Rambova

Valentino demonstrates the famous tango from
The Four Horsemen of the Apocalypse with wife
Natacha Rambova.

As a New York boulevardier

CHAPTER EIGHT

VALENTINO buried himself in his work. He no longer cared about the parts he was getting. So what if he was typed as a heavy? Work took his mind off his personal problems.

Valentino landed the role of a heavy in four successive productions. The first two were produced in Hollywood at the Metro studios—*Once to Every Woman*, starring Dorothy Phillips, and *Passion's Playground*, starring Norman Kerry and Katherine MacDonald; in this one Valentino played Norman's brother.

Maxwell Karger, production manager, then moved the entire cast and personnel of the next production, a location picture, to New York for filming. This starred Margaret Namara, with Valentino, of course, as the heavy. It was called *The Great Moment*.

His return to New York, the scene of his early struggles, was also a great moment to him.

He walked the once-familiar streets again—Fifth Avenue, Forty-second, Forty-ninth, Madison Avenue, and especially Broadway. He thought of those war years. Now peace had come to the world, but the end of fighting did not put the world back together as it had been.

He tried to tell himself that he was in a better position than at any time; that he had some sort of purpose to his life—to climb the ladder of motion-picture success. For his work in *The Great Moment* he was paid three hundred and fifty dollars a week. He felt that he could walk the New York streets with the knowledge that, in a measure, he had achieved something worthwhile.

(His enemy . . . compromise.)

But the remembrance of those fresh, young days after his arrival at the gates of America saddened him. Life then had been intriguing, and his discovery of dancing had been a glamorous adventure. He recalled his trembling curiosity about the world and its mysterious moods. Well, life went on; one grew older.

While the picture was in process of production he heard from the director that Metro had decided to make a super-feature and was preparing to spend a great sum of money. They had purchased the film rights to Vicente Blasco Ibáñez's *The Four Horsemen of the Apocalypse*, and casting for the picture was now in progress. Valentino read the book in Spanish and felt that the part of Julio, the young South American tango dancer, was tailor-made for him.

At once he went to the New York office of Metro and talked to Karger. Karger told him politely but firmly that some of the biggest and most successful stars in the film industry were being interviewed for the part; Karger further informed Valentino that with the latter's experience and reputation as a heavy, he could hardly be expected to handle a role like Julio. Valentino insisted, however, that he was sure he could play the part, that he had waited all these years for this opportunity.

Karger shook his head adamantly. "Valentino, you're doing fine in your present roles and you're getting a nice salary. Why don't you stick to that and make a nice living for yourself? You have established a reputation as a heavy, so why not make the most of it? You're trying to hitch your wagon to a star that is entirely out of your reach. You're not the type for Julio, and you know it. Julio is a romantic, gentle, sensitive youth, with an innocent charm. And how do you reconcile that with your villain type?"

"Why can you not make a screen test of me?"

"Sorry, Valentino. You're wasting my time, and yours. Now please get back to your picture. We have a schedule."

"All right. I will continue with *The Great Moment*. I have

to earn my living. But that Julio part—I think you're making a mistake."

He walked out into the New York streets. There was a cold February drizzle but he was unmindful of that. As in the past, whenever he was burdened with some harassing problem, he set out on a walk to think it out.

He walked until he could not take another step.

The role of Julio Desnoyers haunted him like an irrepressible dream. Wherever he went it seemed that he heard a low voice whispering to him: "You are Julio. You are Julio."

That night in his hotel room he hardly slept.

Early the next day he reported on location and *The Great Moment* continued to be filmed against the backdrop of the metropolis.

When it was finished, he called again at the Metro office. Things were beginning to hum that winter of 1920 with the preparations and groundwork for *The Four Horsemen of the Apocalypse*. Publicity releases announcing that Metro was spending a fortune in the production of this film epic appeared in all the newspapers and magazines. Also reports were published to the effect that the role of Julio was still open and that the hunt for a suitable player was in full swing. "Who is going to be Julio?" was the cry on all sides.

At the Metro office Maxwell Karger was still of the same opinion regarding Valentino's suitability. Karger told him in no uncertain terms again: "You are trying to wade in beyond your depth. Pretty soon we'll find some young star for the part—someone who has made a box office name for himself. We can't afford to take a chance with practically an unknown in such a costly production. You can understand that, can't you?"

Valentino nodded. "I suppose you are right. But I have a feeling that I can be Julio."

He left the office disappointed. The one great chance of his career—and it was slipping from his fingers. But surely Karger was right. Why should they give the part to him? Who was he? What had he actually accomplished in motion pictures? Bit parts. Desultory roles of heavies. Little handouts through the years. But nothing noteworthy—nothing really important or vital to the public.

He shook his head, tried to convince himself that the part of Julio was not for him. Karger had said, "Stick to what you're doing and don't grab for that which is out of your reach."

And so, when *The Great Moment* was finished, he accepted still another part as a heavy in a picture called *The Fog*, in which Eugene O'Brien had the leading role. The picture was filmed mostly in New York. Valentino attended to his work and played his part with his usual thoroughness and sincerity.

He had given up hopes of landing the part in *The Four Horsemen of the Apocalypse*. After all, they had made it plain to him he was not wanted in any other role but that of a villain.

Well, he would go on playing these supporting roles and save his money. Eventually he would get out of the film business altogether and buy the farm he had always wanted. One could not go on forever in a haphazard fashion. Inevitably one tired of the same routine of being out of work, of looking for a part, of getting some bit in a picture, then out of work again, with the same cycle repeated. This time he would carry out his plan to break away from the revolving squirrel cage.

(Compromise.)

He walked past the theater marquees at Forty-second and Broadway, and saw a flashing electric sign announcing Mae Murray in *The Delicious Little Devil*. His own name was not mentioned, though he was the leading man. Out of curiosity he bought a ticket and went in to watch his own performance. When it was over he asked the man sitting next to him what he thought of the picture and received the answer: "Fair."

"What do you think of that fellow Valentino?"

"Who?"

"That fellow who played opposite the girl."

"Oh, that one. Okay, I guess—for a foreigner. But that Mae Murray—wasn't she great? Some dish, eh?"

So there it was. He was not yet known to the public. He was still a nonentity. With this revelation he went out into the New York night. It was cold. He drew the blue Chesterfield overcoat closer about him and started up the sidewalk. Snow flurries, spinning eddies of white coldness, made him homesick for sunny California; made him remember the dreams that hadn't come true.

Oh, if he could only find some quiet place where he could go into seclusion and live in absolute peace and tranquility without this continual struggle . . . for what? Money? He spent it as fast as he earned it and in the end he had as much as in the beginning—exactly nothing. He had not been able to save enough to buy the farm. Then why the struggle? The answer was his burning desire to make people see and feel the beauty of life in all its colorful romanticism.

He walked past the brightly-lit shops and restaurants. People hurried past him in both directions. Some of them, he felt sure, had families to go home to—wives to greet them with warm embraces, children to welcome them with eager arms. A wife . . . children . . . home. He had always wanted that above all else. The marriage he had hoped would give this to him had ended before it had begun. Here he was, the same as when he first landed in New York—homeless and alone, with no prospect of a change.

He walked toward Central Park. The electric street lights cast gilded spotlights at the white flurries of snowflakes performing their dance routines. He moved along the paved walkways and passed the spot where he had tended the rose bushes once upon a time, long, long ago.

He had had great aspirations then, and he wondered whether by now he was not disillusioned and somewhat of a failure. After all these years what had he accomplished? A few roles, unimportant, fleeting. What little notice his name had achieved would soon be forgotten. Maybe he would wind up back on Skid Row, back among the flophouses, the cheap bars, the vagrants.

He walked, with heavy steps, back to Broadway. And suddenly he longed for lights, laughter, music, and a girl.

He felt chilled. Snow drops brushed against his face, tender cold kisses.

On impulse, he stepped into a dance hall—The Dance Box. Here he could find the lights, the music, the companionship of young girls—and they were all so pretty. He could not remember ever seeing a girl who was not pretty. He was so love-starved he could have embraced them all and given each a kiss.

He stood in the stag line for a minute or two, then he purchased a strip of tickets, each ticket good for one dance. He approached an attractive gum-chewing blonde and smiled.

"Dance?" he asked.

"Sure, handsome."

He handed her the entire strip of tickets and he danced once more.

The girl in his arms looked up at him. She seemed intrigued by his dancing. Her cheeks were flushed, her blue eyes shone; she chewed her gum faster.

"Boy, can you glide. You're a dream; do you know that?"

"*You* are the dream," he said.

"Say, you're new here, ain't you?" She nestled close against him. He tried to be nonchalant. "Francine's my name. What's yours?"

His reply was hesitant. "Rudy," he said.

"Cute."

He felt revived, like a man rescued out of unfriendly waters.

The next number was a waltz and he did it full justice. As so many times before, he expressed his feelings in the pattern of his dancing. The girl seemed puzzled. She looked up at him.

"I don't know who you are but you sure can dance. There's something about you—say, you ever been on the stage maybe?"

Valentino laughed and would not answer lest he spoil the magic spell. A few moments later he did ask her, "Ever hear of Valentino?"

"Italian, eh? I danced with lots of Italian guys but never heard that name before." She smiled, "Friend of yours?"

"Not exactly," said Valentino, his eyes twinkling, and at the same time recognizing the proof that his name had not reached the public.

With the girl in his arms he forgot the cold loneliness that always seemed to wait for him.

When he came out in the night he felt much better. There was a new, a reborn, strength within him. A little blond angel who chewed gum had made him happy again and he blessed her, whoever she was. She had given him some badly-needed moments of contentment.

During the final days of the shooting of *Fog*, Valentino slipped back into an atmosphere of deep depression. He could not bear to think that the picture was about to wind up and that he would have to start all over again looking for a minor role as a heavy in another picture. How long, he cried to himself, can I keep doing this? Valentino's exercise in self-pity was symptomatic of the moodiness of his character and the inconstancy of his personality. It wasn't long ago that he had welcomed the fact that he could get these roles and resigned himself to the belief that not everyone can be lucky enough to touch the stars. But now he was no longer willing to settle for this second-class status. The conviction that he could and should play Julio, that it was a part tailored just for him, had become an obsession which burned like a branding iron. Why won't they at least give me a chance, he demanded? Why? Why?

Previously, he had regarded Hollywood's policy of limiting foreigners to villain roles as a simple, if foolish, perpetuation of an old box-office custom. Now he began to see it as a symptom of anti-Italian and anti-European prejudice, and to take it as a personal affront. Mostly, he kept his feelings to himself, but now and again on the set he made sarcastic remarks about American democracy which astonished his fellow performers. None of them quite knew what he was getting at, because Valentino would not pursue the subject further—at least not openly. Since he was a man who had never thought deeply about political or social matters, and only half believed what he was trying to tell himself, he was reluctant to verbalize it. His associates on the set decided that this odd Italian had lost himself in his angry villain role . . . he was already known as the kind of dreamy actor who often forgot where make-believe ended and reality began.

Valentino began again to toy with the idea of throwing over his Hollywood career and fulfilling his early ambition of buying a farm. He must have known that by now the idea was impractical for him and that he was too deeply immersed in show business to break from it. Yet he went through the motions of writing letters to the Italian Agricultural Society to ask them what help they would give him in acquiring good acreage in California. Their answer was the same as before. If he had enough money for the down payment, and was sincere in the interest he had expressed, they would help him to secure the right site. It is doubtful whether Valentino would have pursued his inquiry beyond the conversational stage in any case, but he dropped it abruptly when he received a phone call in his hotel room one morning.

It was the most important phone call of his life.

The voice at the other end belonged to a woman. It was a pleasant voice, but authoritative.

"Hello," it said, "this is June Mathis. I would like to have a talk with you, Mr. Valentino. Could you come down to the local Metro office?"

Valentino gripped the phone as if he were magnetized to it. June Mathis was one of Hollywood's best screen writers. More important, June Mathis had written the script for *The Four Horsemen of the Apocalypse*. Why did she want to talk to him?

He wondered as he dressed with more than his usual meticulous care. He put on a blue serge suit, and fitted a white silk handkerchief in his lapel pocket. Then he donned his blue Chesterfield overcoat, white silk scarf and gray Homburg hat, and went out.

When he reached the Metro office, June Mathis was waiting for him. She smiled, extended her small delicate hand—a hand that wielded so mighty a pen.

"Rudolph Valentino, I'm glad you've come. Shall we go into the private office?"

Karger was there, a perplexed look on his face. He nodded to Valentino but said nothing.

Valentino followed Miss Mathis' slight figure into the inner office. She closed the door. She went behind a mahogany desk and sat down. She looked like a little girl behind the big desk.

She asked Valentino to be seated. Then she studied him for a long moment.

"Perfect," she said.

"I do not understand."

"You are going to play Julio."

(The soldier earned a medal.)

CHAPTER NINE

IN the little Metro office high in a Manhattan skyscraper Valentino sat rigid in his seat, stunned by what he had just heard.

He slowly recovered from the impact of the announcement. He could only stare gratefully at his benefactress, the little lady behind the big desk, who meant to chart a new future for him.

"I don't know what to say . . ." began Valentino.

"Don't say anything now. But listen . . ."

She rose and paced the floor. Once or twice she went to the window and looked down into the street far below. It was winter in New York and the big city was churning with people and traffic. She turned to Valentino, her lips forming into a reassuring little smile.

"You, Rudy, are going to begin an entirely new course of life. This picture, with you in the leading role, will focus public attention upon you. It means that your character, your private life, will be in the revealing spotlight of publicity. You may be acclaimed, idolized. I'm sure you won't let that go to your head and lose sight of the fundamental truths. I must tell you I had quite a struggle to land this part for you. In Hollywood they wouldn't listen to me. They told me I was crazy, that I was jeopardizing the investment of a fortune by selecting someone who was not a proven success. I explained to them that the role of Julio demanded a Latin type, and one who understood and could dance the tango. And you, Rudy, in my estimation, fill the bill. After hours of wrangling they agreed, but with reservations. They as much as told me that if my decision is a wrong one, if it damages the production in any way, my career in Hollywood will no longer be worth very much.

"So you see, Rudy, I've staked everything on your playing this role as it should be played and I count on you—I know that you won't let me down."

Valentino rose. He was trembling. This was a tremendous responsibility. He saw now so clearly that there were others involved in what had been a personal dream for him. Here was a woman who had revolutionized the art of screen writing, who had built up a great career, gambling it all on this one film production involving him. For a moment he felt weak. He was almost afraid to accept the burden she held out to him.

But then he remembered his own dream regarding this role. He had wanted this so badly—now it was his. This was the moment of decision.

"Miss Mathis, I will not disappoint you. I promise."

"Thank you, Rudy. I know you will do your best."

They looked at each other in a common bond of understanding, and June said, "The heads of Metro have given me authority to suggest and to help select the people to play the various characters in this production. I was stymied, I must admit, by the role of Julio. It was obvious that an American type could not possibly do justice to this part. Somehow I never thought of you, perhaps because I always associated you with the heavy roles which you were doing. Then I happened to see a movie, something called *The Eyes of Youth*. Maybe you remember it. You had a very small bit in it. But I was charmed by your personality, by that brooding expression that flits across your face, and there, suddenly, I saw Julio. I contacted the studio executives and they told me you were in New York with Mr. Karger, working in *The Great Moment* and *The Fog*. So I chased you all the way here to corner you before you made any other commitments. And now the next thing, of course, will be the signing of the contract and you will be Julio in *The Four Horsemen of the Apocalypse*.''

"Miss Mathis, I do not know how to thank you. All these years I have been waiting. . . .''

"Well now you can stop waiting and start working on your role. Let's go to lunch and we'll discuss it some more.''

After they parted that afternoon, Valentino was literally bursting with emotion. He wanted to cry out to all the city, "Look at me! I am Julio! I am Julio in *The Four Horsemen of the Apocalypse*!'' He wanted to take all New York into his embrace and thank the inhabitants. He looked up at the theater marquees, envisioning his own name in electric lights, flashing to all his newborn fame. He walked along Broadway, the Street of the Famed, and he felt a kinship with everyone he passed.

Once, back in the long ago, he had looked upon the theatrical empire as an embattled citadel with the gates locked tight against all newcomers. And then along had come a gentle little goddess, by name June Mathis, who had placed within his grasp the golden key.

That night he celebrated. He visited his old haunts at Maxim's, he danced once more with those ladies who were eager to obtain a dance partner. He drank champagne. He laughed. And when he thought of the dark hatred he had only recently nurtured against the entire entity known as Hollywood, he felt a little ashamed.

Two days later, Valentino boarded a train for California. He had with him the script of *The Four Horsemen of the Apocalypse* and while speeding westward, he read and reread the script. He lived the part of Julio, laughed with him, wept with him, and at the end fought with him in that bloody battle of Armageddon.

There were times in that train coach when the other passengers were puzzled by his behavior. He once replied to a fellow passenger, when names were exchanged in the course of conversation, "My name is Julio Desnoyers.''

"Nice name. Spanish?''

"Partly," said Valentino, then laughed to himself.

When the train neared Los Angeles and Hollywood, Valentino had become Julio. He came to understand Julio's feelings, his loneliness as he roamed the great Argentine pampas, and later, when he had gone to Europe, his loneliness even in that gay city of Paris, an existence that in certain aspects paralleled Valentino's.

Who was Julio Desnoyers? He was created in the novel by the renowned Vicente Blasco Ibáñez.

It was the story of a young man who grew up in the house of his grandfather, a rich landowner on the Argentine pampas who looked upon Julio as his favorite in perference to his other grandsons. The grizzled old man found in the handsome Julio the spirit of his own long-lost youth; he laughed with him, and spent many happy hours in Julio's company. The other grandsons were jealous of the lavish attention bestowed upon Julio, but they could do nothing against the all-powerful king of the pampas.

Julio was given everything he wanted, with no responsibility attached. He was encouraged to enjoy life as he saw fit. His every whim was gratified; he grew up in an atmosphere of luxury, and eventually, boredom. He found his diversions in the cafés and dancing places of the Argentine towns and cities, and he gained a reputation as an expert dancer of the tango. Often he snapped and looped a long whip about some heavily painted tight-gowned creature and drew her to him as a dancing partner.

Meanwhile, his cousins of predominantly German blood were busily engaged in practicing soldiering as rumors increased of a war involving Germany.

It was apparent to the members of the clan that the Old Man was planning to leave his entire estate to his favorite, Julio; but after the grandfather's death no will could be found and the estate was divided among the individual members of the family, Julio receiving a sufficiently large share to make him comfortable—if he was careful—for the rest of his life.

Julio found himself drifting restlessly, aimlessly. Now that his grandfather was gone, he had no sense of attachment to anything and so he journeyed to France, the native land of his father. Here he delved into opportunities for pleasure and excitement as he found them.

As was the fashion with a great many rich sons who came to Paris, he took up painting but soon grew tired of it, for he had no real talent or desire to become an artist. In the meantime, he continued dancing at various cafés on the Left Bank, in Montmartre, teaching beautiful young French ladies the technique of the tango.

At the outbreak of the World War in 1914, he met and fell deeply in love with Marguerite Laurier, who returned his love. But when her husband left for the front, she turned away from Julio in loyalty to him. Julio, alone again, saw all about him the young and old going off to the slaughter in the fight for their homeland.

He continued to assure himself that this was of no consequence to him since he was an Argentinian and need not mix in the affairs of the French.

One morning, accidentally, he met Marguerite Laurier on the street. She was in tears; she told him that her husband had been returned to her—blind. This and the other sufferings of an impoverished people struggling for their very lives awoke in Julio a great hatred for the war and its consequences. He joined the French forces and after a brief period of training was sent to the front.

There, in a muddy trench during a charge into an enemy sector, he came face no face with one of his German cousins, now his foe . . . just another soldier, who raised his gun and pulled the trigger, and the handful of dreams that was Julio lay heaped in the mud. . . .

And over the land, created in the beginning to be bounteous and fair, thundered the galloping hoofs of the Four Horsemen: Famine, Pestilence, War and Death.

CHAPTER TEN

WHEN Valentino reached Hollywood, there was a fresh surprise waiting for him. His leading lady in the picture, playing the role of Marguerite Laurier, would be the friend who had given him companionship and encouragement when he needed it most—Alice Taffe, now known as Alice Terry.

He sought her out immediately when he heard the news. They literally fell into one another's arms in a burst of mutual excitement and joy. On the evening before they were to report together on the set, they took a ride around Hollywood. Now the city which had filled them both with such discouragement in the past had an intoxicating allure for them and they wanted to drink it in deeply. High up in the Hollywood hills they left the car, walked together hand in hand toward a rise of land, and looked down at the flickering lights of Los Angeles and the movie city itself.

"Can you believe it?" Valentino exclaimed to his companion for perhaps the twentieth time that evening. "The two of us—co-starring in one of the biggest movie epics ever made? Pinch me, squeeze me, bite me, cut me . . . do something to me to prove it's all real and that the whole idea will not vanish in the morning mist!"

Alice laughed happily. "I don't want to cut you, Rudy; you might become infected and then what would happen to our picture? But it *is* real, Rudy . . . it is . . . it is! . . . And there'll be many more wonderful things happening in the future to both of us . . . but most of all to you, Rudy, because for the first time you have a part in a picture that seems to have been created for your particular talents and will give you a chance to pour out all that emotion that's bursting inside you. When the world sees this picture, they're really going to awaken to the name of Valentino. And Rudy dear, I want you to reach out for all the happiness that can be yours. No more fits of melancholia, no more circles of sadness under your eyes, no more burying yourself in your little room to brood and to write sad poems!''

They talked at length of the early days of dreams and struggles and disappointments, of Valentino's spells of despair and his recurring talk of giving up the film industry to become a simple farmer. She reminded him of all the times that she had tried to instill in him a sense of hope and courage when he had been all too ready to write himself off as an inadequate failure. ''Well, there were so few who had any faith and belief in me,'' Valentino reminisced. ''Just you . . . Norman . . . my mother, of course. When she died, I felt I had lost my anchor, that there was nothing for me to do but drift away . . . that there was no future for me that would amount to anything.''

''But she died still having faith in you, still believing you were destined for great things,'' Alice said. ''You must never forget that, Rudy, you must always strive to justify that wonderful faith. You have the capacity to do it, if you will only learn to take temporary setbacks as an inescapable part of living.''

When they parted at Alice's house, they kissed tenderly. The next morning, Alice observed, they would meet again not as Rudy and Alice but as Marguerite and Julio.

''It will take a great deal of work and self-discipline for me to grow into my part, but it will be no problem for you, Rudy,'' she pointed out. ''You are already Julio. I think perhaps you were even born Julio!''

Alice's opinion was soon shared by Rex Ingram, who had been selected to direct the filming of the picture. In the beginning, he and June Mathis intended to build the picture faithfully around the Ibáñez novel and to portray the characters precisely as they appeared in the book. But when they studied the early rushes, they saw that Valentino was bringing much more depth and fervid sincerity to his role than anyone else in the cast. The romantic wistfulness and the pathetic aimlessness that was Julio's was being etched so vividly into the celluloid it gave them goose pimples. They decided to capitalize on this unique portrayal by rewriting some of the script to make Valentino's role even more important than originally anticipated and, by the same token, to take away some of the strength and importance of the other roles.

Ingram went even further. He gave Valentino leeway to express his emotions without directorial interference. For an accomplished and experienced director to permit such freedom on the part of an actor who was not even a star was unprecedented in Hollywood. Ingram had never done anything like this before, but he felt this was a special situation and a special performance. He later told the Metro studio brass, "I never saw an actor as dedicated to a role as this one."

The force and impact of the picture were immediately apparent to the Metro executives when they sat down to the first showing of the production. They agreed unanimously that it would sweep the country and that June Mathis had been invested with a touch of genius when she insisted on casting Valentino as Julio. The foreigner who only recently had been a very minor entity in their eyes suddenly had grown seven feet tall. They showered him with the kind of adulation which bewildered him. And he began to receive invitations to parties at the homes of the elite of the film capital.

It was Alice who urged Valentino to accept these invitations. He had found himself ill at ease at the few Hollywood parties he had attended previously and had done all he could to avoid follow-up invitations. But Alice felt he was becoming too important a personality to persist in behaving like an aloof and suspicious outlander. "Besides, when you're alone you brood and that's not good for you," she told him. "Go out and have fun. You don't have to take these people and their antics seriously. Go there to laugh—but don't let them know you're laughing *at* them."

Hollywood by now was building up a reputation for parties that were wild and unsavory. Newspaper columns had been filled with descriptions of orgies and debaucheries. Alice assured Valentino that the press was full of fanciful exaggerations. But the parties he attended very nearly fulfilled the lurid reputation of their press clippings. He was repelled by them and although he had shown as Julio that he could vividly act a part he believed in, he was not good enough an actor offstage to depict a man enjoying himself when in fact he was nauseated by everything he saw around him. He decided he would have to stay away from these giddy worshippings of Baal even at the risk of maintaining his reputation as an anti-social oddball.

As expected, *The Four Horsemen* was an immediate success wherever it was shown. The studio decided to release it in stages, so that it was first shown only in the big cities of the East. In the sophisticated centers of New York, Boston, and Philadelphia, theaters fought for the right to exhibit it. Newspaper critics enthusiastically praised and singled out for special praise the new personality named Valentino who played the lonely, handsome Argentine tango dancer. Movie patrons formed long lines at the box office patiently waiting to buy tickets.

Back in Hollywood Valentino was given his next assignment, the lead opposite the beauteous Alice Lake in *Uncharted Seas*. His role was another foreign characterization.

For his work in *The Four Horsemen* he had received three hundred and fifty dollars a week. After the picture was released in the East and tasted initial success, he felt he should be paid more money, for after all most Hollywood stars were enjoying salaries of from one to five thousand dollars a week.

He visited the office of the Metro production manager, Maxwell Karger.

"Yes, Valentino?" Karger's voice was crisp. Always the hard-core business man; his code was ever the balance sheet.

"Mr. Karger, any chance of a raise in salary now?"

"A raise?" Karger shook his head. "My dear Valentino,

you don't realize what *The Four Horsemen* cost. It practically devoured our reserves. And what's wrong with three hundred and fifty dollars a week? Besides, you'll be working pretty steady now."

"Yes, but others in my class are getting so much more."

"They are proven stars—box-office names. In your case *The Four Horsemen* film has only been released in a limited area. Suppose we wait and see what happens."

"Which means no raise."

Karger nodded. "Correct. Take my advice; be patient."

Valentino went out of the office, momentarily discouraged, but soon able to resign himself to the fact that his raise could not be long in coming. When *The Four Horsemen* was released all over the country, it was sure to bring huge mounds of profits into the Metro coffers and the studio would have to be more generous in the matter of salaries.

Even on his present salary, he felt sure he could now begin to build up a balance in his bank account. But instead he found his money going out as fast as it came in. June Mathis had advised him to be careful about handing out loans to people who might not pay him back, but he found himself still unable to refuse them. This habit, together with his zest for buying expensive clothing and the expense of a new hobby (that of acquiring costly antique swords and pistols), kept him in a position where he was barely able to make ends meet.

In *The Four Horsemen*, Valentino had learned the art of expressing deep emotion with a minimum of physical display. He extended and refined this technique in *Uncharted Seas*. This new style added a quiet dignity to the picture. It was a style which Valentino would expand on in the productions that were yet to come and which would become a future trademark of all Valentino movies. It was received so favorably that other actors followed suit and the old method of using emphatic physical gestures and various kinds of straining effects fell into disrepute.

CHAPTER ELEVEN

ALTHOUGH Valentino had gained prestige and attention in Hollywood as a result of his work in *The Four Horsemen*, he had not yet shattered the movie colony's taboo against "foreign types." He was not yet accepted as a star—either financially or artistically—though his acting ability and appeal could not be overlooked.

The studio heads resolved the artistic problem by using Valentino in parts which called for a "foreign type." He was no longer to be wasted as a villain, but lead or second roles had to be found for him which suited a foreign characterization. Hence, his selection to play in *Uncharted Seas*. His type was also to win him the second lead in one of Hollywood's classics, *Camille*.

The immortal Nazimova, the great tragedienne, had seen Valentino on the set of *Uncharted Seas* and decided he should play Armand to her Camille.

Valentino was, of course, ecstatic about playing the role. All he had to do to get it was pass the test—gaining the consent of Nazimova's art director, Natacha Rambova. Natacha made all the vital decisions for all of Nazimova's pictures. For *Camille* she was having a particularly hard time casting the role of Armand. The actor had to be just right.

When Valentino met Natacha Rambova, he wasn't "just right" for the part—he was bundled in a fur-lined coat and was wearing thick-soled, high-laced boots. Flakes of mica (imitation snow) still lay upon his eyelashes. He had just finished shooting a scene in *Uncharted Seas* and had rushed across the studio lot for the meeting with Nazimova and her art director. He was perspiring freely and the make-up streaked his face.

Natacha walked around him, slowly, raised an eyebrow in Nazimova's direction, nodded and disappeared.

"You've got the job!" Nazimova said.

Valentino was happy. He didn't know why he had received the role, but he was glad to get it. From the first moment he saw Natacha, he was entranced. Her dark, flowing hair encircled a delicate face. Her blue eyes were like rare jewels set off by her soft white skin. As Nazimova expressed it to a Hollywood columnist, "You should have seen him! He stood there staring at her as though he had never seen a beautiful woman in his life."

Natacha Rambova was a recognized genius in Hollywood. Perhaps she was accorded the title of genius because many didn't understand her work. She was years ahead of her time in set and costume designs. She was daring and original, tireless and independent. She was good and she knew it. She did not need others to praise her to recognize her own talents.

She was an American, born Winifred Shaunessey in Salt Lake City. Her mother's remarriage—to Richard Hudnut, the cosmetics tycoon—gave Winifred money and the opportunity to develop her latent artistic leanings.

The newly-formed family traveled throughout Spain, France, Italy and England, where the girl spent hours in museums studying paintings, sculpture and tapestries. The girl decided to dedicate her life to art.

Europe pleased Winifred. After attending school in England, she turned to the study of ballet. She became a protégée of the great Kosloff of the Imperial Russian Ballet. He promised to make a great dancer of her, and she spared no effort in constant practice and dedication. She had to be the best. Being merely great represented compromise in purpose. Under Kosloff's direction, she achieved grace of movement. She took the professional name of Natacha Rambova, because she felt Winifred Shaunessey did not have a truly artistic sound.

She grew from an attractive girl into a striking woman. While others thought of playing, be it with dolls or men, Natacha was too busy broadening herself artistically. She met painters—some good, some bad—and learned what she could from them. Fascinated by blending colors, she took up painting, which she found an extremely satisfying hobby.

The Kosloff Group went on tour in America. Natacha was Kosloff's dancing partner and they received great acclaim. But Natacha found Hollywood and felt that in Hollywood there would be an outlet for her creative abilities. She searched for design work with one of the major studios.

On one of her visits to Metro, Natacha met and became friends with Alla Nazimova. Nazimova went to the heads of the studio and persuaded them to give Natacha a chance. Nazimova thought of Natacha as a genius and, for that reason, she allowed Natacha to take charge of casting and production for her pictures. Nazimova never argued with Natacha, who was cold in her fury and usually correct in her judgments.

"I'm so glad Natacha approves of you as Armand," Nazimova said.

Valentino went back to finish *Uncharted Seas*. He was anxious and excited about *Camille*. The picture would be mainly a vehicle for Nazimova, but he didn't care.

Getting *Camille* underway was not as simple as Nazimova had believed it would be. Natacha was in a hurry to get started, but Metro wanted Valentino's chores to be completed in *Uncharted Seas*. June Mathis, the director of the picture, was willing to allow stoppage of her picture for awhile, but Metro stood firm. Natacha was finally able to speed up production of *Seas* by three weeks.

Finally, Nazimova and her group were all set. Valentino was thrilled, mainly because of the opportunity to be near Natacha. He seemed to lose something of his ease of manner in her presence; even his conversational style became somewhat halting, so awed was he by her personality, by the evidence of her artistic integrity. With her, art was supreme, and all else had to bow to it.

Nazimova's husband, Charles Bryant, did not exactly

approve of the idea of co-starring Valentino in *Camille*. He looked upon Valentino with a feeling of uneasiness, not quite understanding the European mannerisms, the suavity of this new star. This apparent jealousy on the part of her husband gave Nazimova a feeling of security; it was proof that Charles was obviously in love with her. But she assured her husband that she had picked Valentino as Armand because she thought he would enhance the quality of the picture. She further explained to Charles that actually Valentino had succumbed to the charms of Natacha Rambova, her art director. This seemed to satisfy Charles.

Meanwhile, Natacha could feel Valentino's admiring eyes upon her whenever he was near. During story conferences, if Valentino was present, he always managed to sit near Natacha, to pull out her chair when she rose and hurry ahead of her to open doors. Natacha was very busy with her work. She had no time for men and was surprised Valentino could not see it. She did not encourage Valentino in his advances but neither did she take the time to discourage him.

She had to admit, however, that she began to feel a certain sense of pleasure in being courted. His eyes, always so tender when he looked at her, made her aware that she was a woman. This alarmed her, and subconsciously she built up her defenses to protect her first love—her career.

The long-delayed production of *Camille* was started.

Valentino followed Nazimova's instructions without protest. The first thing was a new hair-do. Armand, a French country lad, certainly would not appear with slicked-down hair; his hair would be curly, ruffled. Natacha took him to her newly acquired bungalow and sat him on a kitchen chair. She gave him a shampoo that took the glossy straightness out of his hair. Then she applied heated curling irons. Before long, Valentino had curly hair in keeping with the naïveté of Armand. Contrary to Natacha's fear, he did not seem to mind.

As the first sequences were filmed, Valentino seemed to be Armand, just as in *The Four Horsemen* he had been Julio. It was always this way with him. He put his whole self into a role, and he became the living character.

He continued to do little things for Natacha. He began to

89

bring her flowers. Natacha seemed embarrassed at first with all this attention on his part. She was deeply immersed in her work, with little time for romantic interludes, but she thought it expedient not to offend the leading man in the picture.

When she worked late on the set Valentino stayed around until she was ready to leave, to give her safe conduct home. He bought a used Buick and drove Natacha to her bungalow, or anywhere she desired to go.

Once in the car, Valentino would sit behind the wheel and drive slowly, so as to extend the drive to Natacha's bungalow. Natacha sat at the other end of the seat, her dark hair against the back of the seat, her eyes shut, her mind busy with her work at the studio. She rarely spoke to him before they arrived at her house, then she would thank him and say good night. He would tire of the role of chauffeur, she thought. But she was surprised each night to find him still there, patiently waiting for her to get ready to go home.

One night she leaned her head against the upholstery and turned to look at him. Obviously he would continue to make a fool of himself. She couldn't understand why; there must be a great demand for him at social gatherings. Why was he doing it?

"Why what?" he asked her.

She hadn't realized she had spoken aloud.

"Why do you bother wasting your time waiting for me every night?"

"I don't waste my time. You are worth waiting for."

"Life is very short. Time is very valuable. You just sit and wait, doing nothing."

"I do something. I read or I think about you."

"That's a waste of time. I don't want you to think about me, but I am sure there are lots of young women who would be happy to be the object of your thoughts. I don't have time for such things. So you are wasting your time."

"I don't want to think about other women; I want to think about you. It gives me great happiness to admire you; there is much about you to be admired. You are like all the women in the world to me—combined. You have intelligence, beauty—"

"Don't talk that way to me, Rudy. You have to place more value on your time. You have so much to do. Your career is just beginning. You have to develop yourself. Women are beginning to look for pictures starring Rudolph Valentino. That's promising."

"Do you think I do good work for the screen?"

"No doubt about it. But you have so much to learn. You are very young. Just a boy, in fact."

Valentino interrupted her. "I am a man, Natacha. I ceased being a boy a long time ago."

Natacha closed her eyes. He didn't know if she was back in her creative realm or what. He was content with the silence. They had spoken only for a few minutes, but it was a sign of progress.

He drew up before her bungalow, a neat white and green house with a well-kept lawn, rosebushes, and flower beds. He helped her out of the car and walked her to the front door.

"Your flowers are well-kept," he said.

"I like them," she murmured.

"I am very good at gardening. If you would like, I will take it over and produce a lawn as beautiful as its owner."

"You're impossible, Rudy," she said. "How will making my lawn beautiful fulfill you in your art?"

"The most important thing to me is to be with you. When I am away from you, I count each second till I see you again. I don't mind that I sometimes for hours see nothing but the top of your head, and then on the drive home you close your eyes and drift away. You are beside me. That is fulfillment."

She dismissed him with: "If you want to, you can plant some more rosebushes."

Even though she had closed the door, he stood there. A thin crescent of gold was suspended above the horizon, winking stars about it. The gentle breeze blowing in from the Pacific carried the scent of rose petals to his nose.

"Goodnight, beloved," he whispered. He crawled into his car and drove home at a snail's pace.

The next morning on the set, it was business as usual. Natacha greeted him as she always had, with an order to do something or other. He, like the others, hurriedly obeyed the command.

The filming of *Camille* was proceeding smoothly. Under Natacha's strong rule, everyone worked in unison. Natacha was especially concerned with this picture. She wanted it to be a work of art. She wanted it to reach out and stir the emotions of every member of the audience. With Nazimova as the star and Valentino as co-star, everyone felt the casting was superb. The rushes were excellent, and the studio heads were well satisfied.

CHAPTER TWELVE

NAZIMOVA was not normally a busybody. But she was a person who could not stand by and watch someone be hurt. Although she had promised herself she would allow true love, or whatever it was Rudy felt for Natacha, to take its own course, she felt she had to speak to him again.

"We are having lunch together today," she told Valentino. "Just you and me."

He agreed readily. At the studio commissary they chose sandwiches and beverages and walked to a table for two in a corner away from the other diners.

"How are you making out with our mutual friend?"

"I'm making progress. She sometimes talks to me on our way home."

"You call that progress! Oh, Rudy, I wish that I were unattached and that you felt that way about me. I could appreciate it. Natacha? Never!"

"I can be patient when I have to be. She's worth waiting for."

"I don't know if you will listen to me or not, Rudy, but I do have a suggestion. It may help you. One thing I know is how a woman reacts to certain things. I am not sure of Natacha's feminine instincts, but it is worth a try. Are you willing?"

"Let me hear your idea first."

"It's simple. All you have to do is stay away from her for a while. When you first started waiting for her, she took it for granted. Now she expects you to be there. Do the unexpected. Don't be there for a few weeks. Perhaps she will think about it and even miss it. There is nothing that makes a woman think more than to have something she took for granted suddenly disappear.''

''Do you think it will work?''

''I know it would work on me.''

''All right, I'll do it. But what will I do instead?''

''I don't know. Go out and have some fun. Stay home. Whatever you do, don't let her know that you are just teaching her a lesson. I will tell her—if she asks—that you seem to be enjoying a social whirl. Perhaps I will even hint about another woman. Jealousy is a good emotion for a woman who is undecided.''

''You're a good friend. Thank you.''

That night Valentino left the lot with the other actors. He did not return to pick Natacha up. If she felt anything she didn't show it the next day. Her blue eyes looked at him steadily and she greeted him as she had always done.

Valentino felt himself wavering. He was suffering by staying away from her, and suppose she felt nothing more toward him because of his absence? He would then have hurt only himself. But he had thought it good advice when Nazimova offered it. He would continue to follow it.

Nazimova decided it might help if she herself spoke to Natacha. She intercepted Natacha on the *Camille* set.

''Natacha, Rudy is in love with you.''

''Infatuation, nothing else. In his mind he has created an image of a goddess which certainly bears no resemblance to me.''

''Have you tried stopping it?''

''I've tried. I've thought of different things to do, to say. He is so earnest, so persistent. I don't want to hurt him with a point-blank dismissal.''

''Whatever you do, Natacha, don't send him away. It will break his heart. It may interfere with his work.''

A few days later, Valentino approached Nazimova.

''Is anything coming of my staying away?'' he asked.

''I cannot tell for sure. You know the way she is. I thought

I noticed something, but I couldn't be sure. How long has it been?''

"Four days and fourteen hours," he answered without hesitation.

She laughed heartily. "Stick to it. At least another week. If there are no results by then, I'll let you know, and you can do as you like."

Valentino agreed. But when Friday came, he hesitated. The start of a weekend always made him feel more lonely. He returned to the studio lot around nine. There was a light in Natacha's office, as he knew there would be. He sat in the Buick until the light went out, then he gunned the motor and roared off.

He was driving down Hollywood Boulevard when an ice cream soda sign attracted his attention. He parked the car and went into the ice cream parlor. He was drinking his soda when a woman sat in the booth across from him. She looked familiar. The dark hair, the small nose. Of course!

"Teodolinda, how are you?" he said as he sat in her booth.

"Rudolph Valentino! How are you, Rudy? My God. How long has it been since you first came to Los Angeles with Jolson's troupe? Let me look at you! You've matured a bit. If anything, you've become even better-looking. My God, this is a surprise!"

He laughed happily. After months of being rejected, here was a woman who was overjoyed to see him. "What are you doing here?"

"I'm spending a week in the California sunshine before I go back East—for good."

"Are you giving up show business?"

"Well, you might say show business has given me up. I never was much good, just another pretty face among all the others. Let's not talk about me. Tell me about yourself. I've seen you in several pictures. I hoped I would meet you again."

She reached across the table and took his hand.

She continued. "Every time we stayed over for a while in this part of the country, I have looked for you. Once, a few months back, I even went to the Metro lot. I was told you were in New York."

"Yes. We did some location scenes. . . . You look wonderful, you know. I think you have gained a little weight."

She chuckled. "Don't remind me."

"Don't be silly. It looks very good. It is more alluring. Your face has filled out a little more. . . . What have you planned for tonight? Have you eaten? Would you like to go out dancing?"

"It so happens I have nothing planned for the night. It is kind of late, though. Have you eaten? No? Look, I'm staying around the corner in a friend's place. Come back with me and I'll hustle up some food for us. We have lots to talk about."

"All right. Fine, in fact." He paid for their sodas and they walked to her friend's apartment.

"My friend is away. She went to San Francisco for the weekend. I was at loose ends and feeling a bit lonely. I'm so glad I decided to go out for a soda."

"Tonight was my lucky night, too. I might have just gone home after work and gone to bed. Then we would have missed each other again."

"I'm glad we didn't." She stepped out of her shoes, stood on her toes and put her arms around his neck. "You haven't changed at all, Rudy. I still find you one of the most exciting men in the world. When I see you in a movie, I get goosepimples even when you're playing the villain."

"And that's often," he said. He kissed her and she drew him into the kitchen.

"Make yourself comfortable while I cook the steak. Why don't you make us a drink and turn on some music?"

He went to the table with the liquor on it and made a highball for her. "Have you wine?" he asked.

She took a bottle from a cabinet and handed it to him.

After eating, they sat side by side, he drinking wine, she drinking rye. They filled each other in on their lives since their first meeting. His sounded like a success story; hers was different. She wasn't sorry for herself. She said she had never thought she would make good. She didn't have the necessary drive or ambition, she said. She also confessed to liking to have some fun sometimes. Show business stifled her.

"Let's not talk any more," she said suddenly. "I've thought of you so many times. I've remembered that time on the train so often. I find it hard to believe that you are here with me. And what are we doing? We're sitting and talking as though we have not been separated at all. You've kissed me only once, even though we've been together since a little after nine. That's three hours, much too long."

She threw her arms around his neck and leaned heavily against him. He reached behind her head and loosened her hair. The black hair flowing down her back still reminded him of Teodolinda's, and now of Natacha's, too. Nazimova would approve of his actions tonight, if she knew. He kissed Teodolinda tenderly. Soon the kisses were less tender and more passionate. Through half-closed eyes, Teodolinda surveyed him.

"I want to change into something more comfortable," she said. "I won't be long."

Valentino ended up spending the entire weekend with her. On Sunday morning, he suggested that they take a ride together and go swimming.

"No," she said. "I can't be seen with you or I'll have all sorts of problems."

"What does that mean?"

"I told you last night that I love you, Rudy. I meant it. Ever since we first met, I was yours for the asking. I knew you wouldn't ever ask. First, I'm older than you are. Second, I guess I'm just not your type." She put her fingers across his lips. "Don't say anything, Rudy. Please. Let me talk." She lighted a cigarette. "I told you I'm going back East at the beginning of the week. I am. I'm getting married."

"Married!" The word exploded from him. "Married and you are spending a weekend with me, like this. I—I don't know what to say."

"You'll read it on the front page of every newspaper next week. 'Millionaire Weds Show Girl.' " She pulled him close. "This weekend has nothing to do with my marriage to him. If anything, this weekend will make everything more bearable. I don't know if I can make you understand, but I want to try. I have been lonely and I have been poor. By marrying him, I will have a husband and I will be rich.''

"Who is he?''

When she named him, Valentino whistled through his teeth.

"I'll make him happy. I'll be happy. It takes very little to make me happy. The fact that he loves me and has millions of dollars only makes it easier for me. I keep wondering what would have happened if I had met you after I'd been married. Now, with this weekend, I don't have to wonder. This is our good-by. For me, it's good-by to a dream.''

"I'll try to make it a worthwhile weekend,'' he said.

"You have already, my darling. But don't stop trying.''

They parted on Monday morning. Valentino went directly from her apartment to the studio. If they ever met in the future, he would have to call her by a different name, but in his heart, there would always be a secret place reserved for his grown-up Teodolinda, the woman who had twice lifted him up when he felt insecure, the woman who had made him feel like a man.

He was full of fun on the set that day. Once, as he turned away from Nazimova, a smile upon his face, he saw Natacha looking at him. When his eyes met hers, she turned away. He laughed aloud.

Valentino stayed away from Natacha for the rest of the week. On Thursday of that week he opened his paper and saw the headline: MILLIONAIRE WEDS SHOW GIRL. He smiled to himself. There was a picture of his Teodolinda, smiling happily and winking. He felt, somehow, that the wink was meant for him. He cut the picture out of the paper and kept it in his bureau drawer, under his shirts.

The next Saturday morning dawned brightly. The sun shone and the birds sang. Valentino got dressed and drove to Natacha's bungalow. He hadn't seen her for two weeks, except the times they met on the set or around the studio. In the back seat, he had a rosebush, his excuse for seeing her today.

The house was quiet when he arrived. He looked at his

98

watch. It was barely 7:30 A.M. He set about planting the rosebush.

"Who is out there?" Natacha's voice called.

"It's your gardener, ma'am," he called back.

A shadow appeared behind the living room window. "Rudy, you idiot. It's hardly daybreak."

"Because I am up doesn't mean you must be. Go back to sleep."

"How can I with all the noise you are making?"

"I am almost through. I will pack up and leave now."

There was silence. Soon she appeared at the door, wearing a bathrobe, her hair in braids.

"Have you eaten breakfast?" she asked. "As long as I am awake, I may as well make you some. Come in."

He entered the house and smiled cheerfully. "May I wash up?" he asked, indicating his dirty hands.

She stared at his hands for a moment and showed him to the bathroom. She couldn't explain it to herself, but the dirt on his hands somehow made him more real to her. Before this she had thought of him as one of her materials, something with which to create.

"I find it strange to see you with dirty hands," she said.

"Why?" he asked. "There is nothing as clean as earth. Anyway, soap and water will wash it away."

"Do you think soap and water wash everything away?"

"Not everything," he answered.

She broke eggs into a frying pan.

"Then why do you make some of the pictures you do? Don't you want to leave something permanent on this earth? Something you can be proud of?"

"I am proud of that rosebush I just planted."

"I'm not talking about gardening, and you know it . . . I want to leave my mark upon this world. Not just anything, something great. Don't you feel the same way?"

"Yes, I do, but for me it is not as easy as it is for you. You create out of your head and your hands. Your job allows you to do that. I cannot do that. I must work with what is offered to me. If I do a superb job in a bad movie, the movie is not any better. My part of it can be, though."

She set the eggs before him. "Thank you for planting the rosebush. I thought you had forgotten your promise." That was all the indication she gave him that she had missed seeing him. He accepted it as a shout of loneliness.

He was waiting for her again on Monday night. She smiled when she saw him. His heart flipped with satisfaction. On Tuesday morning, he grabbed Nazimova and kissed her.

"You were right, you wonderful woman. It worked."

"You'll have to tell me all about it," the actress said. She pushed him away and whispered, "My husband is on the set this morning. If he saw that, he will be unbearable for the rest of the day."

Charles Bryant had indeed seen it. He *was* unbearable for the rest of the day. Every time he passed Valentino, he glared at him. He took Nazimova to one side and soon the entire crew heard shouting. Natacha arrived at the set in time to have Charles Bryant brush by her and see Nazimova burst into tears. Natacha accompanied Nazimova to her dressing room.

"What's this all about?" Natacha asked.

"Ah, that man. He is so jealous. It is good, to an extent, but sometimes it is overdone. He is now jealous of Rudy."

"Why?"

"I guess it is because he never sees Rudy with another woman. I told him long ago that Rudy was crazy about you. He doesn't believe it, I guess." Nazimova's sly mind was working quickly. "Natacha, you must do me a favor, a big favor. If you don't my work will suffer from the arguments that are bound to occur. Say you will.'"

"How can I say I will until you tell me what you want? If I can, I will."

Nazimova smiled. "There is to be a big masquerade ball. You must get Rudy to take you. Charles and I will be there; he'll see you with Rudy and then he'll get over his jealousy. Say you will—if you can get Rudy to go."

"You know I can get Rudy to go. Okay, I'll ask him tonight when he drives me home. But I want you to know that I'm doing it only for you, and I am going to tell Rudy that, too. I don't mind dispelling jealous notions on Charles' part, but I don't intend to add to Rudy's foolish romantic notions.''

"Thank you, darling. You are a real friend.''

They went back to the set and Nazimova went back to work.

Natacha asked Rudy to take her to the ball. She explained to him the reason for their going together. Rudy said yes. His heart was singing. He could have kissed Nazimova again the next morning, but remembering the scene from the day before, he waited until there was a close-up shot between them and whispered his thanks. Nazimova smiled and wished him luck.

The ball was a gala affair, held at the Ambassador Hotel in Los Angeles. Apparently all the Hollywood celebrities were present—actors, writers, producers, directors and top executives.

The ballroom, bathed in colorful lighting, served as a colorful backdrop for the masqueraders, who arrived in a countless variety of costumes representing the apparel of all peoples down through the centuries.

Natacha came dressed as Cleopatra, Queen of the Nile. Valentino came dressed in the gaucho costume that he had worn as Julio in the early sequences of *The Four Horsemen*.

There was dance music and soon the revellers were weaving about the crowded floor through the various dance numbers—fox trots, collegiate and waltzes. And then came the stirring rhythm of an Argentine tango. Valentino took Natacha in his arms.

The masqueraders stepped aside and made room as Julio and Cleopatra glided across the ballroom floor.

They all watched. Those who had remained dancing stopped and stood aside as Valentino and Natacha moved through the steps of the tango.

The music throbbed out across the hall. Natacha's dancing art meshed with Valentino's and the result was drama, excitement.

Valentino was in ecstasy. In his arms, at last, he held the one woman who thus far had somehow eluded him.

Natacha was breathless. Her blue eyes shone, her usually pale face was flushed.

"Rudy, your dancing—it's wonderful."

"And yours, Natacha, more so."

"Rudy, I'm sorry if I've been rude to you."

After the ball, Valentino took Natacha home. It was almost dawn.

"Rudy, before you leave . . . if you want to . . . you could—" she hesitated for a moment—"kiss me."

"Natacha—darling."

He took her in his arms, held her close, and Natacha Rambova became Winifred Shaunessy again.

Valentino drove up the street toward his apartment, and drove right by without slowing down. He could not go in— not yet. He had to drive around a bit and think about it—the fact that he had kissed Natacha, kissed her right on the lips, good and hard, and the way she had danced, and the things she had said. It was something to think about.

Valentino and Natacha, before they had met, had each seen a studio preview of *The Four Horsemen*. It had already been shown in the East. But now the authentic Los Angeles première was to take place. It was to be an impressive affair, with all the notables of Hollywood present, and with the Mayor and all city officials attending. Valentino invited Natacha to be his guest.

And now, all this—an official première of his first starring picture.

The welcoming of the arrivals at the theater before show time was a glittering ceremony.

Later, as *The Four Horsemen* unreeled upon the screen, there was absolute silence in the packed house. The audience looked on, one unified being, holding its breath.

Valentino, sitting beside Natacha in the darkened theater, realized that his cup of happiness was filled to the brim and overflowing.

And then his unexpected reward. There in the darkness a soft hand touched his own and tender fingers curled about his. It was Natacha's hand. He felt the gentle pressure, and squeezed back hard.

As the picture neared its finish, there were sobs of women

102

all about. With Julio's tragic end in no man's land, the picture was over and the lights went on.

Reality had returned, and Valentino saw the tears in Natacha's blue eyes. There were no words spoken between them; they just looked at each other, hardly hearing the deafening crescendo of applause that followed a brief stunned silence. The audience went wild. The name of Rudolph Valentino was on everybody's lips. All were remarking upon the impact of his performance. The comments came to Valentino's ears as he stood close to Natacha.

"Rudy, you've made a conquest," said Natacha.

He held her hand. It was her opinion that he valued above all; he was happy to know that his performance had touched her.

When *The Four Horsemen* went into general release it was received with the same approbation it had been accorded in the eastern theaters. It was a particular hit with the young generation. Girls and young women saw in Valentino a new kind of soulful sex symbol who both entranced and titillated them. They gushed over him and wanted their boy friends to emulate him. All of a sudden, young men started plastering their hair with pomades to obtain the glistening appearance Valentino projected in this film. And since he had danced the tango, the young set adopted it and it seemed that across the nation everyone in his teens and early twenties was frantically occupied in taking tango lessons.

Sensing the romantic appeal of this new personality, newspapermen demanded choice tidbits about him that they could print. At the moment, there was little that could be honestly provided them as grist for the mill. Valentino's refusal to go to the libidinous parties where gossip paragraphs were hatched en masse presented a publicity problem to studio executives. Having no real fodder to feed the demands of the press, they glibly invented a variety of morsels. Valentino was horrified at the inane and false items he saw in print, but he was told to pay no attention to them. It was the way of the movie business, it would help make his picture an even bigger success, assure success for him in subsequent productions. He was not obliged to take what he read seriously.

Valentino reluctantly went along with what he was told. If Hollywood felt little charades had to be played with newspaper readers in order to maintain public support of motion pictures, he felt obliged not to upset the apple cart.

The beginning of the Twenties was an era of escapism, and the motion picture theater swiftly developed as the most welcome and accessible temple of escape. Every post-war period inevitably results in a mass dissipation of tensions and an uninhibited release of pent-up feelings. World War I had been the bloodiest and most critical war fought to date and so its aftermath almost logically produced the biggest binge of exhibitionism America had yet know. It also created a lust for glamor and romantic adventure, a fascination for the exotic, and a desire above all to flee from the drabness, the sadness, and the harshness that the real world seemed always determined to thrust upon its occupants.

The silent movies could offer what neither vaudeville nor the legitimate stage was able to dispense. The movie cameras could transport audiences on any magic carpet they chose to fly and allow them to share the kind of glittering adventures which the other media of entertainment could not possibly provide. The silent film suggested a Utopian realm where all dreams came true. Because the silent stars did not speak, they seemed much more interesting, much more intriguing to the public than those whose voices could be heard freely on a live stage.

Thus, the silent movies became a shrine of glamor to audiences who flocked in ever-increasing numbers to worship their new idols. Shrewd, pioneering businessman recognized the potential for expansion of a modest industry into an empire. They began to turn out films on an assembly-line production basis for the prime purpose of any corporation—to earn profits for its stockholders. Men like Marcus Loew, Samual Goldwyn, Adolph Zukor, Jesse Lasky and William Fox succeeded in mating art and finance into an entertainment colossus.

This was a strange and critical combination. The actor, despite the monetary rewards, was mainly concerned with the expression of his art. The producer, with the bank looking over his shoulder, was concerned with production and sales. Here, quite frequently, there was conflict when an artist, faithful to his principles, fought against the demands to "use" and "prostitute" his artistic integrity.

Valentino himself was intrinsically an artist. To him the accumulation of money had no appeal, no satisfaction. It was the sense of achieving something of true value that counted to him. When he wanted to farm, it was the successful growing of plant and flower that counted. In the films, it was the perfection of his performance that mattered.

Natacha Rambova, likewise, had no craving to acquire money for money's sake. What mattered to her was that she would be able to express her art form in the way she wanted and receive appropriate plaudits that one of her skill and ambition merited.

But this combination of art and finance, however, was incontrovertible as the way to bring low cost entertainment to the millions. There had to be compromises all along. There were bitter controversies, too; but art without finance would have resulted in nothing, and pictures like *The Birth of a Nation*, *Broken Blossoms*, *Shoulder Arms* and *The Four Horsemen of the Apocalypse* would have been impossible and stars like Lillian and Dorothy Gish, Richard Barthelmess, Mary Pickford, Charles Chaplin, and Rudolph Valentino would have never started to twinkle.

CHAPTER THIRTEEN

WHEN Nazimova's husband and manager, Charles Bryant, returned from the East, she was anxious that he meet Valentino at close range and learn for himself that his prejudice was unfounded. She chose the old Sunset Inn in Santa Monica as the setting.

When Hollywood was in its heyday this bistro hosted many a festive evening. The stars of the screen glittered there nightly, and thus the place became steeped in film tradition. The inn was noted for good food and good prohibition cheer—a service to its patrons that occasionally brought Federal raids.

Nazimova, Bryant, Natacha and Valentino chose a corner table for their dining pleasure. Bryant, a well-bred Englishman, was precise in his decorum, an expert in protocol. He attended his wife with the solicitude of a nobleman's valet. Valentino, continental in his taste, openly admired this, and hoped that Natacha did likewise.

It was a busy night at the inn. Many of filmdom's topnotchers were there—Viola Dana; Bebe Daniels, pert and sparkling; and that new exotic personality, Gloria Swanson. Representing the comedy field were Buster Keaton, diminutive beside his playmate, the bulky Fatty Arbuckle. Also present was that grotesque gagster of the Sunshine Comedies, Slim Summerville.

In the midst of all this flashing talent and box-office nobility, Natacha began to feel the thrill of conquest and reflected glory in being escorted by the handsomest and fastest rising star of them all, Valentino. Her sense of victory was emphasized by the number of young females in the place smiling at Valentino with a moonstruck glow in their eyes.

To Valentino, Natacha seemed happier than he had ever seen her. She laughed, she quipped, she was not at all the self-repressed, self-disciplined ascetic who confined herself to her artistic timetable. For this, he was grateful.

Carried away with determination to make a favorable impression on Nazimova's husband, Valentino began to match drinks with him. Every time Charles proposed a toast, it meant another drink. Valentino had no affinity for anything more alcoholic than wine of Italian vintage and, sparingly, champagne. But this was a special occasion. In due time Valentino's eyes were quite glassy for the first time since Natacha had known him.

"I want you to know that Mr. Bryant and myself are the best of friends. Am I right, Mr. Bryant, sir?"

"That you are, my good chap. I would say we are very close. Have another drink, Rudolph?"

"Thank you, Mr. Bryant, sir."

Valentino stood up and held up his glass. "I give you my good friend, Charles Bryant, the nicest Englishman that ever came to Hollywood and the husband of the most beautiful woman in the whole world." He wavered and would have fallen had not Nazimova lent a supporting arm.

"Rudy, will you sit down?" admonished Natacha.

"I have not finished my toast."

"Never mind your toast. You're making a spectacle of yourself." Natacha's voice was low, but sharp.

Nazimova leaned forward and placed her hand on Valentino's arm. "Rudy, darling, something tells me you've had enough."

"Enough? Your husband and I are close friends. We drink together, as friends should. Right, Mr. Bryant, sir?"

"Right, Rudolph. And call me Charlie."

And they drained their glasses again.

Natacha was growing impatient. This was not like Valentino. He was altogether out of character.

"Rudy," she told him, "why don't you stop? You're getting stinko."

"Natacha, you are beautiful but I am not stinko. Am I stinko, Charlie?"

"Of course not, my friend. As a matter of fact, we're both quite sober."

Nazimova looked at her husband. "Please, Charles, no more drinks—please—be a good fellow."

"We're both good fellows, are we not, Rudolph?"

"Good fellows, Charlie. A toast . . ."

Nazimova was worried. Natacha was not only worried but growing angrier by the minute.

Bryant emptied his glass with the equanimity derived from generations of imbibers. Valentino, on the other hand, was descended from a line of wine drinkers and the bootleg liquor was having its full effect.

Natacha, exasperated, kicked him under the table in warning. But Valentino was unmindful of her protests. Although he had started out to make a good impression on the Englishman, the situation had gone far beyond that.

Natacha's eyes beseeched Nazimova who said, quite calmly, "We'll leave them. They're rather impossible."

So Nazimova and Natacha put on their wraps and walked out of the inn by themselves.

"We'll teach them a lesson," said Nazimova.

"I'm disappointed in Rudy," said Natacha. "I never thought he'd do such a thing."

"Of course, he was only trying to be nice to my husband. shall speak to Charles when he's sober and give him a piece of my mind."

They were about to enter the car when they heard singing. The two men were coming out of the inn, arm in arm, and singing in perfect dissonance:

> "*I left my love in Avalon*
> *And sailed away—*"

Other guests of the inn gave them curious glances. Nazimova and Natacha looked at each other, and shrugged

Men could be such naughty boys.

They all got into the Bryant Rolls-Royce, Valentino and Natacha in the rear. At once Valentino fell into a drugged sleep. Natacha shook him awake. He opened rather filmy eyes and stared at her as through a cobweb. "My darling Natacha. A Venus de Milo in white marble. You know what I mean—"

"No, I don't know what you mean and, furthermore, you're not driving when we pick up my car at the Bryants'."

When they arrived at Nazimova's home, Natacha hurried into her car which was parked in the yard. She stationed herself behind the wheel and started the motor. In a moment Valentino was walking unsteadily toward her.

He raised his voice and it sounded to Natacha rather ridiculous, for he had always spoken in a low and soft tone.

"I am driving you home," he told her, wavering in the moonlight.

"You most certainly are not. I'll drive myself home. Good night."

She raced the engine and the car shot forward leaving a cloud of exhaust. Valentino ran after her, trying to hold back the car.

"Natacha, don't leave me. Stop. I am sorry."

But she never stopped. He was left behind, panting and tired, and still groggy. Nazimova, as always, was gentle with him. "Come, Rudy. We'll put you up for the night. In the morning things will look different."

The following morning he apologized to Natacha for the first and last binge of his life.

With *Camille* finished, preparations were made at Metro for the filming of its next production, *The Conquering Power*, to be directed by Rex Ingram. It was a story adapted by June Mathis from the novel *Eugénie Grandet* by Balzac, and Valentino was selected to star in it opposite his friend, Alice Terry. It was an arrangement that made him very happy.

Natacha was satisfied, but when Valentino came to see her at the bungalow, she had a word of advice.

"Rudy, you go up to the production department and

demand an increase. You're a hit in *The Four Horsemen* and they know it. Neither of us cares about being rich. But if you're a star, then you deserve the same degree of recognition as any other star.

"The trouble with you, Rudy, is you're too easy with them. Stand up to them. Metro is a company that hates to part with a penny, but they change their tune when somebody who is important to them shows he means business."

Following Natacha's advice, Valentino went up to see Maxwell Karger again.

"Mr. Karger, considering the success of *The Four Horsemen*, I feel it's time I got more money," he said quietly.

"Valentino, you people are all alike. Just because you happened to make a strike in one picture, you get the idea that you're permanent box-office."

Valentino was remembering Natacha's advice.

"But Mr. Karger, I must have that increase," he said. "My living expenses have gone up since I've become better known."

"Sorry. The company is not in a position to give any increase at this time. Besides, I'm sure you're living beyond your means. I would consider your present salary of four hundred dollars a week as very generous. I can think of a dozen good actors who would call this pay a fortune."

Valentino could not work up an argumentative attitude about this. He would only say, quite calmly, "I will do *The Conquering Power* at my present salary. After that, I don't know."

The interview was over. Result—no increase.

When Natacha heard the news, she fumed.

"They have a lot of nerve. What do they think we—you are? Still an extra? A bit player? They are taking advantage of you."

"I told them I would do one more picture at the present salary."

"You should have told them to go to hell. We can't let them treat you like a mongrel begging for a bone. But I suppose you'll have to go through with your promise. Let me tell you, Rudy, this is the last run-around Metro is going to give you. After this, they'll dance to our tune. Rudy, we're artists, but we have a right to a say in the kind of picture we will do and our reward.''

Valentino, as was his custom on receiving an assignment, read the novel first, studying each paragraph, and paying particular attention to the character he would portray. He then read the script by June Mathis; and it was during this study period that Valentino underwent a transformation from his own personality to that of the character in the story.

In this case the character in question was smug and over-bearing. He wore a monocle, sported a cane and wore fashion-plate clothes. It was the monocle that fascinated Valentino to the extent that he bought one at an optometrist's for his own personal use. He practiced inserting it over his eye until he became adept at it. Also, he assumed the over-bearing attitude that went with it.

Soon his identity with this character in *The Conquering Power* seemed to be complete and he became, for the time being, an overriding, criticizing, well-dressed boor who scolded waiters in restaurants, cab drivers and other ser-vitors. But to Natacha, in or out of character, he always made sure to be courteous, gallant and obedient to her slightest wish.

One incident of this Jekyll and Hyde affair affected Natacha to a point of alarm.

They were seated at a table in the exclusive Wilshire Arms Café on Hollywood Boulevard. The head waiter handed the menu to Valentino, who raised his monocle to his eye and peered down at the bill of fare in haughty disdain.

"My good man," he addressed the awed head waiter, "I do not see my favorite dish on this card."

"I am sorry, sir. If Mr. Valentino would care to name it . . .''

"Spaghetti and meat balls, you fool. This is insufferable! I shall make formal complaint to the manager. The idea! No spaghetti and meat balls. Incredible! And furthermore, my good man . . .''

"Yes, Mr. Valentino?"

"Where is the Italian wine? This is impossible—

absolutely impossible. My dear Natacha, shall we leave at once? Or shall we remain and suffer?"

Natacha signed, and said, "All right, Rudy. You can come out of it now. Drop your monocle and save your acting for the cameras."

After dinner at the Wilshire Arms and a movie at Grauman's Chinese, Valentino drove Natacha home. Since shooting of *The Conquering Power* was to start early in the morning, Natacha told Valentino that he could only stay a minute.

They stood facing each other in the living room of her bungalow.

"Natacha, you are wonderful."

Impulsively he put his arms about her, held her close, his blood racing. The feel of her body in his arms overwhelmed him.

His mouth found hers in a kiss. Natacha gasped for breath. His eagerness crumbled. Somewhere along the line he had overstepped the bounds. He released her and stepped back.

Natacha patted her smooth dark hair into place. Calmly she said, "Why do two civilized and intelligent people have to maul each other to express their emotions? We're grown up, Rudy. Every time we're alone you act more like a schoolboy than an experienced man of the world."

"It is the the way I feel about you, Natacha. A man wants to touch the woman he loves. It's not wrong."

"Maybe not, but sometimes it's terribly annoying."

"I understand how you feel," said Valentino. "Forgive me, Natacha. There is so much I do not know—about you—and I do not want to displease you in any way."

"Good night, Rudy, dear."

She kissed him on the cheek, lightly.

Then he was alone, driving his old Buick up Sunset Boulevard toward his apartment. The night was close about him. He wondered whether Natacha could ever really love him. A woman in love with a man welcomed his embrace. People were the same, fundamentally, the world over, and love was the same.

Perhaps he was aiming at too lofty a star. He could, for

instance, find some uncomplicated girl who was warm and eager to comfort him; someone, perhaps, of his own nationality who would help him in building a home and filling it with love and children.

Was this madness on his part, hoping for response from one who walked like a Greek goddess, one who was beautiful and wise, yet cold and unattainable? Madness, yes. But an inspiring madness that drove him to love her all the more and to worship her, even as a goddess.

The attraction for Natacha was far more than that of a man for a beautiful woman. Valentino's attraction was psychological. Subconsciously he was seeking the strong will, the love and the protection that his mother had given him. Natacha filled the bill.

She could give Valentino the direction and guidance that he needed. She was perceptive and shrewd and sure of herself. He was none of these things and so he admired what she had.

And finally, Valentino also filled the bill. She was an ambitious, strong-willed woman who saw in Valentino the opportunity for her own success, for she aspired toward greatness.

They made a strange pair, these two. He was merry, childishly intrigued by simple pleasures. She was complex and almost totally devoid of a sense of humor.

Where Valentino was sentimental and affectionate, as shown in his love of children and animals, Natacha was hard and firm. He was a man schooled in the graces, but he was also a man of passion. For her part, she was cold and unresponsive as if there were an imperceptible wall between them. Yet because of her ways, and because of Valentino's, she was what he needed.

CHAPTER FOURTEEN

"VALENTINO, for the midnight entertainment scene you wear a black vest with your evening clothes."

"Ingram, you are wrong. It is a white vest."

"I say a black vest."

"I insist . . . a white vest."

"Black."

"White."

"Valentino, you're pig-headed, stubborn and conceited. When I directed you in *The Four Horsemen* you were a gentleman. But the way you behave lately! You're developing what ails most of the stars, a puffed ego."

"Ingram, you insult me in front of all these fine people. But that has nothing to do with the vest which I say is white."

Production on *The Conquering Power* was momentarily stalled. Supporting players and extras stood about watching the scene which was not part of the script.

Ingram demanded that Frank Elliot, an English actor known for impeccable taste in clothes, be brought to the lot. "We'll leave it up to him, and he will prove to you that you are wrong as wrong can be," the director said.

Elliot was called to the scene. The vest should be white, he said.

Ingram exploded in a violent oath.

"I don't have to take that," Valentino shouted. And he walked off the set.

Rex Ingram's able and sympathetic direction had helped

Valentino bring off his triumph in *The Four Horsemen*. In the filming of that picture, he and Valentino had worked in perfect harmony. Valentino had been given much leeway in his performance, but only because Ingram recognized that this would be good for the picture. Valentino himself had demanded nothing. Yet on the set of this picture, the Italian actor had shown traits of boorishness and rudeness that seemed entirely out of character with his true personality. Ingram decided that the success of *Four Horsemen* had gone to the actor's head. He had been rude and disagreeable in turn, hoping to cut Valentino down to size.

What Ingram didn't realize was that the disturbing factor in Valentino was his penchant for transmuting a movie role into his own personality during the production of a picture. Valentino was no longer the sensitive, philosophical Julio of *Four Horsemen*. He was the arrogant egotist of his current picture. He could not seem to remember where his movie part ended and his real self began.

Natacha's bungalow was located near the Metro lot. Valentino often had lunch with her there. Now he hurried off the set and rushed over to the bungalow, anxious to get her approval for his action. His eyes were still flashing sparks as she opened the door for him.

"That Ingram!" he said angrily, before she could even greet him. "He started a fight and I left the set."

Natacha's eyes opened wide. "My, my, is this the Rudolph Valentino I used to know?" she said dryly. "Sit down, calm youself, and I'll make you some tea. What was the fight about?"

He gave her a word-by-word recital of the incident of the vest. "Not a very important subject to fight about, it seems to me," she said, as she poured the tea. "Still, you certainly showed him there are some things a director doesn't know, although they always feel they know everything."

"What really angered me is that he cursed me right in front of the whole set. I don't like to be insulted. I have a pair of excellent eighteenth-century swords. I ought to challenge the man to a duel." Suddenly, Valentino jumped up and grabbed an imaginary sword. "Ah there, Ingram, you cur, put yourself on guard!'' he said mockingly.

Moving from kitchen to living room, leaping over divans and couches, thrusting forward and back, Valentino gave a convincing demonstration of a duel.

He gave a final thrust and his phantom opponent fell properly dead. Natacha, her eyes sparkling in a way that reminded Valentino of his late mother, applauded his act vigorously.

''Bravo, Rudy! Done like a true enemy of the bloody Borgias.''

''Now you are laughing at me,'' he said, sitting down and patting his forehead with his handkerchief.

''Rudy, you've won your victory. Now you had better forget the whole thing. Anything you do is grist for the newspaper mill, and if this incident gets out of hand, it will mean a series of exaggerated stories about certain alleged duels you fought over fantastic women, and so on without end.''

A few days later, Valentino came over to visit Natacha.

''Guess what?'' he said.

''Tell me. A white or black jacket?''

''No. This time it's a complete evening dress suit.''

''This silly fuss about clothes is going to be the ruination of *The Conquering Power*. What about the dress suit?''

''Well, late last night someone knocked on my apartment door.''

''Rex Ingram?''

''No. His assistant director.''

''Ah, Ingram sent his second asking for satisfaction.''

''Not satisfaction,'' said Valentino, ''but the loan of my evening dress suit. Ingram was invited to attend a banquet of the Metro executive staff and naturally he had no proper clothes. He and I being about the same size. . . .''

''Of course, you didn't give it to him?''

''Why not? He had to have it, poor fellow. I bet he looked good in it, too.''

Natacha sighed. The duel that Valentino had been ready to wage with Rex had gone no further than her kitchen and living room. Casualty: one overturned chair.

"You're a child," said Natacha.

"I am going backwards. First, I am a boy and now I have diminished to a child. Ah, my beautiful Natacha, it's a good thing I'm crazy about you or you would be next on my dueling list."

"You're still a child."

Valentino's expression was that familiar look on the screen—one of prolonged sadness.

"I wonder when you will think of me as a man."

After *The Conquering Power* had been tucked away in the cans, Valentino began to spend time in the small yard behind Natacha's house, usually lying outstretched on the ground, tinkering with his old Buick. When this car finally passed the point of no return, he picked up an old Cadillac, which required even more attention.

He was a man who prided himself on his neatness. But when he indulged himself in his auto maintenance, he let his well-groomed hair become tousled, while his face and trousers became streaked with grease and his white shirt reeked of oil. There were days when he spent four or five hours on the old car. Natacha couldn't understand the fascination it held for him, but he told her he liked to do things with his hands and a creaky auto provided a good outlet for him.

He had time on his hands. His studio had a full production schedule, but there was suddenly nothing for Valentino. Once again, his "type" militated against him. There was just no picture on the immediate schedule that demanded a "foreign" performer. The delay would be short-lived, they assured him. Meanwhile patience was in order.

Natacha, in turn, had been commissioned by the studio to design the sets and costumes for Nazimova's next picture, *Salome*. But at the last minute, the picture had been inexplicably postponed. So she had no work either.

Valentino and Natacha were constantly in each other's company during these trying days, yet there was a strange casualness about their relationship. Knowing her attitude toward emotional expression and uninhibited love-making, Valentino played a waiting game, hoping that some day soon she would start to regard him as he regarded her and would let her emotions flow naturally.

He would kiss her on arriving or departing with a light peck on the cheek or a brush on the lips; any demonstration more emphatic was taboo. He reminded himself constantly of her attitude and behaved accordingly. He went home to his apartment each night and returned to her bungalow each morning.

Valentino bought the groceries for the bungalow until his funds ran out. His period of unemployment was dragging on much longer than he had expected and now both he and his companion were in desperate straits. Natacha refused to ask her parents for help. She had cut herself off from them some time ago to be on her own and she was too proud to admit her need to them.

The fact remained, however, that there was no more money. Natacha had pawned what she laughingly called the family jewels and there was nothing else.

Valentino and Natacha looked at each other one morning over the breakfast table and both had the same thought— food. Valentino thought of his guns. He also thought of the old Robertson Cole ranch, now without any tenant, and a paradise of quail and rabbit, which he had seen on his trips to Santa Monica.

He drove to his apartment and returned with two rifles, oiled and ready to use. They rode out in the Cadillac and stopped at a secluded spot in a pine grove. Here Valentino taught Natacha how to handle and fire a rifle. She was, as in all else, an apt pupil, and learned fast. Soon she was hitting tin cans at thirty paces.

Thus equipped with a rifle apiece they set forth one fog-veiled dawn into the precincts of the Robertson Cole ranch on a hunting expedition.

The houses were few beyond Santa Monica and at this early hour they felt safe from detection. This was a doubly illegal hunt—poaching and shooting game out of season— but their stomachs could not reason with the logic of Nimrod jurisprudence.

Quail were all over the place. With the black canvas top of the car pulled down to the rear, Valentino sat upon it, his feet dangling over it, and took aim. As long as the Cadillac kept moving, the birds did not take to sudden wing, and Valentino fired and bagged eight quail, which was the limit they had set.

They then stopped the car and Natacha, gun in hand, joined Valentino in a hunt for rabbit. They walked slowly across the brush, scrub pine, and fern. After Natacha had bagged one and Valentino three rabbits, they decided to quit at once, for it was growing lighter and they might be caught. They drove home in triumph. Even the Cadillac seemed charged up. They arrived at the bungalow without stalling once.

That noon and evening they feasted on roast quail and tender cooked rabbit.

After supper they sat on a bench in front of the house on the rectangle of lawn. They watched the fireflies twinkling in the deepening dusk, and the city lights going on and becoming a blaze of glory. Automobiles glided by on Sunset Boulevard, and a whispering young couple, arm in arm, strolled by on the sidewalk.

Valentino sat very close to Natacha. She looked into his dark and glowing eyes. He felt happier than ever. He didn't feel lonely now. All those painful weary days of longing and frustration were now safely in the past. Here was a companion for him, a woman who was not only beautiful but a genius in her own right, who knew something of life and of people, who could help him build his future.

He wanted now, more than ever, to put his arms about her, to hold her close, to kiss her delicately shaped lips, to let her know definitely how he felt. He wanted to make violent love to her, but he knew that was not for him now. One such move and the magic spell of their friendship might be broken.

Natacha's eyes were closed. Valentino noted the delicately defined contour of her sensitive face against the starlight. He wondered what she was thinking. Or was she sleeping? He leaned closer to her, his hand gently touching hers.

"Natacha, dear, you are precious."·

"We've had fun today. It's the first time I ever went hunting." Her voice was soft and husky.

"Like it?"

"Lots. But I feel guilty about the killing part. Rudy, isn't it risky? Out of season. And poaching. Suppose we're caught?"

"That makes it all the more interesting. But who is to know? Nobody ever bothers with that ranch anyway."

"There are always the game wardens."

"Very small chance of them catching us. We can always say we are new on the ranch and don't know about the game laws."

Natacha sat silently for a moment. Then suddenly, she asked, "Rudy, are you going to the studio tomorrow?"

"I'd rather go hunting again. There is plenty of game."

"You're right in the middle of building up your career, Rudy," she pouted. "You've got to try the studio again."

His face darkened. "I'm beginning to think the studio has lost all interest in me. They don't really care for foreigners, you know. I think they've decided I was a freak hit in one picture and now they can wash their hands of me."

"You can't take that attitude," Natacha said angrily. "You can't just crawl into a shell and give up because the studio is not doing what you want. You have talent—a real talent, a rare talent. There's something about you that charms and fascinates women. You can achieve tremendous success if you're properly handled. The studio executives cannot see beyond their noses, it is true, but you need someone who will pound on their desks and wake them up to your real worth. You need someone to handle the worldly aspects of your career. You're too much of a romanticist and too emotional a person to do it yourself. You need someone like me to guide your arrangements with studios, to analyze the kind of pictures you are offered, to see that you receive the wages and recognition a star deserves."

"You mean you'd be sort of an agent?"

"No. Just a friend who will help you."

He hardly realized what had happened when she put her

arms about him, and pressed her lips upon his. He took the cue and embraced her, forgetting to be gentle as he returned her kiss.

One thing escaped his awareness—that her kiss was the seal of a bargain, not an avowal of love.

CHAPTER FIFTEEN

THE next day, Valentino presented himself at the Metro studio again, but with the same result. He was received with a great show of courtesy, but was told regretfully they still had no roles that suited his particular "type." It wouldn't be much longer, however. . . . If he would only be patient. . . .

When he returned to the bungalow with the news, Natacha reacted with a violent display of temper. "Those fools!" she said. "I'll make them sorry for this. Don't they realize you're more than just a 'foreign type'?"

She paced up and down the room. Valentino looked at her questioningly. Finally, she said, "Metro has been miserable to you. I don't want you to go back there. It's obvious they have little artistic sense anyway. Tomorrow, you'll begin to make the rounds of other studios. Go to Famous Players-Lasky. They have some bright people there. They may know how to use your talents."

He followed her instructions and went to Famous Players (later to become Paramount Pictures) early the next morning. His reception was very cordial and he left there brimming with hope. They hadn't realized he was available. They thought that with the success of *The Four Horsemen* Metro had put him under long-term contract. They recognized his box-office potential and wanted to exploit it. At the moment they weren't sure where they could use him, but they were going to look over their production schedule and their script properties very carefully. They felt sure they would find a role for him that would do him justice.

He returned to the bungalow in a buoyant mood and his enthusiasm quickly infected Natacha. "See what I told you?" she said. "You don't give up just because one company has no faith in you."

They still had the problem of feeding themselves and so the next morning they went off on another hunting expedition. They returned with an armful of quail. A few days later, however, they were almost caught. "We can't take another chance," Valentino said. "We'll have to try something else."

Natacha remembered that she had once picked mussels with a group of friends on the beach west of Santa Monica. They had cooked them and found them to be delicious. "I love sea food; let's try it," Valentino said.

They left before dawn the next day, drove to the beach and began to scour the rocks offshore. They worked quickly to take advantage of the low tide. The mussels were plentiful along the rocks and they were able to fill three pails before the tide began to wash on the beach. Back at the bungalow, Valentino cooked the sea food in tomato sauce and garlic. The delectable aroma gave him a heady feeling and he serenaded Natacha as he served her. "Sea food properly cooked and seasoned is a food for kings," he said gaily.

He and Natacha were still complimenting themselves on their menu when they sat down to eat it again in the evening. But the mussels began to pall on them when they had to eat them a second day and by the third day, they were happy to see the last of them disappear. Necessity drove them back to the beach again, but this time they went through their chores of collecting the fish and cooking it with the enthusiasm of prisoners awaiting their tasteless penal fare.

When a week passed without any call from Famous Players-Lasky, the emotional Valentino lapsed back again into the familiar mood of depression. He was becoming convinced that this studio, too, was stalling him—that he was back on the same treadmill where he started years ago.

"It's always the same and I am sick of it," he told

Natacha. "Right now I have a good mind to escape the whole business. I have a marvelous plan. You like the outdoor life as much as I like it. There is much good farm land around here. We can start with an acre or two, buy it on installments. Partners—you and I. I can plant the crops. We can get cows, chickens, and have fresh milk, cream, eggs. You can learn to make butter and cheese, as my mother used to do in Italy. No more worrying about getting work, or scavenging for food."

"Rudy, look at me. Do I look like a farm woman?"

"A very attractive one."

"I'm glad to know you aren't serious."

"But I am."

"Do you mean you'd throw away your career?"

"What career? One good picture. Now they've shut the door on me."

Natacha seized his hand. "I don't want to hear any more of this foolish talk of your quitting or of us becoming farmers," she said. "That studio is going to call you, I tell you. Not all studios in Hollywood are run by idiots!"

The phone rang two days later. It was Famous Players-Lasky. Could Mr. Valentino come over right away?

Mr. Valentino was ready to fly there. Natacha helped groom him so he looked the part of a star. "Remember, Rudy, don't let them know you're desperate for work or they'll take advantage of you. And you don't work for less than five hundred a week. You're a very important personality."

"Natacha, for God's sake, do you want us to starve? I'm in no position to dictate terms."

"Don't let them know that! Be cordial, cooperative, sure, but don't let them step on you!"

He went to the production office of Famous Players-Lasky, and they told him, "We have a good book, *The Sheik*, by E. M. Hull. We believe you would be good in the title role of the sheik. Here's the book. Read it through and let us know your reaction. Come back in three days. We'll talk contract and salary then if you are willing. But don't take more time. The plans are to start this picture at once. We've already booked Agnes Ayers and Adolphe Menjou for the supporting roles."

He didn't say a word about five hundred dollars a week. He said only, "Thank you very much. I will be back in three days, you can depend on it."

CHAPTER SIXTEEN

WHEN Valentino brought *The Sheik* to Natacha's bungalow, she looked through it, reading a paragraph here, a page there. She then threw the book down in disgust. "Trash! Absolutely and completely—just plain, unadulterated trash! A story fit for half-witted morons. *The Sheik*, indeed! You take that book back to them and tell them to find someone who doesn't care what he does to earn a living."

"But, Natacha, you don't seem to realize that a little while back you were urging me to find work. Well, here is work. Think what the money will do for us. You said you wanted to stop poaching and hunting out of season. Well, here is our chance to live decently."'

"But why such trash? I tell you this story will ruin you. Whoever sees it will laugh at you in those Arabian costumes you'll have to wear. Why, the whole thing is just too ridiculous. Whatever you've built up will be wrecked. *The Sheik!*—Those people at Famous Players are crazy if they think they can get away with this. How could they be so crude as to sink good money into this farce?"

"Maybe they know what they are doing."

"If this is the best they can come up with, then they certainly do not know what they are doing. I'd rather starve than prostitute my art for this. I'm sure you feel the same way."

"You mean you want me to tell them no?"

"Exactly. I won't let you jeopardize your career. I won't

let you make a ridiculous buffoon of yourself."

He dropped the subject for the rest of that afternoon, and decided to wait for a propitious moment to push it again. That evening, as they sat down to a meagre supper, he saw Natacha looking at their empty larder.

"I think it's about time we stopped deluding ourselves," he said softly. "I've been offered work and I've got to take it."

"Are you forgetting that you're supposed to be an artist?" she flared at him.

"We can't eat art, for God's sake," he shouted, surprised at his own vehemence.

Natacha burst into tears. He was immediately contrite, but as she buried her face in his handkerchief she mumbled that of course he was right, and of course, she'd been acting the fool.

"I've been beastly," she sobbed. "I can't stand for you to compromise yourself, but I know that you have no choice and that you must take the part. You're sick of quail and mussels and so am I."

He dried her eyes. "I'm ashamed of myself," she confessed. "I can't remember when I've ever cried before. I pride myself in never letting my feelings get the best of me."

"I wish you'd cry more often."

"Yes, I know, you want me to be truly feminine, but I'm just not that way, Rudy, and I never will be. Come on, let's go over your script now and see if we can bring anything to this potboiler."

As a novel *The Sheik* was considered mediocre. The plot of the story—the kidnapping of an attractive English girl by a desert chieftain—was trite. The writing was dry, unemotional. There was no distinctive quality to the book. Ordinarily, it would have taken its place with the legion of the nondescript, gathering dust on booksellers' bargain tables.

When the filming of *The Sheik* began on the sand dunes of Oxnard, California, only Valentino showed enthusiasm and spirit. He acted the role of the sheik with his usual thoroughness. He was probably the only member of the cast who brought meaning to his part, investing it with a verve and

127

dash the book never had. The director and the supporting players went about their business in a matter-of-fact way, shooting the scenes in haste—sometimes with only one take, for the sake of economy and speed. To them it was the routine of earning a living, with regular pay checks.

The production department was just as anxious to get the film over with and to start on something more appealing. In story conferences, it was the general feeling among the studio heads that they had made a rash move in selecting this story to be filmed, especially with an actor like Valentino, who actually was not too well proven in box-office appeal. True, he had made a success of his role in *The Four Horsemen* for Metro. But that could have been a lucky break that comes once in a lifetime. Both he and *The Sheik* might backfire badly at the box office.

Whenever Valentino went to visit Natacha at her bungalow she made no bones about the fact that she still considered him to be working in a trash production. "It will set our industry back ten years," she insisted.

"You are probably right, but I am enjoying my work. Gives me a chance to ride a horse and fight in a film. That fascinates me."

"I see that it does. Agnes Ayers may have something to do with that. But enjoy it while you can, Rudy, dear. When this film is released it will be laughed out of the theater."

"Natacha, you don't have much faith."

"In the picture—no. In you—yes. You're too good to be wasted in junk."

"I had no choice. You said so yourself. I could not afford to say no. And I'm even getting the five hundred a week you told me to ask for."

"Yes, yes, Rudy, I know that. But it doesn't seem fair that they won't give a part or a picture that's really worthy of you."

Production on *The Sheik* ended on October 15. Valentino was already wondering what his next move would be. When he had signed the contract for *The Sheik* it was with the understanding that he would be kept busy with succeeding roles; but the prospects did not look encouraging. If *The*

Sheik proved a fizzle then his screen career might well be finished.

That evening he drove, by himself, up Santa Monica Boulevard. He stopped the car at an uninhabited spot, at the edge of a deep pine grove. There were very few autos passing at this time. He got out and walked—something he had not done for a great while—to think things out.

The sky was star-studded and now the Pacific breeze, laden with the scent of orange blossoms, caressed him as with gentle fingers. It was a caress that immediately reminded him of his blue-eyed, beautiful, but somewhat cold-blooded Natacha.

He had to do something about her. The two of them could not go on much longer in an in-between status. Their relationship had to take one direction or the other—an end to the friendship or a beginning of a real life together.

It came down to the inevitable. He would ask her to marry him. He was still legally married to Jean Acker but he could ask her to hurry the divorce along. There was only one thing that worried him—the prospect that Natacha might say no. But that, he felt, was the chance he had to take, and soon.

Natacha greeted him at the bungalow with a kiss on the cheek, then made some tea and set the table with sandwiches and fruit. Valentino, searching for the right moment to ask the question, gave a rather pitiful imitation of a man enjoying a cup of tea and a sandwich.

Natacha was unusually quiet as she washed the dishes. Valentino, as was his practice, took the dish towel and did the drying. When he finished, he threw the towel down, came close to Natacha and forced her to look at him.

"Natacha, we've been through some good times and some not-so-good times together. If I would ask you to marry me—"

"Rudy, darling, I was wondering how much longer you were going to wait."

"You mean—?"

She nodded. "Yes, Rudy. But you're a married man, you know."

"Jean will hurry through with the divorce once I explain to her. And you will not be sorry, Natacha. I will do everything to make you happy. You know I will."

"Yes, I know."

He took her in his arms and she dropped a dish and it broke into many pieces. There at the sink Valentino played a love scene that was not part of any script, but to him it was the most important scene of his life.

Later, for the first time, Natacha, the aloof, the unattainable, gave herself to him. He should have been soaring on the wings of exaltation, yet long after she had fallen asleep he remained awake, thinking. He was nagged with a sense of disquiet. This was the only woman he had ever met to whom he wanted to give his heart and soul completely, without question. She was going to marry him, yet she had never really said she loved him. She had tried very hard to match his passion, but he had instinctively detected withdrawal on her part as their bodies met, and she was passive when he had forced her to accept his love-making.

He would have to be very patient, he realized, before he could break down her reserve.

What made Valentino the screen's greatest lover? Psychologists, sociologists, and everyone with an interest in motion pictures have argued the question for years without arriving at one answer.

Certainly, his impact was accentuated because he was a complete departure from the usual movie type. The fact that he played his roles with fervid intensity, that he made his characters seem real because to him they were very real indeed, heightened his attraction.

And although the motion picture moguls were very late in realizing it, the fact that he was a "foreign type" added immeasurably to his glamor. In the Twenties, when escape was so important and unreality so attractive to moviegoers, this first "foreign lover" seemed much more appealing and alluring than the all-American types they had seen so often.

Whatever the assessment of Valentino the actor, there is

no doubt that the actor was happier than the man. The real Valentino was confused and insecure. His life with Natacha was pretense, pretense that the woman for whom he had undying love loved him equally in turn. Valentino was happy only when he kept himself from facing up to the truth.

CHAPTER SEVENTEEN

FROM the first showing of *The Sheik* in New York, Chicago, San Francisco, and other first-run cities, it struck the country like a thunderbolt. It was, in effect, a one-man invasion of America. This was not an invasion of the military to conquer a city or a land. This was an invasion of a single individual, a young man who had dreamed of settling down to a quiet, peaceful life on a farm.

The electric lights on the marquees of a multitude of theaters proclaimed to all, RUDOLPH VALENTINO IN "THE SHEIK," and city after city fell before the tidal wave. In a few weeks the invasion was complete. From coast to coast, from the far reaches of the Canadian northlands to the Latin countries below the border, the personality and magnetism of Valentino had made a complete and thorough conquest—not for the time being, not for a month or a year, but for generations yet to come.

At once the real, living man became a legend. There was no gradual evolution, no hesitation or doubt. In the space of the first two or three weeks that *The Sheik* was exhibited, Valentino had become a myth.

He came riding a horse across the desert to win not only the heart of the beautiful English Lady, as portrayed by Agnes Ayres, but also the hearts of all the fair ladies of the land. It was as if all the women of America—not just the young set this time—fell like ninepins at his feet.

In *The Four Horsemen* he had drawn a sympathetic reaction from the audience who admired his acting. They wept with him. They were saddened by Julio's final rendezvous with destiny. But here was a new Valentino with no vestige of the pathetic helplessness of a Julio. Here was a dashing, bold figure who leaped upon the screen in a white-hot aura of action and fierce, primitive love-making. Before, as Julio, he had loved simply and quietly, careful not to overstep the bounds of propriety. In *The Sheik* he loved boldly and brashly, with a reckless abandon that swept the viewers along, forcing them to thrill to Valentino's look as much as did Agnes.

With this picture, Valentino became a person of enormous prominence on the American scene. He had introduced an entirely different prototype of young male romantic. This one was bold, direct, with a primitive behavior pattern toward the weaker sex. Girls began calling their boy friends "sheiks" and the word was adopted for permanent usage in the language. Young men treated their girls like harem slaves and the girls loved it, adored it, clamored for more.

On the dressers of the women of America the photograph of a new face brightened their boudoirs. It was the face of Valentino under the burnoose he wore in the film. Young married women started asking their bewildered spouses, "Why can't you be like Rudolph Valentino? He can drag me into his tent any time." This adulation of Valentino on the part of the women began to stir up in the American male a growing resentment, perhaps jealousy. A condition soon existed where the women worshipped Valentino as a god while the husbands condemned him as a menace to their own self-confidence and amorous capabilities. The only way to counteract Valentino was to act like him, they decided.

Meanwhile, offers poured in from all the major studios. Now he could have the choice roles that had been denied foreigners for so long. His fan mail increased a thousandfold, and during the concluding period of 1921 and the beginning of 1922 Valentino's name began to appear in the newspapers more and more. He was discussed, analyzed, criticized, written about in exaggerated news items and magazine articles that twisted, distorted and yellow-journalized his character and activities until the real man was almost completely lost in the maze of fantastic fables and sex-drenched verbiage.

Natacha read the newspaper stories, heard the glowing comments of her friends, and of people in the street, and found herself puzzled. They had not laughed the picture out of the theaters as she had predicted.

Instead, frantic women were fighting to get into the theaters, almost tearing down the doors in their frenzy, and Valentino was warned by the studio not to make any personal appearances at any time. They didn't want him to place himself in bodily jeopardy in the path of well-wishers and autograph fanatics.

Valentino was bewildered as much as he was pleased by this unexpected success. He considered himself no different than he had been during the period he had lived through rejections and failures. Why were Americans so fickle and inconstant?

Natacha's reaction bewildered him, too. He had no doubt that she was enjoying his success, that she was happy for him, yet she seemed to resent the fact that it was *The Sheik* which had brought him the prominence she had predicted for him.

"The public should be congratulated for seeing your real qualities despite the shoddiness of that picture," she told him. "It's just a shame that you have to be associated with something so inartistic it should never have gotten out of the cutting room."

To Valentino, it seemed ridiculous for Natacha to keep insisting that an enormously successful picture was trash. Perhaps *The Sheik* was an inartistic as she said . . . and then again, perhaps it was not. Perhaps Natacha kept saying these things because her pride would not permit her to say that she had been wrong in trying to keep him from appearing in it. He sighed. He did not want to fight with Natacha or argue with her, but he wished she could accept the good fortune that had come his way without carping and with a full heart. What a complex person she was!

Valentino's next assignment for Famous Players-Lasky was to co-star with Dorothy Dalton in *Moran of the Lady Letty*. His salary would be boosted to seven hundred and fifty dollars per week.

Natacha disapproved of this picture, too. "Rudy, dear, you're doing the same thing—accepting anything they throw at you. You made a big hit in *The Sheik* and they know it. Now you can ask for better roles. Don't be afraid of losing your job, like a clerk or a laborer. You are an artist."

"But even artists need money, Natacha. Seven hundred and fifty a week is nothing to sneeze at."

"If it's only a question of money, why not open a store on Hollywood Boulevard? Rudy, I thought we had this settled."

Valentino was patient. "Natacha, again I ask you, do you want me to tell them no? Before I do that let me remind you we are engaged to be married. I have a responsibility now; I must provide for our future. We can start a bank account and save and build a home like other people."

Natacha pouted in silence for a few minutes, then she looked up at him, her blue eyes pained.

"Very well, Rudy. I suppose you're right—since you look at it that way. We are still in no position to bargain, I suppose. Take that role. But when we're better set financially, it will be quite different. If they think they can stick you in any third-rate story and ruin your career and stifle your artistic expression, they're crazy."

The tension eased when Natacha resumed her work for Nazimova, designing the sets and costumes for the resumed picture, *Salome*. This assuaged the injury to her ego and she regained a sense of tolerance. It gave her the opportunity for the expression of her artistic temperament and thereafter the conversations she had with Valentino were more subdued and reassuring.

Valentino was the chef of the little household whenever he dropped in for luncheon or dinner. The Italian dishes he concocted were increasingly tasty now that they had money to buy whatever was needed. While busy with the skillet and pan, he sang his favorite song, "Santa Lucia," changing the name to "Santa Natacha." Their spirits were light and gay.

One evening she ran her pale, tapered fingers through Valentino's perfectly combed hair, mussing it up completely.

"Why do you do that?" he asked with a smile.

"Rudy, if I ask you a little personal favor, would you do it?"

"Of course. Ask."

"Your hair—"

"What about my hair?"

"I want you to wear it sort of mussed up a bit. You know, don't comb it down so flat and perfect until it shines like black satin."

He looked at her, half in irritation, half in surprise.

"Babykins, my dear, I will wear an apron for you, I will go around without a shirt for you, I will even go barefoot for you, but please don't ask me to wear my hair windblown."

"But why not?"

"Because, Babykins, the way I wear my hair, I do not have to worry about keeping it out of my eyes. It is part of my philosophy—to be neat."

"I think you're stubborn."

"Would I ask you to stop using lipstick? Or to stop wearing those ridiculous high heels? Of course I would never dare."

"You're impossible," she said. "But you are handsome."

He took her in his arms and held her close, as though to keep her from re-entering her ivory castle.

"When are you going to fall in love with me?" he asked.

"I do love you," she said.

"Then how can you even notice my hair?"

She kissed him with a sigh.

That same October, Natacha's parents wired from New York that they had just arrived from Paris and were coming to Hollywood for a visit.

"I wired mother about our engagement," Natacha told Valentino. "Isn't it nice of them to come to see us? They're

136

so anxious to meet you personally after seeing you in *The Four Horsemen*."

Natacha met Mr. and Mrs. Richard Hudnut at the station while Valentino was on the set of *Moran of the Lady Letty*. The greeting was warm, and her stepfather told Natacha, "You're almost as beautiful as your mother."

At last they saw the bungalow Natacha had described so fancifully in her letters. Her mother caught her first glimpse of it from the narrow walk, and discovered its Lilliputian size. As she told Natacha a year later, "Actually, my dear, when you so proudly showed me the house I thought it was so pathetic—it was so small. And then you showed me the inside—oh, those miniature rooms! I often wondered how you managed. You had just about enough space for the table and chairs in the kitchen, and the sofa took more than half the floor in the living room. And that doll-house bedroom, with the bed barely squeezed into the space! Also, that red and gold rug painted on the living room floor—your own handiwork. It was all so precious. But what did it matter? It was your own home and you were proud of it and that made me proud of you."

Having seen the house, Mrs. Hudnut winked slyly at her husband, a signal to withhold any comment which might prove embarrassing.

"We're on pins to meet the prospective groom," said Mrs. Hudnut.

"Rudy will be here any minute now. He's on location not far from the studio."

"Seems like a nice chap," said Mr. Hudnut. "I could use a young man like that in my business."

"I'll remember that offer," said Natacha. "But I want you to remember, that Rudy is an artist, and artists—well, you know how we are about business." She turned to her mother. "Mother, dear, come to the bathroom and freshen up."

When Natacha opened the door of the bedroom, there was a snarling sound as Zela, the lion cub, glared at Mrs. Hudnut.

"My God! A lion!" Mrs. Hudnut exclaimed.

"Just a cub, mother. She won't harm you. I'll get her out, so she won't bother you."

When Mrs. Hudnut returned to the living room, Natacha led her to Valentino's two prize police dogs in the garage.

"You and Rudy do love animals," said Mrs. Hudnut.

"Adore them. It's one taste we have in common."

Natacha took her mother's hand. "Come this way, mother."

Natacha led her mother to the back of the garage and pointed to a box with a screened opening. "Isn't she a beauty, mother?"

"A snake!"

"Not just an ordinary snake. This is Mathilda."

"Good heavens, child! Why a snake? I can't stand those slimy creatures."

"Mathilda isn't slimy at all. She'll eat out of your hand. Look at her—striking color effect, don't you think?"

"Please, Natacha. I—I feel faint. Perhaps I had better get out of here."

Natacha led her mother out of the garage.

"We have a rare species of lizard. Rudy brought him home from Oxnard when he was filming *The Sheik*."

"How marvellous, but not now, Natacha, dear. I still feel rather—"

"Squeamish, mother? Rudy also bought a horse—nobody wanted him, poor thing, because he was skin and bones. But we're fattening him up. Want to see him?"

"No, child. A few more beasts and you can charge admission to your own private zoo."

Valentino arrived in time for dinner and was delighted to find Natacha's parents waiting for him.

He embraced Mrs. Hudnut without hesitation and planted a kiss on each cheek. Then he promptly embraced Mr. Hudnut and planted a kiss on each of *his* cheeks—a Continental salute.

"Well," said Natacha's mother. "Let me look at Julio in the flesh. Even more charming and handsome than you are on the screen."

"I do not deserve such praise, Madam. I thought the daughter was attractive, but the mother—oo-la-la—"

Mr. Hudnut winked at Valentino.

"That's the way to do it, my boy. Hand them a line. They love it."

"Thank you, sir."

"Rudy, this calls for a drink," said Mr. Hudnut. "What are you offering?"

"You'll enjoy it, sir. It's a special brand of wine fermented from the grapes of southern Italy by an ancient winery."

Valentino brought out the decanter and they sat down at the diminutive table in the dining room, so close that they pressed against each other. Toasts were drunk.

Valentino seemed at his gayest and Natacha was proud and triumphant. This now top-ranking star who, apparently, had won the affection of her parents almost on the instant, was, when one came down to it, her very own property. Natacha was very acquisitive when it came to art.

Dinner was served. These dishes had been prepared by Natacha herself, following Valentino's recipes closely and his detailed written instructions given to her the evening before. The menu:

> Main course:
> > *Bisteca Milanese*
> > (Beefsteak Milanese)
>
> Dessert:
> > *Pesca con Vino Rosso*
> > (Peaches with Burgundy)
>
> Wines:
> > California Grape
> > Italy Grape

The meal went well. The conversation flowed easily. Valentino was fully aware of the evening's importance. He had a family, at last. He was no longer alone, secluded in a room, hemmed in by four walls. He had his own people now. It was like coming back after a long journey.

And he owed it all to Natacha. Tonight she seemed more of a woman than an artist. After all, she had prepared a fine dinner, provided him with a decorative, comfortable house, and given him parents. Valentino glanced at her with pride. This was the kind of wife he wanted.

Soon they would be married, and their home would be filled with the gay sound of children. The Hudnuts would visit more often, and at Christmas—

Natacha's voice broke into his dream.

"Rest assured I'm going to see that Rudy makes proper use of his ability. His talent has hardly been scratched."

Perhaps the least-known facet of Valentino's make-up was his intellect. It was vastly superior to that ordinarily associated with movie stars. He may have been lacking in worldliness, he was not shrewd enough to play the "angles," but he had a wide range of knowledge. This was evidenced in part by his books, books a library would be proud to own. Many were excellent examples of the engraver's art, selected judiciously by Valentino.

The books were in Latin, French, German, Spanish, Old English, Greek, Russian and, of course, Italian. Valentino had read all the books he owned, and was thoroughly familiar with their contents. He had a precise, retentive momory.

The range of Valentino's interests was shown in his collection of costumes of every nationality and every period. With these, Valentino collected books on customs and costumes of nations.

He generally read histories in two languages, English and Italian, so as to be sure of his facts and to weigh the impact on his mind.

As an appendage to his costume collection, Valentino owned specimens of every spear, dart, sword, cutlass, and side arm, all of which he prominently displayed on red velvet. Alongside these stood pieces of carved ivory, old silver, jade and onyx statuary. And he knew the story behind every piece he owned.

Rudolph Valentino was more than just a celluloid idol.

Valentino and Natacha Rambova arrive in Paris by plane from London during their international dancing tour.

Valentino loved to get into greasy coveralls and tinker with his high-powered cars.

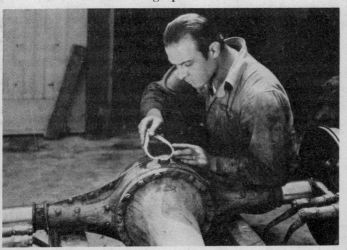

With Nita Naldi,
leading vamp of the 20's, in *Blood and Sand*.

With Agnes Ayres in an exotic
love scene from *The Sheik*, the film that established
Rudy as the screen's greatest lover.

With Lila Lee as Carmen in *Blood and Sand*.

Sporting beard and beret, he poses in his Mercedes-Benz.

At the wedding of Mae Murray to Prince David Mdvani, for whom he was best man.
(Bottom) With Bebe Daniels in *Monsieur Beaucaire*

With Gloria Swanson in *Beyond the Rocks*

In his costume as Gallardo in *Blood and Sand*, Valentino celebrates the fifth annual "Paramount Week." Although Famous Players-Lasky became Paramount Pictures in 1917, to insiders it remained "Famous" for years to come.

In *The Young Rajah*

Posing for a newsreel photographer. Valentino wore a beard during the filming of *The Hooded Falcon,* his wife's production which ended in a fiasco.

CHAPTER EIGHTEEN

THAT evening after dinner, they visited the Auditorium Theater in Los Angeles and saw *The Sheik*.

Mrs. Hudnut was properly impressed. On the drive home her husband nudged Valentino. "You sure have what it takes! How do you do it, boy?"

Natacha interposed. "I wouldn't give two cents for that story. It was Rudy who brought those people into the theater."

Later, at bedtime, Natacha at first insisted that her parents sleep over. They could sleep on the bed while she used the couch.

Mrs. Hudnut remarked that the bed was too narrow.

Mr. Hudnut's eyes twinkled. "That bed seems wide enough to me."

Mrs. Hudnut's eyes also twinkled. "My dear Richard, anyone can see that this is definitely a single bed."

To settle the argument, Natacha phoned and made a hotel reservation for them.

On the following day, Valentino and Natacha went to the hotel and helped the Hudnuts pack. Valentino drove them to the station.

On the platform, waiting for the San Francisco train, Natacha stood close to her mother. Mr. Hudnut put his arm through Valentino's.

"I like you, son. Look here, why don't you pay us a visit in

Frisco as soon as you finish this picture you're doing? Promise?''

"I will be delighted, sir."

"And look, son, any time you want to start calling me Dad, it's okay with me. And one more thing. Just in case you ever quit the movies—even for a while—our company is wide open to you. Cosmetics is a big industry. You can pick your job. Will you remember that?"

"I will—Dad."

"Good boy."

The train pulled into the station and there was a flurry of kissing and good-byes. Rudy and Natacha waved till the train was out of sight.

On the way home Natacha drove while Valentino scanned the evening paper. He read the gossip columns, since he was finding mention of his name with increasing frequency. There was an item: "Since that torrid tango dancer with the slithering hips has put on a sheik's kimono, our womenfolk are leaving dirty dishes in the sink."

Valentino's face darkened. His eyes narrowed in silent fury. Natacha glanced at him. "What is it?"

"Those parasitic gossipmongers—why don't they leave me alone?"

"Remember what I told you, Rudy. From now on you must school yourself to be indifferent."

Moran of the Lady Letty was completed on schedule in the latter part of November. Valentino took a vacation by himself and, with Natacha's blessing, visited the Hudnuts in San Francisco for two weeks. On a clear November day, with the air sunny and brisk, he walked to the spot where he had met Norman Kerry that fateful day when Norman had suggested a try at Hollywood.

Valentino recalled his brief bond-selling career. He recalled his penniless state, the gnawing hunger, the feeling of not being wanted.

And now? He tried to comprehend, to assess his present status. It was difficult to believe it, but *The Four Horsemen* and *The Sheik* were playing to capacity houses here in San

142

Francisco; and he had been told it was the same elsewhere.

He had become a star. His name blazed in electric lights wherever there was a theater; his dream had materialized. With fame had come money; he was earning a substantial amount each week, with more in the offing.

People would say he now had everything. Yet he knew he had not accomplished the thing that was most important to him. He had not yet won the love of Natacha. Her physical aloofness remained a source of irritation for him.

He was also nagged by the fear of disappointing her in her artistic demands. His conception of art was his own feeling for beauty and the natural rhythm of life. He wanted to interpret his impressions in his own way, whether in acting, dancing, writing poetry, or growing flowers. What more could anyone want for him? Yet he knew Natacha had her own unshakeable ideas about art and how he should perform. She wanted everything done her way, and although he tried to accommodate her at all times, she tended to be unreasonable.

At the same time he knew there could be no other woman for him. He would have to speak to Jean Acker again about pushing through the divorce, for he had to marry Natacha before something came up to make her change her mind.

As soon as Valentino returned from San Francisco, he started work on *Beyond the Rocks*. He signed a regular contract with Famous Players-Lasky which gave them an option on his services at a salary of a thousand dollars a week. He would co-star in this picture with Gloria Swanson. She was the new queen of the movie colony and the opportunity to play opposite her was considered a plum.

Natacha, as Valentino had almost anticipated, criticized the story of *Beyond the Rocks*. She found it inane and pointless. But the fact that his co-star was the fabulous Gloria Swanson mollified her somewhat.

They made their decision to buy a house, since the bungalow was so small. They picked out a large house on Wedgwood Drive, in the Whitly Heights section.

They pooled their resources, scraping together whatever cash they had available to make up the down payment. Valentino put in the thousand dollars he had saved toward the possible purchase of a farm. This left them with little money for the purchase of new furniture and equipment—Natacha wanted nothing from the bungalow—but Valentino assured her that with his increased salary it would not take long to furnish the house.

He felt certain that Jean Acker would obtain her divorce by spring, at which time he and Natacha could be married. He decided to move Natacha into the new house for Christmas so they could enjoy the holiday together in a festive setting. Their private menagerie—Zela, the lion cub; the police dogs; the rare lizard; the skinny horse; and Mathilda, the snake— moved with her. To keep up appearances, Valentino himself took an apartment.

The only furniture in the Whitly Heights house was a chair and a bed. But on the day before Christmas, Valentino had a truck deliver a Christmas tree big enough to fill a room. It was the first tree either of them had had a chance to decorate for several years and they went about their chores with gusto. They hung stockings on the mantelpiece and each filled the other's stocking with candy and novelty jewelry. Natacha decorated the entire house with holly wreaths, fir branches and paper cut-outs of Santa and his reindeer. What excited Valentino more than anything else was Natacha's blithe, uncomplicated spirits. He had never seen her so happy. Tonight, he reflected, there would be no weary arguments about art, no tirades about the tawdriness of Hollywood productions, no lectures about the parts Rudolph Valentino should or should not essay.

After dinner, Natacha lit the candles on the tree. The time had come for opening the presents. They decided there was no point in waiting for the morning. There was a new tie for Valentino; also a box of monogrammed handkerchiefs; and finally a set of automobile wrenches for his work on the car.

For Natacha there were an emerald brooch and a gold compact with the inscription: "From Rudy to Natacha with Love."

"Thank you, Rudy," she murmured. "That was sweet of you. Merry Christmas, dear."

"Merry Christmas, Babykins, and thanks for those splendid gifts. And here is something special for you.''

He took her hand and gently placed a diamond ring on her finger.

"An engagement ring!" said Natacha. "Rudy, you *are* precious.''

She came close to him and clung to him, and Natacha Rambova had given way once more to the blue-eyed colleen, Winifred Shaunessey

It was a long, lingering kiss, passionate, tender, fulfilling; and at last Valentino released her.

She looked at the ring. "Rudy, first the brooch, then the compact, and now this ring—you must have spent a small fortune.''

"Not exactly, Babykins. The fact is I did not spend any money at all. I just told them I was Rudolph Valentino and they gave me anything I wanted—to pay for in the future, of course. Wonderful system.''

"Rudy, to buy on credit costs no less than cash—usually more. Besides, it puts you in debt. Part of your salary should be saved in the bank, as you once said yourself.''

"You are right, Babykins. I will begin tomorrow. From now on my slogan shall be, 'To the bank.' ''

"You, Mr. Valentino, are impossible.''

"And sometimes I do impossible things.'' He smiled mysteriously. "Now, the surprise gift of the evening,'' he said.

"More?''

"Close your eyes,'' he commanded.

He stole out of the room, and returned in a moment. When Natacha opened her eyes again, he pointed to the fireplace. There was the tiny head of a Pekinese pup protruding from one of her stockings on the mantel.

"Rudy, how wonderful!'' She took the trembling pup in her arms, and leaned over to kiss her fiancé. "This is a Christmas I will never forget,'' she said. She was trembling and her eyes were bright.

If Valentino had finally reached the heart of this complex woman, this would truly be a holiday he would never forget.

CHAPTER NINETEEN

AFTER the holidays, preparations were begun for the production of *Blood and Sand*. This was to be another story from the pen of Ibáñez, and the scenario, once more, was written by that gentle little lady who had first opened the gates for Valentino in *The Four Horsemen*—June Mathis.

Valentino's salary for this film was to be a thousand dollars a week.

In *Blood and Sand* Ibáñez tells of a young Spaniard, Juan Gallardo, who is fascinated by the bull ring and climbs to the top as a famed matador. He marries his sweetheart but he meets and succumbs to the wiles and sultry charms of an aristocratic siren who drives him to neglect and desertion of his wife. This woman tires of him in short time and turns to another lover, spurning the distracted Gallardo. He cannot forget this woman, and he will not go back in remorse to his wife. In the arena he falters because of this anxiety within him and is gored by the bull. He is carried to the chapel at the arena and here he lies in deathly pain. His frantic wife hurries to him. He dies in her arms while the roar of the crowd is heard outside as they witness another struggle between a beast and a man.

Here was opportunity for the portrayal of a wide range of emotions, human hopes, desires, passions and frustrations. And for once, Natacha had no biting criticism to offer. At last, she said, Rudy had been given a film with a real artistic potential.

The studio imported costumes and bullfighting equipment from Spain and Mexico, including photographs and diagrams of the *corridas* in Madrid and Seville.

The technicalities were probed and data was gathered to give the picture authenticity. While these preliminary operations were going on, Valentino continued to shoot the final scenes of *Beyond the Rocks* and by January 25, 1922, that production was wrapped up. It became a fairly successful box-office attraction, though in quality not at all up to the standard that Valentino had set for himself.

He therefore immersed himself in the new picture. He studied the technical aspects of the bull ring, the procedures, the movements of the participants and their reactions; also the behavior and emotions of the spectators. Natacha helped him by discussing with him the details of this ancient sport.

During these days Valentino moved and lived in a new world of his own creation, the world of the toreador. He was introduced by the studio to a retired matador who, during the filming of *Blood and Sand*, was employed as Valentino's dresser.

From this one-time hero of the *corrida* Valentino learned much of the details of the sport, the native understanding of it. He learned how to handle himself in a bull ring, how to maneuver the *muleta*—the square of red cloth—and how to deliver the *coup de grâce*, the plunging of the thin sword into the bull's shoulders.

He learned the work of the picador, riding in on horseback, to prod and enrage the bull with the lance; also the footwork of the *banderillero* as he dances into contact with the lanced bull and inserts into the animal's bleeding hide the sharp-pointed darts decorated with crimson and blue ribbons, the *banderillas*.

And now Valentino, over and over again, under the tutelage of the old matador, practiced all this, side-stepping and dancing away from the bull's charge to avert being gored.

Also, over a glass of that rare Italian wine in the Whitly Heights home, with Valentino and Natacha as fascinated listeners, the matador recounted thrilling tales of his younger days when he was king of the *corridas* and the idol of all Spain.

Soon Valentino had blended himself into the character of the leading role, and he became to all intents and purposes Juan Gallardo, the toreador. He assumed that fatalistic outlook—he conducted himself as though he lived for the moment. He even ate as a toreador would eat, always considering each meal the last one.

He read books on the history and art of the bull ring; Natacha worked with him, coaching him, giving her own views on the subject.

One night, in the living room, he was practicing with the cape, using a tablecloth. Natacha took the part of the bull and as she charged him, Valentino would step deftly aside, sweeping the cape in a graceful arc.

Finally they rested and refreshed themselves with ginger ale and cookies. Her usually pale face flushed from her exertions, Natacha suggested, "It would help the picture greatly to film it in the original locale."

"You mean Spain?"

"Of course."

"But the studio has already scheduled it for local production."

"Insist on Spain. Tell them a story about bullfighting needs the background of the land of real bullfighting. California is not the place for *Blood and Sand*."

So Valentino went to the studio and told them he wanted the picture shot in Spain. At Natacha's prompting, also, he asked that George Fitzmaurice be made his director. He was refused on both counts. Fred Niblo was named the director and he was told the studio could not undertake the expense of taking a company to Spain. The Hollywood sets had served as adequate backgrounds for every kind of picture under the sun . . . pictures with Greek backgrounds, British backgrounds, Chinese backgrounds and what not had been filmed on the studio lots. What was so special about a Spanish story that demanded an authentic setting? Valentino's job was to act, anyway, not to find far-off countries as sites for Hollywood movies.

148

Valentino accepted all this with his usual sense of resignation. But not Natacha. She was irate over the "stupidity" and "near-sightedness" of the studio executives. And once again Valentino had to struggle through a production with his fiancée's carping voice ever-vocal in the background.

The production of *Blood and Sand* was well under way when, on March 4, 1922, Valentino was granted his interlocutory decree of divorce from Jean Acker with the admonition by the Court that it would not become final until a year later.

Valentino walked out of the courtroom trying to comprehend that he was free at last. He had the legal right now to marry Natacha. The long wait was over. In his excitement he almost forgot the one year.

He waited for Natacha at the house until she came home from the Nazimova set, and he broke the news to her.

"Wonderful," she said. "But it's still a matter of a year."

"How can they do this to us? There must be a way to get around that," said Valentino.

"Yes. Others seem to have done it," said Natacha, "by going to another state or even to Mexico."

"Then let's do the same."

"Not so fast, Rudy darling. *Blood and Sand* is a great responsibility and we stay put until you finish that picture."

"If you say so, Babykins."

Mr. Gilbert, Valentino's attorney, advised him that it would be wise to obey the law and wait the year until the divorce action became final.

However, Valentino and Natacha had no intention of waiting. In their minds it was legal to get married in Mexico as others before them had done.

The last sequences of *Blood and Sand* were completed during the second week in May. Since Natacha's work on Nazimova's *Salome* had ended at about the same time, they made hasty preparations to take the trip. They planned to go to Mexicala, just across the border in Mexico. They were accompanied, to act as a witness, by Douglas Gerrard, Valentino's close friend. First they motored to Palm Springs.

There they picked up Dr. White, another friend, and proceeded to Mexicali.

The marriage took place on May 13 in the Mayor's house. News of their arrival had preceded them. There was a string orchestra on the porch of the house, supplying the ceremonial music, while in the yard of the home was the town band pounding out stirring martial renditions with great gusto.

At once the whole town seemed to wake up from its siesta, and under a cloudless blue sky and warm Mexican sun a full-fledged fiesta was soon in progress. There was singing, much dancing and the drinking of native wines and liquors, including the inevitable *tequila*.

The Mayor made a speech in which he thanked the couple for their consideration in honoring this humble village and bringing to it a holiday spirit. Mexican dishes were served in generous quantities, and the band serenaded Valentino, his bride, and his friends.

The fiesta continued with dancing, singing and drinking, and it lasted through the hot hours of the day and well into the cool twilight. Finally, with the band playing louder than ever, and the people calling out fond farewells, the newlyweds were escorted to the border by the Mayor and the Chief of Police in their official automobile, a steaming, rattling Model T Ford.

Final farewells were exchanged and the Valentinos motored to Palm Springs. Gerrard returned directly to Los Angeles from Mexicali.

As soon as the newlyweds stepped into the hotel in Palm Springs, they received a long distance telephone call from Gerrard in Los Angeles. He frantically beseeched them to come home immediately because certain legal complications had cropped up.

Valentino and Natacha were alarmed and exasperated. Why weren't they left alone? Didn't they have a right to their own private lives? Why weren't they permitted to begin their honeymoon?

It was a long and anxious trip back with Valentino at the wheel and Natacha sobbing against his shoulder. They arrived in Hollywood well past midnight on Saturday, and drove to the Whitly Heights home.

There a reception party was waiting—uniformed police.

A copy of the charge was read to Valentino. He was being arrested for bigamy, having broken the one-year decree.

"Please," begged Natacha, "there must be some mistake. This is terrible. This will ruin us."

"Sorry, Mrs. Valentino. We have our orders from the District Attorney himself."

"We broke no law. Rudy is a free man. He has his divorce papers."

"I'm sorry. We'll have to take him with us."

It seemed obvious that for political reasons the officials were grabbing this opportunity to make a good showing of speedy justice. They were sure that the star could not possibly lay his hands on the bail money of ten thousand dollars until Monday. That would keep him in jail at least two days.

Mr. Gilbert, Valentino's lawyer, conferred with Natacha in her home.

"It is advisable for you to leave Hollywood. The publicity will be disastrous if you stay, and your remaining here can only make things worse."

"I suppose you're right."

"I would advise your leaving at once."

Natacha asked Douglas Gerrard and other people she knew whether they could put up the bail. Nobody seemed to have enough cash they could tap.

However, Garrard knew that his personal friend, Dan O'Brien, the Chief of Police of San Francisco, was vacationing in Los Angeles. Gerrard phoned him.

"Sorry, Doug, about Valentino in jail," the Chief said. "But I'm afraid I can't go that much bail. I don't have the money. You know I'd help if I could."

"Dan, we can't let that poor fellow remain in jail."

"Wait a minute," O'Brien said. "I know somebody. He's mighty good at saving money—Tommy Meighan. I'll call him."

When told the bail was for Valentino, one of the era's great stars, Meighan commented: "Swell chap. I'll get the money." He hurried to the bank, which was open a half-day Saturday. He soon appeared at O'Brien's hotel room and handed him a certified check for ten thousand dollars.

That Saturday afternoon Valentino was freed to await his hearing in court.

CHAPTER TWENTY

THE worst was yet to come for Valentino.

His honeymoon was shattered and it looked as if his career was about to be shattered also. The newspapers were having a field day telling the story of Valentino's disregard of the court order.

He felt the whole world was laughing at him and Natacha. Crowds of people flocked by their house out of curiosity, and cranks telephoned them. The situation became intolerable. Then the boom was lowered. "Rudy," Natacha said, "I'm leaving you."

He couldn't believe his ears. He tried to talk, but his throat was tight.

"Mr. Gilbert has advised me to leave Hollywood until things are settled," she said. "He said it would be disastrous if I stay. I think he's right."

"No, Natacha. No. Stay with me . . . we'll fight this together. What would I do without you?"

But Natacha was adamant. Her decision had been made. She tried to spell out the horrors they would have to face if they stayed together and finally Valentino could understand that it would be for the best if Natacha didn't have to go through the police court hearing. He could understand, but he couldn't fully accept it.

The next day, she was packed and ready. She was going east to her parents. Valentino drove her to the station.

"Some day," she said, as they waited on the platform,

"we will finish that honeymoon."

He tried to speak to her, anything—but his mouth trembled and his throat was all choked up. He had to look away. He didn't want her to see the tears in his eyes. He tried desperately to stifle the sobs that were coming up almost of their own accord. Her eyes were moist, too.

"Rudy, don't you believe your own words? Remember you told me everything would be all right."

"I am sorry. I—I lost myself."

She wiped his eyes with her kerchief.

"When the train comes, turn around, dear, and face the other way. Don't look this way until the train is gone."

He nodded. Words were impossible. She put her hands on his shoulders and kissed him.

"Rudy, no more tears."

The train was approaching. As she directed, he looked the other way. The porter took her bags and she boarded the train. The locomotive hissed out of the station.

There were reporters and pressing crowds of people. He heard some of their remarks: "Where's your sweetheart going?" "Did you two lovebirds have a quarrel?" "Come on, Rudy, are you two really married, or what?" "Did the bride run out on you, Rudy?"

He fought his way through the hecklers, got into his car and drove away.

He drove out on Hollywood Boulevard and did not stop.

The sunset was a blaze of orange and golden flame. There was beauty all about him in the boundless vineyards, the citrus groves, the redwood forests, the blue hills in the distance.

But he saw nothing of that.

He drove on and on, the ache within him as unceasing as the throb of the motor. . . .

At the Police Court hearing, Valentino's lawyer, Mr. Gilbert, argued that his client's marriage to Natacha had never been consummated. Without further ado, the case was dismissed. Valentino was free again to pursue his career and private life—with the provision that he observe the one-year period of grace and live separate from Natacha till the end of that time.

Famous Players, now sure that Valentino's pictures would not be barred by court order or through censorship, decided to cast him in *The Young Rajah*. Valentino wasn't too happy with the script, but it had been written by June Mathis, and in deference to her he voiced no objections about his part. If Natacha had been there, she would have been unsparing and unrelenting in her criticism. With her gone, he was able to be more relaxed in his work, and free of the tensions which her strong personality and opinions generated. Yet without her, he felt miserable and bitterly lonely. There were ·women aplenty available to Rudolph Valentino. Many beautiful actresses threw themselves at him. But none of them interested him. For him, there could be only one woman. So he retreated into the cocoon he had occupied before he had become so deeply involved with Natacha.

The press had gone all out in reporting the Mexicali marriage of Valentino and Natacha and its aftermath. The stories had been dressed up to titillate the gossipmongers and those who wallowed in the cesspool of scandal. Valentino had become accustomed to the inane little falsehoods in motion picture columns, but these lurid headlines enraged him. When he was told that this sort of publicity was very good for him and that it was making him a more important personality than ever before, he threw up his hands in disgust. "The last thing I want is to be famous *this* way," he said.

Reporters who interviewed Valentino always came away with a deep appreciation for his mind and his personality. The only trouble was that they wrote very little of what he told them. They felt their readers were not interested in the subjects Valentino talked about, but would rather read about the things he disliked talking about, which they could make up to suit their convenience.

For instance, Valentino almost always began an interview with a talk about the things in his astonishing collections. There were his specimens, exotic enough and colorful enough to adorn a museum. There were his books of many languages, his costumes of every nationality, his encyclopedias on the customs and histories of nations, his collections of armor and firearms, and his statues. The range of his knowledge and interests impressed the coterie of pressmen who came to see them. But they would then exasperate the star beyond measure by printing almost nothing of what he had said. Instead they would devote their columns to a garbled report of his tangled romantic situation.

It was the era of a new form of idol worship, and the idol could be a writer, a boxing champion, a band leader, a Channel swimmer, a baseball player, or a screen star—F. Scott Fitzgerald, the father-confessor of the flapper and the self-appointed chronicler of the "lost generation"; Jack Dempsey, the Manassa Mauler of the boxing ring, idol of the roaring crowd; Paul Whiteman, the King of Jazz; Gertrude Ederle, the first American woman to swim the English Channel; and Babe Ruth, the King of Swat. Valentino had become an idol of motion pictures, and he was the kind of idol people wanted to gossip about. So the newspapermen felt they were doing the job the public demanded when they confined their stories on him to his personal life.

As the separation between himself and Natacha lengthened, he began to miss her more, not less. He could not adjust himself to the loneliness that had once been so much a part of his life, and he refused to cultivate new interests or new friends. He wrote her long letters almost every day and when a day or two passed with no letter from her, he grew frantic and began to worry that she was forgetting him in the absorption of her new surroundings. He talked to her now and then, on the long-distance phone, but this only seemed to make the separation more unbearable to him.

He had a number of complaints about the picture he was doing and he wrote about these in detail to Natacha. Back would come her letter urging him to shake his fist at his producer and director and demand they comply with his artistic recommendations. Because he missed her so much, he felt more obliged to do what she requested than if she were right there beside him. So he became involved in one argument after another with those who gave him direction on set and with those who sat in the front offices. When he lost these arguments—as he inevitably did—he would write Natacha at length, telling her that she was right in her complaints that artists were being pushed around by the men in the counting offices. For their part, the studio chiefs were becoming increasingly annoyed at Valentino's belligerence. They blamed it on the influence of Natacha and there were some who felt that the distance between them was not nearly great enough.

In one poignant letter, Natacha wrote that she was afraid that their abortive marriage plan had done irreparable damage to his career. He replied that there was no basis for her fear. "If anything ruins my career, it will be the pictures which the studio keeps on giving me and nothing else," he wrote her angrily.

By the time *The Young Rajah* was completed, Valentino and Famous Players were at swords' points. Natacha had become so much a part of him, that he was completely unstrung without her. He saw his studio as a heartless persecutor, determined to block him from achieving the artistic highroads that Natacha had plotted for him. This was the studio that had rescued him after Metro had relegated him to limbo, but he could spare them no gratitude. He had, he told himself, paid off that debt with interest. He insisted that the studio give him the absolute right to pass on all stories assigned him, and to accept only those he felt would further his career and improve the quality of the film medium.

"If you don't give me that right, I will know you want to use me only as a pawn, cashing in on my popularity for an immediate return, but giving no thought to my future," he told company officials.

The studio, for its part, was proving just as belligerent. They felt Valentino had to be sat on, otherwise he would stimulate all contract players into making demands that would strip away the authority and power of the studio chiefs. They told him his job was to act, nothing more. When he told them he had offers from other companies who would pay him a better salary and permit him more freedom besides, they reminded him that he had a contract with them and that it was as unbreakable as an iron chain.

Angered, Valentino decided to test the contract. He walked off the lot, saying he intended to make a new deal with another company. Famous Players went to court immediately, and despite the protests of Valentino's lawyer, got an injunction which barred the actor from appearing in any motion picture.

Natacha wrote him she was very proud of him. But he was unemployed again, and cut off from his income. He had saved only a little money and that would be gone very quickly. There was no point in his remaining in Hollywood right now, because he had nothing to do. He decided to go east, to see Natacha.

In order to avoid newspaper notoriety, his friend Douglas Gerrard brought him a full black beard which he was to wear on the train. In this way he hoped to pass unrecognized by the reporters. At Valentino's request, Gerrard would go east with him.

As always happened in these cases, the secret leaked out, and Rudy was met by reporters and scandalmongers at every station along the route to New York.

"Come one, Rudy, that beard doesn't fool us. Give us the lowdown. Are you going to meet your wife?" "How about the year's waiting time, Rudy?" "How long are you going to stay with Natacha?" "Come on, Rudy, take those whiskers off. We know you." This was the type of remark flung at him by batteries of reporters and sob sisters whenever the train pulled in at a station.

A cab brought Valentino and his friend Gerrard to the Hudnut country home, a twelve-hundred-acre estate of mountain landscape, breathtaking in its natural beauty—wooded slopes, crystal clear streams, indigo blue lakes.

Natacha came out of the house at the sound of the auto horn, and when she looked at Valentino and saw the huge black beard covering his face, the dark-lensed goggles shielding his eyes, the soft gray hunter's cap drawn low over his forehead, the tweed golfer's suit he wore, the golf bag flung over his shoulder, she burst into the loudest and longest laugh that Valentino had ever heard from her.

"Oh, my heavens, is that you, Rudy?"

"Of course." He removed his beard and the goggles.

"Rudy!"

"Babykins!"

They embraced, then stood apart, looking into each other's eyes. Finally Natacha turned to her parents who had come forth to join them. "Mother, Dad—I want you to see this. Rudy, put the beard and goggles on again." He did, and the Hudnuts were quite amused.

"Son, mighty glad to see you, beard or no beard," said Mr. Hudnut.

He gripped Valentino's hand. Then Valentino took Mrs. Hudnut's hand and kissed it in courtly fashion. Mrs. Hudnut beamed.

Natacha herself now removed Valentino's beard, saying, "Don't you think he looks better this way, mother?" Then she turned to Gerrard. "I'm truly sorry, Gerry. I've neglected you terribly. Come into the house and I'll make it up to you with the finest Scotch-and-soda you've ever tasted. Or champagne, if you like. Come along, Rudy. You and I have a long session awaiting."

CHAPTER TWENTY-ONE

THE stay at Fox Lair proved to be an experience that Valentino would never forget.

The summer days were idylls replete with pleasure and laughter. The trio—Valentino, Natacha and Gerrard—were always either on the golf links or in the lake, swimming. Natacha was at Valentino's side throughout the daylight hours, and in the cool of the evenings they took long walks on needle-carpeted pathways through pine glades and along the banks of the lake.

On such a night they strolled along the edge of the waters, peering into the still depths and admiring the reflection of the myriad stars. Gerrard had diplomatically remained behind on the veranda, sipping a Scotch-and-soda with his host.

Valentino and Natacha walked slowly, arm in arm. They were silent as they listened to the thrumming of insects, the call of a whippoorwill close by and the echoing answer of one in the distance. The tranquility and sheer beauty of the scene reawoke in Valentino the innate longing to live on the land, away from the press and confusion of crowded cities.

"Rudy, these days are precious. But there is one thing that worries me."

"Nothing should worry you. We have each other."

"That may not be as perfect as it sounds."

"I do not understand."

"Rudy, as far as your career is concerned, it's a mess and you know it. I feel that I'm responsible."

"You?"

"Of course."

"But how? Please—you must not talk like that—"

"Rudy, let's be truthful about it. Since you've known me, you've had trouble with the studio. Now there's an injunction and you can't even earn a living."

"I feel I've struck a blow for the actor's side of the industry. And I'm sure Mr. Gilbert, my lawyer, will work it out all right. I could not go on the way the company handled my assignments."

"You are right, Rudy. But I feel I've influenced you too much. I know the studio people insinuate that I manipulate you like a puppet."

Valentino's eyes implored her. He said, "Once you told me to be indifferent to people who don't know what they're talking about. Now I can tell you the same thing. I have learned much about values from you. Perhaps I've done what you wanted, but I've done the right thing."

She pressed his hand. She moved closer to him and leaned against him as they walked. They reached a mossy bank and sat down upon it. Valentino threw some pebbles into the placid waters. They watched the reflection of the stars break into numberless tiny irregular hexagons of light.

"Babykins, did you ever stop to think you are my wife?"

"Almost your wife."

"Ah, that wedding in Mexico."

She sighed. "The gods were jealous."

In the last week of August the Hudnuts left the estate to the caretaker and, with Valentino, Natacha and Gerrard accompanying them as far as New York, they sailed for Europe.

Natacha established her residence in New York with her aunt, Mrs. Werner, in an apartment on Sixty-seventh Street, not far from the residence of Valentino who had moved into the Hotel des Artistes, situated on the very same street. Gerrard had gone back to Hollywood to resume his screen career.

From August into the succeeding months Valentino and Natacha lived at these apartments, observing carefully the one-year requirement of separate residences; and Valentino,

161

because of the strictness of the injunction, was unable to accept any engagements entailing acting.

Meanwhile a strange phenomenon was taking place. Despite the adverse publicity in connection with the legal involvement between Valentino and Famous Players, his pictures were increasing their hold upon the imagination of the public. The theaters in which they were exhibited were always packed. People would see the same picture several times, for each viewing disclosed some new facet of his personality.

And it was strange also, that while *The Four Horsemen*, *The Sheik* and *Blood and Sand* were packing them in solid and grossing millions for the producers, Valentino was on the streets of New York, penniless, not working, getting into debt, and wondering how long the litigation would endure.

And because of the tremendous success of the Valentino personality, at once the major studios began grooming chosen male stars to fill the gap caused by Valentino's absence from the screen.

Actors like Ramon Navarro, Ricardo Cortez, John Gilbert, Rod La Roque, Gilbert Roland and Nils Asther were publicized as the new Valentinos, but the public considered them on their own merits and found none of them to be adequate replacements for the original.

The mannerisms and Latin appearance of Valentino were imitated in every degree of simulation but audiences still regarded Valentino as original and unique.

During these critical days Valentino had the feeling that he had bounced back to the park-bench-sleeping period in New York, back to the days of sweeping barroom floors on the Bowery.

But there was a difference. In that bygone era his name had not attained godly power that spellbound multitudes.

During the autumn and winter days which followed he spent many hours with his loved one, browsing in the public libraries, exploring the great art collections in the museums.

Natacha found work, occasionally, in the design department of a dress salon or for an interior decorator. Valentino's clothes—which he always wore so neatly—began to show the first signs of seediness.

But while he was with Natacha he forgot his economic plight and he laughed at his own predicament. He enjoyed each precious moment in her company. He felt confident in the guiding star of his destiny; his faith was calm, mystic.

He dreamed of great achievements yet to come, artistically, as Natacha would want it. His one purpose in life was to work toward the goal of Natacha's ideals, for these now were also his own ideals. His fulfillment was in pleasing her.

Frequently, they went down to Roseland Ballroom to dance like school kids. On one such occasion Valentino forgot to wear his dark glasses and an observant blonde recognized him as he and Natacha danced toward her.

"Goodness, it's Valentino! Rudy Valentino!"

At once the crowd congregated. Dancing was forgotten and they all stared at him as he continued to dance with Natacha, not yet cognizant of what was taking place. Then the music stopped and as Valentino and Natacha started toward a seat, they were surprised to see all the dance couples standing before them en masse. They were friendly, laughing, calling out greetings.

Valentino acknowledged this with a smile.

Voices were heard—"Come on, Rudy, give us a tango." "Please, Mr. Valentino, dance for us." "Rudy, a tango!" Then a chant started: "We want a tango. We want a tango."

Valentino and Natacha exchanged resigned glances. They nodded at their fans and smiled. Then they took position for the tango. The band took up the cue, broke into Argentine tango music, and once more Valentino went through the dramatic tango sequence of *The Four Horsemen*.

In the middle of December, that winter of 1922, Valentino and Natacha first came face to face with psychic manifestations and spirit séances. Their interest was stirred when a friend of Natacha's died, and the friend's daughter told them she was receiving messages from the departed by means of rappings under the table. The daughter, whose name was Joanne, insisted that both she and her mother had received these messages for years from other departed friends. Valentino asked if she could bring a message from his mother. Joanne assured him it would be entirely possible as soon as she had initiated him into the intricacies of her craft.

That Valentino should have allowed himself to believe in spiritualism is not surprising, since for all his intelligence he had always been a dreamer and a mystic. What is surprising is that Natacha, too, allowed herself to be caught up in this pseudo-science. With her shrewdness and her sense of the practical, she might have been expected to laugh it off as nonsense. But this was a point in her life when she, like Rudy, was in a state of drift. The Mexican marriage that had backfired, Rudy's break with his studio, their unsettled situation—all these things had left her stripped of her usual self-confidence. This girl claimed that séances could help foretell her future and give her an insight into what she might expect. Well, it sounded silly, of course, but there was no harm in trying it and seeing what came out.

Valentino and Natacha worked as a team while Joanne guided them into her world of the occult. Soon they were receiving messages from Valentino's mother, from departed relatives and friends, all of whom sent homey messages. This was all well and good, the impatient Natacha said, but what about those tidings for the future? Joanne went back to work. She taught them automatic writing, invested them with symbolic master spirits and acquired for herself a spirit named Meselope. Through Meselope, she now predicted that the injunction against Valentino would be lifted in a short time; that they would take a long journey and visit countries, followed by a shorter journey through this country. Valentino would also acquire a new attorney and a manager.

Through the winter months, they found themselves attending more and more séances. While millions of movie fans across the country were finding their escape in watching Rudolph Valentino movies, the great star and his fiancée were finding their own escape from a vexing world by sailing off into the realm of phantoms.

CHAPTER TWENTY-TWO

In February, 1923, a man named S. George Ullman came into Valentino's life with a heaven-sent idea of how the out-of-work actor could extricate himself from his desperate financial plight. Ullman was the sales manager of the Mineralava Company, a firm which produced a beauty clay used on women's faces. He was a man with an eye toward the spectacular in advertising, and when he read an item in a New York newspaper which described Valentino's state of insolvency he conceived the notion of utilizing the actor as a super-salesman for his clay. The newspaper story noted that Valentino's lawyer had been trying to effect a settlement of his contract dispute with Famous Players but without success. It also pointed out that Valentino had been borrowing money from his lawyer and others to live on in New York and that he was close to fifty thousand dollars in debt.

Ullman made inquiries into the injunction Famous Players had secured. There was no question that it prevented Valentino from performing for any other motion picture company. But Ullman also saw a loophole—the injunction did not say anything about dancing. The company therefore could not stop Valentino from making as much money as he was able to by performing with his feet. Ullman, after making an appointment with Valentino on the telephone, outlined this plan to Valentino and Natacha. They would go on a nation-wide seventeen-week tour as a dance team. They would be paid by his company. After each performance, Valentino would make a brief talk about the virtues of the beauty clay and point out that the clay was responsible for his dance partner's beauty and her exquisite complexion.

The idea didn't appeal to Valentino until Ullman mentioned that his company was prepared to pay him a salary of seven thousand dollars a week—seven times the salary he had received as the star of a picture which had swept the country! This salary was higher than Ullman had been prepared to pay when he first sought out Valentino, but it took only a brief meeting with the star to convince him that Valentino would be worth every bit of that money to the Mineralava Company.

"I had familiarized myself with Valentino's pictures and I knew that he was attractive to women," Ullman wrote later. "But until I met him, I had no idea of the extent of his magnetism. . . . To say that I was enveloped by his personality with the first clasp of his hand and my first glance into his inscrutable eyes, is to state it mildly. I was literally engulfed, swept off my feet, which is unusual between two men. Had he been a beautiful woman and I a bachelor, it would not have been surprising. I am not an emotional man . . . I have in fact, often been referred to as cool-headed, but in this instance, meeting a real he-man, I found myself moved by the most powerful personality I have ever encountered in man or woman."

Ullman decided that if Valentino's in-person appeal could magnetize a businessman like himself at first meeting, there was no reason in the world why it would not hypnotize thousands of women into scurrying posthaste to the nearest store to order Mineralava. He was also aware that the unusual dispute between Valentino and Famous Players had made the star's activities a matter of important news interest and that he would be able to extract maximum publicity mileage out of a Valentino dance tour. Because of these factors, the offer he made to Valentino represented the highest sum anyone in America had ever paid to a dance team.

Once Valentino heard the seven-thousand-dollar figure, he was ready to sign at once. Natacha, however, had other ideas. She told Ullman he would have to wait a few days for their answer and after he was gone, voiced strong objections. "I want you to be known as the greatest actor of our time, and for you to appear professionally as a dancer again would be a step backwards in your career," she told Valentino. "Besides, when you tell people to go out and buy beauty clay, you become an ordinary commercial purveyor, not the great artist I want you to be."

"But my darling, you heard the man say seven thousand dollars a week," Valentino remonstrated. "There is no other way for me to earn money like that and we cannot live without money. My debts are mounting like pyramids. Would you have us starve?"

The argument between the two was a repetition of what had taken place in Natacha's bungalow during the trying period when Metro could not find any parts for Valentino and the two were reduced to near-starvation. Natacha had argued then that nothing mattered but that Valentino should not compromise with his artistic desires; Valentino had insisted that the elemental necessity of filling their stomachs took precedence over everything else.

Natacha's rigid point of view had not changed since then. She could be, and often was, impractical to the point of sheer folly. Valentino, too, was a dreamer who frequently let his emotions take precedence over the realities and the financial practicalities. But he at least realized that when one reached a point of penury it was time to sublimate one's pride in favor of other considerations. And although her personality was stronger than his and he was so deeply in love with her as to be willing to defer to her judgment and prejudices in almost all matters, he felt he could not yield on a question that was so vital to him. If Famous Players had shown any signs of a willingness to compromise their dispute and permit him to return to acting, he probably would have succumbed to Natacha's pressure and would have either rejected Ullman or put him off. But Famous Players remained obdurate and so Valentino felt he had to be firm with Natacha and ignore all the arguments she raised about artistry coming first.

In addition to the financial considerations, Valentino was interested in accepting Ullman's offer for another reason. He had been chafing at the bit over his inactivity and he was afraid that if he remained too long on the sidelines, the public that he had captured with his performance in *The Sheik* would forget him. He much preferred that the public view him again in a powerful motion picture than as one half of a tango team, but it was better to be doing some kind of public performance than nothing at all.

After several days of argument, Natacha's resistance was finally overcome, and the two signed their contract with Ullman. The final weapon that Valentino used as a convincer was the couple's new-found addiction to spiritualism. Joanne's prophecy was that Valentino and Natacha would take both a short trip—presumably meaning a trip around the country—and a longer trip. Ullman's offer had come soon after the prophecy was made and Valentino maintained that this was the "short trip" Joanne had talked about. Following their tour, they would have enough money to take a "long trip"—a vacation trip to Europe. They had often talked of making such a trip and soon they would have the financial wherewithal to realize this hoped-for excursion. To reject Ullman, Valentino pointed out, would be to turn their backs on a prophecy which had excited and intrigued both of them. It could even lead to all kinds of ill fortune.

Once the agreement with the Mineralava Company had been consummated, Valentino became Natacha's tutor in the art of dancing the tango. She was naturally graceful and had a number of years of dance training as a young girl, so that there was not much that her sweetheart had to teach her. They decided that their program would consist of the same Argentine tango number that Valentino had performed in *The Four Horsemen of the Apocalypse*, followed by Russian and Oriental dance numbers. Ullman advanced them the money to purchase costumes to glamorize their appearances on the dance floor. Watching the two rehearse, the sales manager thrilled to their artistry.

"Valentino was a man who lost himself completely in whatever performance he was called on to do, so that when you saw him on the floor he struck you as a man who brought the deepest passion and sense of romance to his every step,"

e pointed out. "Furthermore, his obvious love for his part-
er heightened the ardor of his movements. Natacha was in
o sense the romantic that Valentino was, but she loved to
ance and when she was on the floor she seemed to lose the
oolness that was normally her métier and became not a
eserved beauty, but an exotic and most desirable woman.
After watching them for a few times, I became more con-
inced than ever that they would captivate their audiences
nd justify the tremendous investment I was making in
hem."

Early in March, 1923, Valentino and Natacha packed their
elongings and left New York by train for Chicago. They
vere accompanied by Mrs. Werner, who had acceded to
Natacha's request that she join them on the tour to take care of
Natacha's wardrobe and act as all-round helper. Ullman,
who had gone ahead to Chicago, met them at the station with
he news that he had made arrangements with the railroad
ompany to hire a private car for them. The tour would begin
n Omaha, Nebraska, and then fan out across the Midwest
nd Far West, taking in both large cities and small towns.
'We've got a beautiful, large railroad car and I guarantee
ou the accommodations will be better than you can find in
ny hotel," the sales manager told them.

During the next few days, Ullman mapped out the fi-
al details of the tour with Valentino while Natacha took on
he job of arranging the decorations and furnishings for
heir private car. On March 13, two days before they were
cheduled to leave for Omaha, a telegram came from Valen-
ino's lawyer with the news that the lovers had been waiting
o long to hear. Valentino's final divorce decree from Jean
Acker had just come through and now he and Natacha were
ree to marry.

Bursting with excitement, Valentino literally carried
Natacha out of her hotel room and rushed down to secure a
marriage licence at Chicago's city hall. There, he was treated
o a rude jolt.

The clerk told him that though the state of Illinois recog-
ized the validity of a California divorce, it required a waiting
eriod of one year *after* the issuance of a final California

decree before permitting a remarriage.

The couple headed back toward their hotel rooms in a state of deep depression. Valentino was almost in tears. "To wait so long and then to be told that our marriage is still not permitted . . . it's unfair . . . it's unfair . . . ," he kept murmuring.

They took their problem to Ullman. The sales manager told them not to worry, he was sure that other states bordering Illinois had different laws and that the couple would simply have to find out which of these states would permit a legal marriage. Valentino then remembered that a man named Michael Romano who had once done some legal work for Metro was now an Assistant District Attorney in Chicago.

"We became very friendly while I was working on *The Four Horsemen*," he recalled to Ullman. "I'll go right down to see him now. I'm sure he'll be able to help me."

In the District Attorney's office, Romano listened to Valentino's problem and smiled reassuringly. "The solution is simple," he said. "Tomorrow morning, you can drive down to Crown Point, just across the state line in Indiana. There's no extra waiting period in Indiana and any Justice of the Peace will be happy to marry you."

So in Crown Point, Indiana, on March 14, 1923, with Ullman and Mrs. Werner as witnesses, and a cost of a five-dollar fee, Rudolph Valentino and his beloved Natacha Rambova at last became man and wife.

It was not the kind of wedding and not the kind of start in married life that the romantic Valentino had envisioned. He and his bride had to rush from the ceremony right back to Chicago. Two hours later, they had to be aboard the private coach that was to take them to Omaha. There would be no honeymoon for them until their engagement as a touring dance team was over. Over the clicking of the train wheels Valentino whispered to his wife, "I won't feel really married to you, Babykins, until we can be alone together on a ship to Europe with nothing to think about except our love."

As the train reached the outskirts of Omaha, the wind began to howl like a banshee and a sudden rush of snowflakes lashed the windows of their coach. The storm continued through the daylight hours. By nightfall, when Mr. and Mrs. Rudolph Valentino were to present their first performance in the Mineralava tour, the storm had grown into a full-blown blizzard and Omaha was blanketed in snow. Traffic in the streets had come to a a standstill.

Backstage at the auditorium, Ullman paced the floor like a father in a maternity hospital. The prospect of launching his tour before a half-empty house filled him with dread. Valentino was almost as nervous and downcast as the sales manager. Only Natacha retained her sense of imperturbability. "The people will come, never fear," she said confidently. "They may be late, but they will get here."

Natacha proved to be a prophet. The opening curtain had to be delayed for half an hour, but when it finally went up the house was filled to overflowing. People had come by the thousands by foot and sleigh, defying every obstacle, to see the man they knew as *The Sheik* and his beautiful bride. When the couple danced their first tango the applause was thunderous and it continued that way for the rest of the evening. After their final number, they did two encores to satisfy the demands of the packed house. Even Valentino's curtain speech in which he made his sales plea on behalf of the beauty clay was greeted with an ovation. Valentino was notoriously poor at reading prepared speeches which were put before him, but he was able to make brief, informal talks with a feeling of sincerity that drew good audience reaction. The crowd's warm response to his speech and the manner in which the people of Omaha had turned out on one of the worst nights in the history of their city augured well for the Mineralava tour.

Valentino proved his unique drawing power on every stop after that. Every one of his performances played to a full house and crowds mobbed him on the streets afterward. Large crowds also made it a practice to gather at railroad stations in towns where publicity preceded his arrival. Even at sidings where the Valentino train stopped to let other trains pass, the word would spread that the Sheik was aboard, and knots of people would run out to wave and shout his name. The majority of people who came to see him were, of course, women, but he also drew a heavy turnout of men. The women came to ooh and ah over him; the men came to eye him enviously, and to see if they could learn and emulate the secrets of his romantic appeal.

Surprisingly, Valentino also proved a tremendous attraction to children. They showed such interest in his appearances that in Wichita, Kansas, and in smaller midwestern towns, city officials actually closed the schools to permit the students to attend his matinee dance performances. Sometimes, the turnouts at his shows were so great that people fought for seats and created ugly incidents. Twice, when these incidents threatened to blow up into full-scale riots, Valentino hurried out on stage and made an extemporaneous talk which cooled the fire of the troublemakers. The charm and poise he displayed in dousing these audience conflagrations before they got out of hand made an enormous impression on sales manager Ullman. When one of these near-riots occurred in Montreal, Valentino got the crowd to behave with an eloquent appeal made in two languages—English and French.

Valentino's charm was such that he was even able to mesmerize an audience in San Antonio which was enraged because their show was held up for two hours. When Valentino and Natacha had unaccountably failed to show up in the theater by curtain time, Ullman kept the orchestra playing and, made a number of appearances out front to assure the crowd that the show would begin soon. It was an unusually hot night, and as time passed without any sign of the dancing team the sweltering audience began to mill around in the aisles, threatening to tear the theater apart unless Valentino appeared. Ullman went out on stage again, but was chased off by a volley of boos, curses, and warnings of a physical assault.

At 10:30 Valentino and his wife finally arrived at the theater and said they would go on immediately. Ullman warned him against going out. "The people are in such a violent mood that the moment they see you they may attack you," he said. Valentino pushed him aside, however, hurried to the stage in his street clothes and began explaining to the audience that a maddening traffic snarl was responsible for his late appearance. He made little jokes about the traffic stiuation in San Antonio and generally handled himself so well that the crowd's ugly temper subsided. They even began to laugh and shout, "Okay, Rudy, now do your stuff." When he and his wife went into their dance numbers, they received as rousing a reception as they had received anywhere else.

The stunning success of the Valentino tour as well as the nationwide publicity it triggered caused a swift realignment of thinking among the brass hats at Famous Players Studio. They had several secret meetings and soon after tendered an olive branch towards Valentino's attorney. Up until that point, they had maintained an ironclad opposition to the idea of taking the star back on any terms except their own. But when he demonstrated through these dancing appearances that his name was indeed box-office magic, they realized that the only way they could capitalize on this magic for their own profit was to get him back on their lot. They had hoped to bring him to his knees by financial pressure, but now that he was earning much more through his dancing than he had ever been paid in motion pictures, they had lost one of their principal weapons in the fight.

The fresh negotiations between the studio and Mr. Gilbert, Valentino's lawyer, dragged on for a few weeks. Valentino and Natacha were both anxious for a quick settlement and when the issue became protracted, they decided that the lawyer had outlived his usefulness to them. Valentino sent him a letter dismissing him and arranged to have Max Steuer, a New York attorney, take over his legal affairs and act as his representative with the motion picture company. At the same time, he asked Ullman to give up his connection with the beauty clay company and become his business manager at the end of the tour.

"Natacha and I are both delighted with the way you've handled everything on this tour and we have faith in your business ability," Valentino told him. "I need you as my business manager and I am sure this will provide you with a much greater future than you could have with your present company."

"I'm very flattered," Ullman told him. But he added that he couldn't possibly accept the offer. He had a family to support and he felt the motion-picture industry was too unstable for his tastes. Besides, Valentino was still under injunction preventing him from appearing on the screen or stage and there was no positive assurance he was going to go back on the Famous Players payroll when his dancing tour ended.

"Think it over," Valentino said to him.

A few weeks later, Ullman abruptly changed his mind. When he told Valentino he had decided to handle his business affairs after all, Valentino said airily, "Oh, I knew all the time you would agree to my request." The startled Ullman demanded to know why Valentino had been so confident. The star looked at his wife and they exchanged broad smiles. "It was all part of the prophecy," they explained. They had been told in their sessions of spiritualism that Valentino would get a new lawyer while on his tour and that he would also get a new business manager. And by now their faith in the occult was so complete that they had a sublime belief that everything predicted for them would assuredly come true. They did not realize that wherever possible they were also directing matters in such a way as almost to insure the validity of their prophecies!

By the time the Valentino tour ended, Steuer had reached a tentative agreement for Famous Players to terminate its injunction and put Valentino back on the payroll for $7500 a week. This was a fantastic sum compared to what they had been paying him when he breached the contract. But Steuer was able to argue successfully that Valentino was now earning seven thousand dollars a week as a dancer, that he had exhibited a box-office magnetism on his tour which few personalities in America could equal and that therefore, Famous Players would have to give him an increase over his dancing pay to get him back.

Natacha was still not satisfied, however. "You must demand the right of approval of the stories they give you or you cannot go back," she said. "Remember, you did not leave them because of the money question. You cannot live up to your obligations as a great artist if you allow them to have control over all creative matters.''

Valentino relayed this demand to his lawyer and instructed him to refuse to sign anything unless this condition was met. Famous Players was furious, but in the end they capitulated. When Valentino, Natacha, Mrs. Werner and Ullman returned to New York, the final details were ironed out. Valentino would get $7500 a week from Famous Players when he began working on the first of two pictures they had in mind for him. They would be filmed in the East, at Famous Players' studios in Long Island City. Valentino would have the right to select the stories for his pictures if he chose and in any case would have the right of story approval. Because of certain technical difficulties, production of the first of these pictures would not start till the fall, so Valentino and his wife could take the vacation trip to Europe they had always talked about. It would be the honeymoon that their dance tour had prevented them from taking earlier.

Valentino's victory was complete. It was a victory that went beyond anything he could have imagined in his most fanciful dreams. He felt he owed it all to his wise and beautiful wife and to the wraiths of the world of spiritualism, to which he was now totally committed. That night, he and Natacha gave a gay party and as they drank their champagne and plied one another with toasts, he said fervently, ''This is the happiest, the most sublime, and the most perfect night of my life.''

In their marital bed, Natacha received her husband with more satisfaction than ever before. She still experienced a shiver of fright as he held her firm, full breasts and rained deep, passionate kisses up and down the curves of her body. But she seemed to gain warmth and confidence as he guided her patiently in their love-making. It would not be long, he felt, before he would be able to melt her coldness completely and evoke in her an ardor that would equal his.

CHAPTER TWENTY-THREE

THE Valentinos' excursion through Europe was a glorious idyll which Valentino later told his friends would live in his mind until the last day of his life. He and Natacha drifted from capital to capital, traveling slowly and luxuriously. They toured England, France, and Italy. Everywhere, mobs of Valentino fans turned out en masse to greet the Sheik and to pelt him with hysterical cries of adulation. Yet despite the frenzy with which they greeted this new screen idol, European moviegoers turned out to be thoughtful and considerate people. They would besiege Valentino for the first day or two after his arrival in each city, but then, having satisfied themselves, would leave him alone so that he and his bride could enjoy their honeymoon. The couple rented cars to roam through the European countryside, took long walks through parks and forests, swam on the picturesque beaches of south France, visited the historical sites, the elegant cabarets, and the palaces that they often read about in books but never before had been able to see. They were lionized by European society and nobility and invited to parties where they met the most distinguished representatives of the artistic, literary, theatrical, and political worlds.

In their spare moments, Valentino wrote poetry—both love poems and poems that derived from his interest in spiritualism. A typical one that exemplified his romantic nature was titled simply "You."

You are the history of love and its justification.
The Symbol of Devotion.
The Blessedness of Womanhood.
The Incentive of Chivalry.
The Reality of Ideals.
The Verity of Joy.
Idolatry's Defense.
The Proof of Goodness.
The Power of Gentleness.
Beauty's Acknowledgement.
Vanity's Excuse.
The Promise of Truth.
The Melody of Life.
The Caress of Romance.
The Dream of Desire.
The Sympathy of Understanding.
My Heart's Home.
The Proof of Faith.
Sanctuary of my Soul.
My Belief of Heaven.
Eternity of all Happiness.
My Prayers.
          You.

Another one called up to him the memory of his mother, and of family love. It was titled ''Three Generations of Kisses.''

> *A Mother's kisses*
> *Are blessed with love*
> *Straight from the heart*
> *Of Heaven above.*
> *Love's benediction*
> *Her dear caress,*
> *The sum of all our happiness.*
>
> *Till we kiss the lips*
> *Of the mate of our soul*

We never know Love
Has reached its goal.
Caress divine
You reign until
A baby's kiss seems sweeter still.

That beloved blossom
A baby's face
Seems to be
Love's resting place.
And a million kisses
Tenderly
Linger there in ecstasy.

Were I told to select
Just one kiss a day,
Oh, what a puzzle!
I would say.
Still a baby's kiss
I'd choose, you see,
For in that wise choice
I'd gain all Three.

These poems and others he wrote were later published in a book called *Day Dreams*.

Because he had read a great deal of Walt Whitman poetry and had gone out to Long Island one day to visit the house where the famous poet was born, he decided to write one poem in tribute to Whitman's memory. He titled it "Glorification to Walt Whitman."

The arms of the earth broke through the sod
With clenched fists in derision
For clay knows not the might of God
It has but earthly vision.

The finger of God wrote in the sky
A sign of mighty fire

> *Reach up to me for I am life*
> *But Earth could reach no higher.*
>
> *With strength of muscle, with might and main,*
> *Earth struggled, strained and tried*
> *But God stretched forth His hand of love,*
> *And Earth was glorified.*

For Joanne, the girl who had inducted Natacha and himself into the spiritualist's faith, he wrote a short piece of verse called "To Meselope, Joanne's Spirit Guide."

> *The serenade of a thousand years ago*
> *The song of a hushed lip,*
> *Lives forever in the glass of today,*
> *Wherein we see the reflection of it*
> *If we but brush away*
> *The cobwebs of a doubting faith.*

Rudolph and Natacha held their own little séances like the one Joanne called up for herself when she gave them their prophecy for the future. Valentino's "spirit guide" took the form of an Indian Chief and he gave him the name of "Black Feather." Through a process of disciplinary concentration and a state of virtual self-hypnosis, he convinced himself that Black Feather was bringing him an assortment of messages from the dead, and particularly from his dead mother. Natacha eagerly awaited to hear about the messages he was receiving and translating to himself. Like Valentino, she had come to believe that spiritualism could really provide advance information about their lives and careers. The two also found spiritualism to be an exciting hobby, as well as a means of draining away tensions.

The Valentinos spent ten memorable days at the sumptuous chateau owned by Natacha's mother and stepfather in the Riviera seacoast town of Nice. They lolled on the beach and swam in the sun-dappled waters of the Mediterranean by day, and at night joined the Hudnuts at gala parties. Neither

Valentino nor Natacha cared much for gambling, but they went to Monte Carlo twice for a lark. Both times, Valentino found himself in good luck at the gaming tables and won a great deal of money. Whenever he found the occasion to gamble in the future, this luck stayed with him to the extent that some of his friends insisted that his séances were held for the purpose of getting tips from the spirits—and that the spirits told him how to load the dice in his favor.

From the Riviera the vacationing couple drove in a Voison into Italy. As he drove toward Milan, Valentino was swept with feelings of nostalgia. Ever the sentimentalist, he found tears stinging his eyes as he passed remembered landmarks. Watching him, Natacha once murmured slyly, "I wonder what would have happened to Rudolph Valentino if he had remained in this country instead of coming to America?"

"He would now be a happy farmer with a fat wife and six children," Valentino answered. "He would be a poor man—but very happy."

"Aren't you happy now?" his wife wanted to know.

"Can you question that, Babykins? When things were at their worst in Hollywood, I often thought of returning here to live. It is lucky for me I could never afford the return trip. If I had, I would forever have lost my chance to fulfill myself as an artist. And worst of all, I would have never have met you, my darling. No, Italy is past; it can never be my country again. But sentimentally speaking, it will always have a little corner of my heart."

His sister Maria was working in a clothing store in Milan and he had written her to meet him at the Hotel Perugia. He found himself feeling strangely nervous about the impending reunion.

"I wonder whether I shall recognize her. Eleven years is a long time," he said several times to Natacha.

"Of course you will know her," his wife assured him. "Relax and enjoy the ride."

The sun rose higher and the dust began to cloud up the highway. They could barely see the farm workers now or the horses, or the chickens in the hen yards.

Buildings and streets hove into view. Milan at last. He

drove through the clean streets. Milan was a beautiful city, a busy place, industrially and culturally. He drove up to the Hotel Perugia. He hurried out of the car. Natacha waved him on to go in without her and greet his sister.

He entered the hotel lobby, his eyes straining for the sight of her. He saw many women there but he could not recognize any of them as his sister.

Then suddenly he did recognize her. How could he have forgotten those dark, thoughtful eyes? She saw him at the same time.

"Maria!"

"Rodolfo!"

They came toward each other. Valentino embraced her closely, kissed her cheeks, her eyes, her hands. She had grown into a fairly attractive young lady, but without make-up and in a cheap, ill-fitting dress, she gave the appearance of a peasant girl.

"Little Maria."

"Not so little any more, my brother."

His eyes were moist.

"I thought I wouldn't know you. I thought you might have changed, but you are the same."

"Rodolfo, I am proud of you. You are a great man. Everybody in Italy knows about you. You are a famous moving picture actor in America. I go to the cinema. I see you on the screen and I make believe you are near me."

Remembering Natacha outside and wondering what she would think of Maria, he looked at her closely. "*Mama mia*, your face—you should use powder, rouge, lipstick. You must make yourself attractive, glamorous. And clothes. That dress—it is an injustice. We shall correct all that—my wife and I will make of you a fine lady and you will have all the young bachelors in Milan running after you. Tell me, how is Alberto?"

"Fine. In Taranto he has a business. He comes to Milan to see me sometimes at the clothing shop."

They talked about Castellaneta and the old days. Their uncle now lived on and managed the farm. They discussed the neighbors, the relatives.

181

He escorted her out to the car, introduced her to Natacha.

"Babykins, this is Maria. Maria, this is Natacha."

Natacha stepped out of the car. She put her arm about Maria and kissed her on the cheek.

"I want you to make Maria beautiful—" Valentino said, "you know, how we do it in Hollywood. The works."

Maria drew back, her dark eyes fluttering. "But it is not to the liking of the Lord, all this powder and rouge. And paint on the lips—that is not moral."

Valentino reassured her. "Maria, you are still living in the past. Even the good Lord recognizes that a woman should look her best. The Lord approves of beautiful things. Isn't that so, Natacha?"

"Of course. Relax, Maria dear, and everything will be just fine," Natacha promised.

Valentino and Natacha spent two days with Maria, then left her to continue their trip through Italy. They promised to visit with her again when they drove back north. In Florence, they stopped at a palace that was the residence of Baron Fassini, a close friend of the Hudnuts. He guided them through his city and through the hill towns that surrounded Florence. He took them to view the great art treasures of the Uffizi and the Pitti Palace galleries and he and Natacha discussed volubly the fine points of each painting while Valentino listened in attentive silence and in admiration of his wife's store of artistic knowledge.

The Baron also volunteered to follow them in his limousine to Rome and act as their guide in the Eternal City. He took them to the Catacombs, where the early Christians buried their dead; the Coliseum; the Forum; the Pantheon; St. Peter's Basilica; the old castle of San Angelo; and the Vatican.

A highlight of their stay in Rome was a visit to the location set of *Quo Vadis?*, which was then in production with Emil Jannings starring in the role of Nero. The filming was going on in such an atmosphere of ludicrous confusion that the Valentinos had all they could do to contain their laughter. The director was Italian and could not speak or understand any other language. There was an assistant director who was

182

Spanish and could speak and understand only his native tongue; a leading lady who was English and could speak and understand no other language; a French actor to whom any other language but French was a strange gibberish; Negroes, cast as slaves, from West Africa who knew only their tribal tongues; and Jannings himself, who stuck solely to his German.

The result: a chaotic mélange of voices—guttural, nasal, cackling, crowing, groaning, and rasping—unintelligible to each other—a babble of "sound and fury" that—as Valentino told Natacha later—could happen only in the moving picture industry—"and my heart goes out to *Quo Vadis?* in sympathy."

South of Rome at that time of year the sandy roads were blanketed with clouds of dust that stung the eyes and choked the lungs. Natacha was so disturbed by it that at her husband's suggestion she went back by train to her parents' home in Nice while he continued on to his birthplace in Castellaneta. He stopped first in Taranto for another reunion, this one with his brother Alberto. His brother accompanied him to their boyhood home on the outskirts of Castellaneta.

When Valentino saw that white-walled farmhouse and the patch of green land about it, it all seemed so small, so lonely, so bereft of any of the glamor and color he had so often attached to it, he felt as if something precious had been lost to him forever. Wandering through his old haunts, he shed a tear or two in remembrance of the boy who had played here in the long ago and acted out charades in which he played the great swordsman.

That boy, he thought regretfully, had never realized his dream. But then he *had* realized a dream which so many other youngsters nourish in childhood and never attain. So how could he complain?

Later, Valentino visited the graves of his mother and father and placed some flowers on them. He held back the sobs as he offered a silent prayer for his dear departed parents.

He then visited with his uncle, but after an hour found himself growing restless. He found he no longer had much in common with his uncle and had little to say to him. For that matter, he was ill at ease with his brother, too. He had always admired Alberto, yet now his brother seemed like a disturbingly simple and untutored person and his account of his prosaic life in Italy had no interest for him. Mass adulation had spoiled him, Valentino reflected, and he felt ashamed. Yet the mood of impatience was too strong for him to contain, so he got up abruptly and announced that he had to leave. He used the excuse that he had important matters to discuss with motion picture people in France and that it was necessary for him to get back there as soon as possible.

He dropped Alberto off back at Taranto and said good-bye with the casual promise that they would soon meet again. In Milan, he picked up Maria and took her with him to spend a week at the Hudnut chateau in Nice. Maria was delighted to see her brother's wife again and after she had washed away the dust of the road, carefully followed Natacha's instructions for applying cosmetics. When she came down to dinner, the Hudnuts complimented her on her new attractiveness and Valentino felt a rush of gratitude toward Natacha for providing Maria with a modern bloom that took her out of the peasant class.

When it was time for Valentino and Natacha to return to America, Maria broke down in sobs. Valentino held his sister close and soothed her by telling her he would be returning often to Europe to see her. This was a promise he meant to keep, yet significantly he said nothing about taking Maria to America. He had often written to his sister in the past that he would bring her to America as soon as he earned enough money to take care of her. He had the money now, but the old promise had conveniently faded from his mind. Maria was part of his old world; she seemed to him to have no place in the new world that belonged to Rudolph Valentino, the famous star.

CHAPTER TWENTY-FOUR

THE Valentinos returned to New York in November, 1923, settled down in style at an expensive suite at the Ritz-Carlton Hotel and swiftly plunged into preparations for Valentino's return to the screen. The first story Famous Players had selected for him was *Monsieur Beaucaire*, Booth Tarkington's story of the French Revolution. Under the terms of his contract, Valentino had the right of story approval. He quickly approved the script because he was anxious to get back on the screen after an absence of almost two years. Natacha, however, demanded that certain changes be made, and the studio quickly complied. They were as anxious to get started as Valentino was.

With his usual propensity for throwing himself completely into a part, Valentino soon became the living, breathing incarnation of Tarkington's costume character. But he soon found Natacha becoming even more deeply immersed and involved in the production than he was. As an art director for Nazimova, Natacha had shown undisputed artistic talents, but she had never been permitted a voice in the actual production. This was an irritant she no longer had to put up with. She had always been intensely interested in becoming an important creative force in motion pictures and she now resolved to use the terms of her husband's contract and his importance to the studio to achieve her ambition. She came on set every day in a capacity that was supposedly advisory but quickly became much more than that. She intruded on every department with suggestions, criticisms, requests—and then demands—for changes. At times she insisted on directing the cameramen and even on directing the director.

Needless to say, she aroused the ire of most of the production people, but she was able to get away with her tactics because of her husband's unswerving support of everything she did. At this point, Valentino was not only deeply in love with his wife but convinced that she had an artistic genius few people could match. Whenever open controversy threatened to break out, Valentino quickly threw his weight behind Natacha and the burgeoning dispute simmered out. The studio executives had sent orders that Valentino was not to be upset or goaded into another walkout, so that his involvements in his wife's behalf was enough to force directors, cameramen, designers, costume makers, and everyone else to control their tempers and defer to Natacha's wishes.

If the studio expected that Natacha's zeal for controlling a production would dissipate after one picture, they were guilty of a serious miscalculation. She assumed an even greater role in the production of *The Sainted Devil*, which Valentino began almost immediately after finishing *Beaucaire*. Once again, her husband's almost worshipful support of her opinions and ideas enabled her to carry them out. It also kept production personnel, ordinarily jealous of any intrusion of their prerogatives, in line. Only one open clash occurred during the filming of this second picture. This involved Jetta Goudal, a French actress who had been cast in an important role in the picture. Like Natacha, Jetta was beautiful, strong willed and outspoken. She resented the "advice" Natacha was giving on set and said so loudly and bitterly.

The result was that she found herself out of the picture.

Angered over her dismissal, Miss Goudal gave out a story that Mrs. Valentino had had her fired because Valentino had become infatuated with her. It made juicy headlines but nobody in the motion picture industry gave it any credence whatever. Everyone acquainted with Valentino knew that his love for Natacha was so complete that he had eyes for nobody else. In fact, many of the Famous Players executives began to whisper that they hoped Valentino *would* become attracted to a woman other than his wife. "If that happens, maybe he'll stop lapping at her heels and behaving like a puppy dog," they gossiped.

Stories of the hold Mrs. Valentino had over her husband inevitably leaked out to columnists and began appearing with frequency in print. Valentino merely shrugged them off. One day a newspaperman discovered that Natacha had made her husband a present of a slave bracelet which he wore devotedly around his wrist every day. He wrote a story about this bracelet in such a manner as to make Valentino look ridiculous. It upset the studio executives, but Valentino pointedly ignored it.

Jibes about the bracelet began appearing in other papers and goaded small boys into chasing after Valentino and chanting that he had become a slave to a woman. As the insults mounted, even Natacha became disturbed and suggested to her husband that he take the bracelet off. Valentino refused. "This bracelet is a symbol of your faith in me and our love for each other," he said. "In time, other men will be wearing such bracelets and no one will laugh. I've started styles before—slicked-down hair, long sideburns, the mannerisms of the Sheik. Eventually, this will become another style." (Valentino's prediction came true, but not until many years after his time. During World War II, GI's began to wear these bracelets as ornaments and as identification devices.)

Both *Monsieur Beaucaire* and *The Sainted Devil* proved tremendous box-office hits when they were released and the result was to convince Valentino that his faith in his wife's judgment had been justified. Many of the production personnel who had worked on the two pictures had come to dislike Natacha so much they secretly hoped the pictures would fail. They were certain that failure would result in her banishment or perhaps her voluntary withdrawal from the activities on the movie set. Now they muttered that the public was so eager to see the dashing Valentino on the screen again that they would have welcomed his new picture no matter how badly it was produced. They may have been right, but there was no way they could prove their point and certainly Valentino was not disposed to place any credence in this argument.

But if Valentino was completely satisfied with Natacha's role in his motion-picture career, he was becoming increasingly restive about her role as his wife. She seemed to have lost the softness and the femininity that had made their honeymoon trip such a glorious adventure. Not only was she involved in his movie-making all day long, but she kept talking about it at night when they were at home alone together. She had even begun writing her own motion picture story which she intended to use as a vehicle for his "greatest production." She was so absorbed in her ambition to be author, artist, producer, director, and all-knowing critic that she had little or no concern for anything else. She had lost all interest in the spiritualism which had so recently intrigued her. She had learned enough about the complexities of motion picture making to convince herself that this was truly the all-consuming interest in her life.

Her face was as beautiful as ever, but the restless and intense look of ambition was beginning to become etched on her features. Her manner had become curt and coolly efficient. Perhaps if Valentino had not opened the door and provided her with the opportunity that had long fired her, she might have finally let her ambition die and devoted herself to her husband's happiness. But instead there was a veil—though gossamer-thin and sometimes hardly discernible—gradually descending between Natacha and himself. He would have done anything to halt its final descent.

He felt that though they were married, they were not close enough as man and wife, with no reservations. It was something he could not fathom but he could feel and sense it. It seemed to disturb the balance of the seesaw on which they sat.

This contained the seeds for destruction of the "perfect" marriage. But Valentino was not ready yet to say anything to his wife about his disquiet. He was still too much in love with her and too fearful of the possiblility of losing her to speak out. He showed his annoyance in only one minor way. He stopped using the name "Babykins"—the pet name he had always favored for her. Natacha's only reaction was to tell him some months later that he had been wise to do this. It was out of character, she said, for a woman in her important position to be called by a childish pet name!

CHAPTER TWENTY-FIVE

FOLLOWING the completion of *The Sainted Devil* and with the agreement of all parties, an independent producer named J. D. Williams took over Valentino's contract from Famous Players. The terms remained the same—Valentino and his wife would still have the right of choosing the stories for the star's pictures. Williams set up a company called Ritz-Carlton Pictures, Inc. which would produce the pictures, while Famous Players retained distribution rights.

The story Natacha had written for her husband—under the nom de plume of Justice Layne—was called *The Hooded Falcon*. It was set in early Spain in the time of the Moors. It was to be a spectacle film and an expensive one at that, with the final cost figured at between eight hundred thousand and a million dollars. Valentino's drawing power was considered so impressive, however, that Williams did not blink at the cost. He even reacted favorably to a suggestion by Natacha that she and her husband go to Spain to collect authentic costumes and props. The couple were told they could spend up to forty thousand dollars for this paraphernalia as well as for film to shoot background scenes.

Valentino was delighted with the prospect of another trip to Europe. He hoped to use it to reawaken the feelings his wife had shown him on their honeymoon tour. Natacha, however, was so stimulated by the prospect of getting her own production on the screen—and with no expense spared to bring out the maximum in artistry—that she allowed herself to think of nothing else. Much of her baggage was taken up with books on Moorish history during the centuries of their domination of Spain, as well as volumes on the social and economic life of the Moors. She intended to read them on the boat and pick up many more books in Spain.

Meanwhile, her husband had filled his own suitcases with a motion picture camera, several still cameras and a number of heavy cans of film. "If you people intend to pick up books or costumes in Spain to add to what you already have, I'm afraid you'll never come home," Mrs. Werner told them jokingly. "Your baggage will weigh your ship down like an anchor and you will never get out of your European port!"

The Valentinos went to France first to meet Natacha's mother. Mrs. Hudnut had decided to go to Spain with them and help in Natacha's "research." The three took a train to Madrid, spent several days in the city, and then went on the Seville, the fabled city of the bullfight, or *corrida*. Valentino felt as if he knew the city, for the bullfighter Gallardo whom he had portrayed in *Blood and Sand* had been discovered (by the author of the original book) living in a small house in Seville. On Sunday, Valentino escorted his wife and mother-in-law to a *corrida* which was being held to benefit the Red Cross. On the way to the bull ring, he visited the Gallardo house. It was by now a moldering, foul-smelling hovel with no atmosphere of any kind, but nonetheless Valentino came out of it insisting that the spirit of Gallardo had manifested itself to him. For the rest of that afternoon, he assumed all the characteristics and mannerisms of his old Gallardo part.

The Spaniards took the bullfighting in stride as they always do, but for the Valentino trio—and particularly for Natacha and her mother—it was a brutal, if hypnotic, experience. The blood of the slain bulls spilled all over the ring and after a while became mixed with the blood of the brilliantly costumed toreadors. The final score came to four gorings, one broken spine, six smashed ribs, and several near-fatal tramplings. The roar of the Spanish crowd washed over everything, the spectators distributing their cheers equally between the toreadors, who were able to score clean thrusts through bull-flesh, and the bulls, who were able to rip holes in the bodies of their human adversaries.

Natacha suddenly grew pale, and clung to her husband as though she were going to faint. Two bony, underfed and over-age horses had come out into the bull ring—ridden by picadors. Two charging bulls rushed to meet them. The picadors lanced the bulls, urging them into a rage and to attack. In the space of a few minutes, the bulls made repeated assaults with horns ripping into the defenseless, feeble horses. These horses staggered about the ring with their entrails dragging along the ground. Attendants ran in, stuffed the entrails back into the horses' bellies and sewed up the gashes. The assaults were repeated until the horses fell dead.

The exhibition sickened Natacha and enraged Valentino to the point where he later complained to the authorities and urged them to rid *corrida* of "a disgraceful and cowardly act."

Natacha was amazed by the attitude of the spectators who cheered the picadors and the conquering bulls until the arena trembled with the continuous roar.

"Please, Rudy," Natacha implored. "I've had enough."

"Same here," said Mrs. Hudnut. "Disgusting."

"They should pass a law preventing horses in the ring. Everything should be on foot," Valentino said.

Valentino was still play-acting his Gallardo part as they came out of the arena.

"Perhaps," he told Natacha, "I shall become a matador, but with fair play. I will give the bull an honorable battle and there will be no disgrace."

There was silence as they boarded a horse-drawn carriage to return to the hotel.

"Darling, did you hear me?"

"I heard you, Rudy," said Natacha. "You are Gallardo. In Italy you told me you were Julio."

She winked at her mother and Valentino put his arm about his wife's waist. "It's a good thing you're beautiful, my love, or I'd beat you every day."

Their stay in Seville was fruitful. Natacha made additional purchases of props for *The Hooded Falcon*—wearing apparel, swords, knives, utensils, tapestries. Her husband, in turn, used up a couple of cans of film taking both close-ups and long shots of Moorish architecture. They spent several nights in cafés observing the performances of Moorish and Spanish dancers. One beautiful Spanish dancer so impressed them with her haunting rhythm and style that the touring couple stood up to lead an ovation for her and then demanded several encores.

Their next and last stop in Spain was the tradition-steeped southern Spanish city of Granada. Here Valentino took pictures of the city's magnificent citadel and its palace, the Alhambra, while Natacha scoured the shops for more authentic props and for Moorish furnishings and utensils. She was taking copious notes of everything she saw that might have some bearing on her planned production and by the time they were ready to leave Spain she had to get a special bag to store her notebooks and memoranda packets. She flushed out dozens of books on Moorish history and tradition from old book stores and spent many hours in the libraries looking through additional historical volumes.

They returned to France to drop off Mrs. Hudnut and to travel through the northern provinces, an area that they hadn't seen during their honeymoon trip. Nita Naldi, the actress who had appeared with Valentino in *The Sainted Devil*, was taking her vacation in France at the same time and she joined them on their tour of the provinces. Nita also made arrangements to return with them to America aboard the S.S. *Leviathan*.

CHAPTER TWENTY-SIX

In New York, the Valentinos found that Williams was making preparations to move his company to Hollywood. "We just don't have enough space to do spectacle films like *The Hooded Falcon* in the East," he explained. "Rather than do some pictures on the West Coast and some here, I've decided it would be better for us all financially if we operated entirely from California."

The Valentinos still had their Whitly Heights home in Hollywood and Valentino had always loved California's year-round sunshine, so their trek to the West Coast was a pleasant experience for them. They had left the movie colony under bitter circumstances, but their return was in the nature of a triumph. Quick to stomp on personalities who it sensed were on the way down, Hollywood was equally disposed to fawn on those screen idols who were riding an upbeat wave. Once again, the elite of the colony showered Valentino and Natacha with invitations for "exclusive" affairs. And once again, Valentino and Natacha made it plain that Hollywood social events held no appeal for them. Even so they took an exquisite delight in the fact that the cynical powers in town who had once snubbed them were now beating a path to their door.

At the studio, however, the Valentinos found that the currents were not flowing as smoothly as they would have liked. Williams was having trouble getting the proper studio space and equipment for the production of "spectacle" movies. And June Mathis, who had agreed to turn Natacha's story into a working screenplay, had not yet completed her script. Williams therefore decided to postpone *The Hooded Falcon* and put Valentino immediately into a picture called *Cobra*. Neither Valentino nor his wife thought too highly of the story and Natacha had several arguments with Williams over it, but in the end consented to do it.

Cobra required some prize-fighting scenes, so Valentino proceeded to "live" his part by sparring with champion Jack Dempsey, who was then making a movie in Hollywood. Dempsey later said of Valentino, "He was no cream-puff, that fellow. He could hit you with a good punch and take a good one too, without folding."

As in the other Valentino pictures, Natacha was all over the lot in *Cobra*, exercising her privilege of controlling the production and imposing her judgment on the director and his assistants. An undercurrent of rebellion soon festered—more serious than anything that had developed on the *Monsieur Beaucaire* and *Sainted Devil* sets. Stories reached the newspapers and film magazines in more lurid form than ever before. Fed by fellow actors in the picture, the production staff and the studio workers, these accounts denounced Natacha's "ruthless tactics," her "selfish domination" of her husband and her "insatiable ambition." Natacha accused four members of the company of spreading the news stories and threatened to have them fired. This added turbulence to already-troubled waters. Valentino again aligned himself completely with his wife, but Williams complained to him that Natacha was "interfering" too much.

"You're an important star and we want to oblige you, but your wife is assuming too much responsibility," he told Valentino. "She's not competent enough to run all phases of production, even though she thinks she is. If your pictures begin to go sour, you'll have your wife to blame."

When *Cobra* was released, its box-office pace was sluggish. In the end, it brought in a fair return, but it was well below the receipts Valentino had drawn for his first two Famous Players pictures. The results came as a rude jolt to the actor. For the first time he came to believe that Natacha had arrogated too much responsibility to herself and that her self-centered ambition might be hurting his career.

Ullman had also been disturbed by the bitter sniping on the *Cobra* set, but had diplomatically avoided saying anything to Valentino for fear of coming between husband and wife. The picture's near-failure now convinced him that he must act, however, and so he urged Valentino to do what he could to divert Natacha's interests. Valentino responded by taking his beloved for a rest in Palm Springs. There, he began to talk to her of the advisability of her spending more time at home, of his love for children, and his desire that they should begin their family.

"It's unthinkable, Rudy," she flared at him. "I'll be glad to have children someday, but now is not the time. Have you forgotten my story of *The Hooded Falcon*? This will be your greatest picture. You need me more than ever now to direct and shape your career, and to protect your artistic intersts. I have lost all my respect for Williams. He doesn't care what kind of picture he throws you into."

Once again, the force of her personality was too strong for Valentino and he dropped the subject of her having children and spending more time at home. When Williams came out to visit them a few days later to discuss June Mathis' now-completed script of *The Hooded Falcon*, Natacha placed the blame on him for the poor returns on *Cobra*. "Why haven't you tried to obtain stories for my husband of the caliber of *The Thief of Bagdad* or *The Black Pirate*?" she lashed out. "Why do other stars rate the best productions while Rudolph Valentino, who towers above them in personality and ability, is persistently given second-rate stories?"

Williams left them in an angry mood. Two days later, while the Valentinos were sitting in their bungalow going over the Mathis script, their telephone rang. Valentino picked it up. It was Ullman calling from Hollywood.

Natacha watched her husband closely as he listened on the

phone. She saw his face grow pale, his eyes fill with disappointment.

"Rudy, what is it?"

He put down the phone slowly and turned around as in a daze.

"Sweetheart, please—please don't let youself go. It was Ullman."

"Well?"

"Ullman says he's just received a notice from Williams—"

"Yes?—yes?"

"Williams has informed Ullman that he's not going to produce *The Hooded Falcon* and admits to breaking the contract."

It is strange, but when the very heavens seem to be tumbling down, there is always that moment of quiet, that single space of calm in the storm—a moment long enough to make one see that nothing is really disturbed on the earth itself. Through the large east window, Natacha could see the expanse of the desert in the light of the descending sun, and a lone blue cloud on the horizon. Through the west window she noticed the San Jacinto mountains rising steeply and majestically to the heights. She kept staring at that mountain for the longest time. Then, at last, she turned away, turned her face into the divan and let the sobs come.

"No crying, dearest. Who cares about that old movie? Besides, there will be plenty more for you to produce. We don't need Williams or any other money-bags. We'll have our own company with George as manager. Ullman is a shrewd businessman, believe me. Now, you stop wasting those precious tears. Williams isn't worth it. Okay? No more tears?" He sat down beside her, took her in his arms, held her close and tenderly.

She said, "Rudy, maybe the newspapers are right in what they are saying about me."

"Now stop that kind of talk. Don't you ever think anything like that again."

The following day, after they had returned from a canter on the desert, Valentino received another phone call from

George Ullman. This time the news was quite different. This time Natacha could see that the expression on her husband's face was a pleased one.

"Please, Rudy, don't keep me hanging. Good news?"

"Terrific, my love!" He put his arm about her and led her into the steps of a tango.

"Sweetheart, listen to this: Joseph M. Schenck, head of United Artists, has a contract all drawn up for us. George just told me on the phone. This is what I've dreamed of—to become part of United Artists—they have the biggest stars and the best company in Hollywood."

"Darling, that's wonderful! Now we will be able to accomplish something of real value. You'll get the best in story material, along with Douglas Fairbanks and the others. For me it opens up a new world to create. Rudy, I'm so happy—"

"George wants me to come right to Hollywood and sign the contract."

"Please hurry, dear. I'll wait for you on needles."

"Now don't get too excited. Try to be calm. A kiss for the road?"

"All the kisses, Rudy." She threw her arms about him and her lips found his.

He went out into the March sunshine and got into his Isotta Fraschini. He drove the hundred and fifty miles to Hollywood in three and a half hours.

George Ullman met him in the front office of the studio and led him at once to the private office of Joseph M. Schenck. Schenck was the chief executive officer of this company of stars which had been organized in 1919 by Hollywood's "Big Five"—Mary Pickford, Douglas Fairbanks, William S. Hart, Charlie Chaplin and David W. Griffith. He extended his hand to his visitor and said immediately, "You belong with us, Valentino, and we're glad to have you."

He pushed a contract into Valentino's hands. "I've already examined it, Rudy," Ullman told him. "Financially, it's the best deal you've had yet and you'll be more than satisfied."

"Well, then I can sign this without even looking at it."

"Better wait, Rudy, there's a clause in there that Mr. Schenck had better explain to you."

Schenck smiled calmly. "It's a few words we put into the contract in order to have smooth sailing once we're making pictures."

Valentino shook his head. "I don't understand."

"Very simple, Rudy," said Schenck. "It merely states that one Mrs. Valentino—your wife, of course—is to have no voice whatever in the selection, the casting, the production, the editing, or the distribution of any of the photoplays in which you appear. Very simple, but indispensable to the peace and efficiency of U.A."

Valentino stepped back as though struck by a blow.

"No . . . no. I won't sign."

"Now, Rudy," said Schenck, "this is your career. You'll join the company of the most famous names in the film industry. When it comes to the selection of story material we have the most competent people you can find. Your wife is a charming lady and very talented in art design. But she is not qualified to direct and produce the pictures we make and we know her reputation for insisting on doing these things."

Valentino's face was strained. He stared at the square of paper with its maze of fine print on Schenck's desk. The contract was the open-sesame to his most important opportunity in motion pictures. But even now Natacha was waiting for the good news—a contract that would include her. This clause would horrify her and its implication embitter her. . . .

Valentino turned to Ullman for help.

"George, what shall I do?"

Ullman's voice trembled. "Rudy, I could advise you on matters of business—anything—but this is one time you will have to make up your own mind."

There was a fateful silence—so still each tick of the clock on the wall was a hammer blow.

Schenck was waiting. "Of course, Rudy, I need not tell you—if you don't sign this contract you are tossing away your opportunity to make truly outstanding pictures. Your wife should want what's best for you."

The moment of decision . . .

199

Ullman slouched down in his chair, his face drawn, his hands gripping the upholstered arms. Only Schenck was calm, collected, seemingly impersonal, but fully aware, nevertheless, of the crisis.

Valentino's eyes were filled with anguish. In all kinds of predicaments he had usually kept his composure, for that was part of his philosophy. This was one time when his philosophy was of no avail. His hand shook as he accepted the pen from Schenck and scrawled his name on the dotted line, directly under the clause.

He felt as if he were another Judas Iscariot. But he also felt that Schenck was right in the things he had said and that Ullman, too, agreed with Schenck.

Schenck gripped his hand, congratulated him. Ullman came forward to wish him the best. "It took courage, Rudy."

Valentino hurried out of the office as though the place were tainted. He got into his car and drove back on the road to Palm Springs in the gathering darkness—a darkness that was not only of the night.

He drove into Palm Springs and he drew up in front of their bungalow. He moved toward the door with leaden feet. Then he was inside, facing Natacha.

"Darling, you've signed the contract!" Natacha's voice was triumphant.

"Sweetheart, I've done something I'm ashamed of . . . I'll break the contract. I won't go through with it."

"Rudy, are you mad?"

"There is a clause in that contract—"

"Rudy, a contract is a series of clauses."

"But this clause refers to you—"

"About my duties?"

"No. It states that you—that you shall have nothing to do with the production of the films. Nothing at all."

Natacha's eyes froze into blue ice.

All of a sudden the sparkle and the warmth had flickered out of them.

"And you signed that?"

"I must have been crazy."

"Rudy, you always said you loved me—and you signed
—"

"Look, it—it was a mistake. When Mr. Schenck spoke to
me, I lost my head. I'll break that contract. I won't go through
with it—unless they take that clause out."

She regained her composure, drew herself up tall, straight
and cold. "You'll do no such thing, Rudy. You signed a
contract and you'll go through with it. After all, it means your
career. You belong with United Artists. A wife should not
hinder her husband's career—"

"You mean you don't mind?"

"That doesn't matter. I'll find something to do."

"You can still work with me privately. As far as I'm
concerned nothing need be changed."

"Of course, Rudy. Of course."

He came toward her, wanted to embrace her, but she shied
away.

"Please," she said, "I'm very tired and it's late. I think I
will go to bed."

She entered the bedroom and he was left standing there,
lost, defeated, not sure as to what he should do. Only Natacha
had been able to free him from his loneliness—and now the
loneliness had come back. It would be a long night.

CHAPTER TWENTY-SEVEN

THE first picture selected by United Artists for Valentino was *The Eagle*, adapted from the novel *Dubrovsky*, by the Russian writer Alexander Pushkin. His leading lady in this was the Hungarian beauty, Vilma Banky, an exquisitely charming girl, who had been discovered by Samuel Goldwyn. Louise Dresser was cast as Catherine II.

Work on this picture proceeded during the summer months of 1925 and, though it seemed strange at first to Valentino, his wife was conspicuously absent from the scene of operations. During this period they lived in their Whitly Heights home, but a marked coolness had set in between them. Natacha would take long drives alone in her car. She would be gone, sometimes, for four or five days at a time, and this upset Valentino terribly. But he never dared ask her where she went. Mrs. Theresa Werner, Natacha's aunt, had moved into a home on Sycamore Street just a few blocks away. She visited frequently and became Natacha's sole confidante.

One weekend, Valentino managed to persuade his wife to go down to Palm Springs with him. He arranged to use the large house of his friend Dr. White. During the ride out to the desert, Natacha scarcely spoke to him. After they reached Dr. White's house, he saddled one of the doctor's horses and asked his wife if she would join him in a ride up one of the mountain trails. She refused and said she would wait for him in the house. He rode off in a mood of bleak despair. He knew he had done a terrible thing to Natacha's pride. He wished he could make it up to her, but he didn't know how. His feeling of sympathy and pity for his wife was mixed, however, with a tinge of exasperation. She must have known that his career in motion pictures could not survive the kind of internecine warfare that had been waged on the set of *Cobra*. The set of *The Eagle,* by contrast, was a model of efficiency and equanimity. If she were on the lot, battling with his director, cameraman, and producer all over again, the picture could never achieve the greatness that was expected of it. Couldn't she see this side of the picture?

He rode back to the house, expecting Natacha to greet him with stony silence. To his surprise, however, he found her sitting on the floor, her face alive with enthusiasm for the first time in weeks. She was surrounded by a mass of magazines and books. "I've been collecting articles and advertisements on cosmetics," she said. "I just got the idea the other day. I want to write a story and produce a picture about the cosmetic world." This theme, she felt, would have interest for every female in the land and therefore a movie based on it would be a certain box-office success.

"Rudy, I can't just sit around. I've got to be working and this will be just fine for me. I'll produce this picture myself."

Valentino sat down on a chair opposite her.

"How much would it cost?" he inquired.

"Not more than thirty thousand dollars. I just called Nita Naldi on the phone and she promised to play a part in it. I'll get Nazimova and others to help."

Valentino said, "You don't mind if I call George Ullman and have him come over and discuss this?"

"He's just the man."

When Ullman arrived, they at once went into the subject more thoroughly. Ullman agreed that it was a good idea for Natacha to be occupied, but he cautioned her to hold down the cost as closely as she could to her original figure of thirty thousand.

Once the capital was supplied, Natacha set to work. She rented studio space, assembled the cast and swung into production. She decided to call her picture, *What Price Beauty?* She ran into many production and story headaches and the cost soon ballooned well past the thirty-thousand limit that Ullman had set. Valentino ordered his business manager to give Natacha whatever extra money she needed. Before the picture was finally completed its cost came to nearly $100,000. When it was released, it brought in only a trickle at the box office. Natacha demanded and got more money to advertise and publicize the film. But the public wouldn't buy it. It was soon evident that Mrs. Valentino's creation was a pathetic failure.

At virtually the same time, *The Eagle* was completed. It was sneak-previewed in a hinterland theater and received unanimous tributes from the audience. All the United Artists executives, from Joseph Schenck down, told Valentino he had given a brilliant performance.

Natacha Valentino's morale dipped to its lowest ebb. She began to avoid all the restaurants and other public places frequented by movie personalities. She would fly into a towering rage when people told her, "It was too bad about your picture, but at least Rudy is a success in *The Eagle*."

She took to staying away from home again for days at a time, never explaining where she went. She never thanked her husband for the money he had put up for her picture—money which had gone down the drain. She never congratulated him on his success in *The Eagle*. It was a success he had achieved without any help or advice from her and she couldn't forget it. When Valentino implored her again to have children and begin their family, she scoffed at him. "So now you think that I'm good for breeding and have no talent for anything else," she said bitterly.

Valentino tried by every device possible to assuage his wife's bitter feeling of defeat and rejection by the motion picture world. But nothing he did seemed to make any impression on Natacha. He brought her gifts of jewelry and furs, but she didn't bother to wear them. Then he sought to placate her with the most expensive gift of all—a princely new estate—in Beverly Hills. It was called Falcon Lair. It included a seventeen-room Spanish hacienda and eight acres of rolling land in the heart of the expensive colony. Natacha had often said she wanted to live in the same community as the movie elite. Now her neighbors would be Marion Davies, Mary Pickford, and Douglas Fairbanks, Harold Lloyd, Thomas Meighan, and others of like status.

Valentino spared no expense in decorating and furnishing his beautiful home, embellishing it with Oriental carpets, tapestries, priceless fabrics, mementoes and *objets d'art*. He knew how she would want it to look, and he had it furnished and painted in the colors she liked. He was sure she would be pleased and thrilled by all this. . . .

But Natacha did not spend a single night at Falcon Lair. She refused point-blank to go there. She grew more and more despondent. She was dissatisfied with her life, with her husband, with herself, with Hollywood.

On a day in the first week in August, Valentino came home to their Whitly Heights house from a morning of last-minute retakes for *The Eagle* and found her packing.

"I'm sorry, Rudy, but let's face it. I've been a mess since we've come back from Spain. I must go away, Rudy. I must be alone, maybe to find myself again."

"I see."

He came near her. He took her hand and held it.

"I won't beg, Natacha. But please listen to me. While you're away think of the happy times we've had. All those precious days—in California, in New York and in Europe. Think of us being together through good times and bad, and then maybe you will know what to do. Where will you be?"

"I don't know exactly. New York, perhaps."

"Why don't you go to Nice and spend some time with your mother at the chateau? You always loved it there. In fact, I wish I were there right now."

"I might do that."

Like part of a bad dream, he helped her close the suitcases and the trunk. He helped her, but his heart was heavy. Why didn't he fall down on his knees and plead that she stay? He still loved her, although by now he realized that she had never had a sincere love for him—that she had seen him only as a means of realizing an insatiable desire and projecting her own future in motion pictures. But despite this unswerving love and his strange need for this strange woman, he felt he had to remain a man. And a man does not beg.

Valentino moved her luggage out of the house, their house, and placed it in the Isotta Fraschini. Then he helped her into the car and they drove to the station.

They were dismayed at seeing the station platform packed with people—reporters, fan magazine writers, friends and the curious. Valentino wondered: how did they get wind of things so fast? It was a harassing experience—people calling to them, making snide remarks and wisecracks. It was humiliation, it was torture, but they had to go through with it with an outward calm.

Mrs. Werner and Ullman, too, were taking the same train to New York, and they promised to look after Natacha. Ullman was going on a business mission for the opening exhibition of *The Eagle*. At the same time he would attend to Natacha's financial needs.

The train hissed into the station and the luggage was put into the baggage car. Valentino helped Natacha up the steps of the coach, and as they waited for the train to move their eyes met in one brief moment of appeal—a moment that could have changed the whole course of their future, had either of them made a definite move of surrender.

He impulsively kissed her and she did not protest. He kissed her again and again.

This was the moment. Why didn't he suddenly sweep her up into his arms, even as he had done that proud English lady in *The Sheik*, and carry her back to Falcon Lair and hold her captive forevermore?

The train was pulling out and Valentino ran along with it still holding Natacha's hand. As the train gathered speed they were forced to release each other. Valentino waved to her and she looked back at him. He watched her until she entered the coach, and he saw her no more, nor ever again.

Reporters crowded about him, firing questions, some of them mocking, ruthless, while his heart was breaking. . .

"Please," he beseeched them. He moved through the crowd

206

seeing nothing but the blue eyes of a goddess.

He finally reached his car, struggled into it, and drove away from the station, along Sunset Boulevard, out of Hollywood, into the countryside; and that loneliness he had always fought against from the beginning began to enfold him once more. He wanted to cry out against it . . . he wanted to run away from it . . . to find laughter again, and music and dancing. . . .

Valentino's business manager and one of his very few friends, George Ullman, was better qualified to analyze the ruin of the Valentino love-match than any other observer.

This is what Ullman said: "It is my opinion that when Natacha's dictatorship was taken from her, it was not long before her love and loyalty to Valentino began to fail.

"When she ceased to collaborate, she also failed to cooperate with him in more ways than one; and a man as proud and sensitive as Rudy could not fail to detect her fading interest.

"From a passionate interest in his future and a desire to promote his best interests, and what from her was true love, Rudy began to observe that her fancy was straying into other paths and fastening itself to other objects and interests.

"It caused her husband the most profound anguish, not only hurting his male vanity, but injuring him in his deepest soul. He felt for the first time that his love was not appreciated, and he began to suspect that he had been married, not for himself alone, but partly as a means to an end. That end was, first and foremost, Natacha's overpowering, unalterable determination to be a figure which the motion picture industry could not ignore. That she aspired to take first place as a director and producer of super-pictures is not, in my opinion, too great an ambition to lay at her door.

"Cleopatra is her greatest prototype in history. In fact, if I believed in reincarnation I could easily imagine that the soul of Natacha Rambova, with all of her physical perfections and her mysterious fascination, had once inhabited the body of Egypt's queen, and that the Nile and its desert sands had once been her natural habitat.

"That Natacha yielded to this overpowering urge of ambition must not be held against her by the analyst, for, from her earliest childhood, traits cropped out whenever the smallest opening appeared. Vital, dynamic, and capable of long stretches of work which were surprising in one of such delicate physique; these were qualities which never could have been entirely stifled without wrecking her. She was a victim of her own ambition."

Alone at Falcon Lair, after Natacha Rambova left him

Valentino could have been another Tom Mix, had he cared to. He was an excellent horseman and loved the plains.

Ex Libris
Rudolph Valentino

Valentino's bookplate

With Jack Dempsey and friend in the famous Hollywood restaurant, The Brown Derby

With Marion Davies, famous silent screen star

The screen's greatest lover with Vilma Banky in *Son of the Sheik,* his last film.

Film czar Will Hays congratulates Valentino at a Hollywood preview of *Son of the Sheik*.

Haroun, Valentino's Irish Wolfhound meets Centaur
Pendragon, one of the star's four horses.
(Below) Crowds watch the Valentino funeral
procession in New York.

Valentino's coffin leaves the funeral home on its final journey. Among the honorary pallbearers are Frank Menillo, Nick Schenck, Douglas Fairbanks, Marcus Loew, Joseph Schenck, and Adolph Zukor.

RUDOLPH VALENTINO
1895-1926

CHAPTER TWENTY-EIGHT

AFTER that first impact of parting, Valentino could not do anything but drive his car aimlessly along the roads in the vicinity. He could not rest, he could not concentrate on work or play. It would take him a long time to come out of the shock. He knew that the wound inflicted upon him might never heal.

Ullman agreed with him: "When the wife a man loves leaves him, it's bad, very bad. But if you could see her again, talk to her . . . maybe . . ."

But at this time there was no medicine that he could take to ease the agony of the separation. It was as though half of him were cut off, leaving the other half writhing in anguish.

He had schooled himself, during his early struggle, in a philosophy of meeting the vicissitudes of a human world with quiet faith. This philosophy was defined on the screen in his various characterizations. As Julio in *The Four Horsemen* he had succumbed to his fate with the calm heroism of the soldier. As Gallardo in *Blood and Sand* he had endured his goring and death with a fatalistic grace worthy of the toreador. But this crisis in his own life he could not meet with calm heroism or with fatalistic grace. He could not escape the torment through resignation.

The loneliness he had suffered in those early days had been harrowing enough, but now it was heart-sickening, and even his work could not ameliorate it.

He began to seek some sort of relief. He tried to immerse

himself in writing poetry; but that seemed to emphasize the situation.

For the first time since he had met Natacha, Valentino sought out other female companionship. His attention turned to the first attractive female available—his co-star in *The Eagle*, Vilma Banky.

He found her twinkling beauty, her wistfulness, her dancing ability soothing. They would take long walks together or go on long drives in his powerful car. But these moments of happiness would be interrupted now and then by haunting memories; and then his eyes would attain that faraway look and his knuckles would show white on the steering wheel. To Vilma it was as though he were seeing something in the great distance, beyond her own range.

She could speak only a few words of English, so he conversed with her in German, another language he had familiarized himself with in his school days. At rare times, when she said something funny, he broke into a laugh, and this surprised himself. He did feel a certain sense of freedom. There was no demand, no strain of trying to please. They just accepted each other as they were. To Vilma, with her European background, the male sex was all-important; to her it was only natural to cater to her escort's wants, to comfort and please him.

Vilma was sensitive and lived on her own dream clouds— but she was possessed of an old-world wisdom. She would have permitted herself to fall in love with Valentino had he so much as given her a hint of encouragement. But perhaps this very solicitude on her part failed to intrigue more than his casual interest.

It had been Natacha's initial indifference to his advances, her independence of spirit, that had challenged him and awakened his admiration and then his love. As for Miss Banky—she was just a refreshing interlude. . . .

While arrangements were being made for the New York première of *The Eagle*, Valentino became more and more a familiar figure in the Hollywood social milieu. He had always scorned these parties, but now began to attend them regularly. He learned to laugh and quip and tried to acquire the knack of small talk. He even learned the dubious "art" of throwing some parties of his own at Falcon Lair.

Now that he was more or less unattached, there were women who fastened their husband-seeking sights in his direction, hoping to gain his favor. Presently he stopped seeing Vilma and went out dining and dancing with others.

One of these was the dark-haired, exotic Polish siren, Pola Negri. He found her volatile and highly entertaining. They became a dancing couple at parties and night clubs; they were seen together at the theater and at concerts. But this romantic new duet was cut short for the time being by Ullman's suggestion that, since Natacha was in New York and the première of *The Eagle* was about to take place in that city, Valentino could attend the première and also try to see Natacha.

Valentino went to New York. On arriving at Natacha's apartment, he was advised by the superintendent that she had just left the country and that her mail was to be forwarded to an address in Paris. Valentino's pent-up excitement flickered out. So she had gone to Paris after all—perhaps to establish a residence for divorce action. He fought down his disappointment, tried to affect a gay mood and escorted a pretty starlet to the première of *The Eagle* at the Strand Theater.

The opening proved a rousing success. Queues of people stretched for two blocks in each direction, waiting to gain admittance. Notables of the city attended; also the elite of the stage and screen. Both critics and audience decorated Valentino with garlands of praise. United Artists executives assured him his fame was climbing to a new peak.

Here in New York—as in Hollywood—he went out to parties; he had to forget. He had to drive out the feeling of loss and fill in the empty hours.

He wined, dined and danced with a succession of society belles and the more earthy showgirls who competed for his attention. He slept two hours in the mornings. He ate heavily and he drank wine and whiskey without his former caution. He had always been careful about his health and had developed a splendid physique—a physique that, for the first time, he was abusing.

Coming out of his suite in the hotel one day, he suddenly stopped in the corridor and leaned against the wall, gripped by a throbbing pain. He saw a doctor for the first time in months and got this word of caution: "There's nothing wrong with you except that you've been drinking too much and eating too many fried foods. Don't deliberately ruin your health. No woman is worth it."

Encouraged by United Artists, Valentino traveled to London to attend the English première of *The Eagle*. One of his devoted British fans, Lady Curzon, made arrangements for him to meet the Royal Family and sponsored him on a fresh round of parties and receptions.

Natacha had still failed to show him the courtesy of writing, but he went on to Paris anyway, hoping to find her. He had been told that she was registered at the Plaza Athénée—the same hotel at which they had stopped on their honeymoon trip. But when he arrived, he found he had missed her again. She had apparently learned that he was coming and had left abruptly to stay at her mother's chateau in Nice.

To forget this fresh rebuff, he indulged in yet another round of parties. Once more the circuit of cafés and bistros, with showgirl Jean Nash, with the loquacious Peggy Hopkins Joyce, with the Dolly Sisters, with the vivacious Mae Murray, and with others—a voluptuous can-can girl from the *Folies-Bergère*, an exotic dancer from Montmartre, a petite French actress from the Place Pigalle.

He got into the newspapers again—this time the American press found something appetizing to report. They began to describe the lavish parties that playboy Valentino was throwing in Paree. They pictured him as a gay Lothario carousing about with a champagne bottle under one arm and a French courtesan in the other, with no concern for tomorrow.

Now and then he would get dizzy spells. Mae Murray, with whom he danced a great deal, warned him gently, "Rudy, please take care of yourself. You look awfully pale."

"I'll be all right, Mae. I've no time to get sick, you know.

I'm always ready to dance or to go to a party. That's my life now."

"Please, Rudy. You must get some rest."

"No time, Mae. I just want to dance. You and I will do the tango. Let's go to another café—there's a good one I know, the Rivoli in Montparnasse—"

And so it went in Paris. But finally, he felt impelled to go on to Nice.

When he arrived at the chateau Mrs. Hudnut welcomed him warmly. Mr. Hudnut embraced him like a long-lost son. "Rudy, we want you to stay here as long as you like. This is your home," he said.

"Natacha?"

Mrs. Hudnut's eyes were misty.

"I'm sorry, Rudy."

"You mean—"

"She's gone. She left for New York two days ago."

Valentino's face turned chalk white.

"She must have known I was in Paris and she wouldn't stay," he said angrily. The Hudnuts said nothing, but Mrs. Hudnut's eyes filled with tears. He turned abruptly and walked out. He knew now for certain that Natacha would never return to him.

Later, he learned that Natacha had not gone back to New York after all, but was still somewhere in France. And it was in a French court that Natacha appeared to secure her divorce from him.

When Valentino returned to Paris, he suddenly thought of his own family again. He had left them behind in Europe after completing his honeymoon trip because he felt they could not be a part of his life as an American star. But now that he had lost Natacha, he felt a hunger to have loved ones with him. So he brought Maria, Alberto, and Alberto's family to visit with him first in Paris and then in London. Alberto and his wife had an eleven-year-old son who took to his uncle Rudolph at once.

When Ullman sent him a cable saying it was urgent that he return to America to start on his next picture, he decided he would ask his sister, brother, sister-in-law and nephew to live with him. His sister Maria refused to come. She was afraid to live in America, she said, and she had made some good friends in Paris. If her brother would pay for a training course, she would like to get a job as a seamstress and make her home in the French capital. Valentino respected her wishes, opened a sizeable bank account for her, and told her that his home would always be open to her if she ever changed her mind.

Alberto and his family were anxious to come to America, however, and so they sailed with Valentino on the S.S. *Berengaria* just after the beginning of 1926.

When Ullman met Valentino and his party at Pasadena instead of Los Angeles—to avoid publicity—he welcomed the star like a long-lost prodigal. "Rudy, I've got great news for you. United Artists bought Mrs. E. M. Hull's sequel to *The Sheik* for you—*Sons of the Sheik*. They've adapted it to the screen by eliminating one of the twin sons of the story, and now it's *The Son of the Sheik*."

Valentino said nothing. Ullman peered closely at him. "You don't look too hot," he said. "Tell you what, Rudy, you're going to take a little rest, then go into training— horseback riding, lots of walking, swimming, handball. You must get back into your usual good physical trim. That night life in London and Paris didn't do you or your bankroll any good. It's the old story—you can't run away from life. Sooner or later life catches up."

"I know, George, I know. Don't worry, I'll behave now."

During the drive from Pasadena to Beverly Hills, Valentino began to think about his new picture *The Son of the Sheik*. He remembered the last Sheik picture and the impact it had made. What would happen this time? Would the public accept it as before? The world was continuously changing. Would people stand for another Sheik production? Five years was a long time and the public's taste changed quickly. He told Ullman, "Why can't I do something like *The Sea Hawk* or *Ben-Hur*? Natacha always wanted them to give me roles like that. George, I'm afraid of another Sheik picture. Maybe we'd better have a talk with the production department and have that story replaced by something new and more important.''

Ullman shrugged. "Rudy, the preliminaries are already under way. If it's a flop, then the studio will suffer the consequences. As far as you are concerned, your fans will understand and look forward to a better picture in the future. We must take a chance.''

"Then you agree with me that a Sheik film at this time would be a bad gamble?''

"I admit it's a gamble, Rudy—good or bad, I don't know. But it's time we got back to work.''

They entered the driveway of Falcon Lair, drove up to the house and Valentino and his family got out of the car. Then Ullman drove away.

Alberto, his wife and their son had been amazed at the vastness of the country on their trip from New York and Valentino had enjoyed the tremendous impact of America on them. Now they were equally amazed at the size of Valentino's estate. Alberto's son ooh'd and ah'd as he pointed out the acres and Valentino, watching him, began to laugh. Then suddenly, his eyes filled with pain. He clutched his stomach.

Alberto rushed to him. "What hurts you, my brother? Do you want a doctor?''

"No—no doctor. I'll—I'll be all right. Something I ate. Natacha was always warning me about too much spice. I'm always a pig when it comes to food. I'll be all right now. Do me a favor, Alberto, and do not tell Ullman about this. He'll pester me as though I were a sick child.''

The pain had gone and Valentino put his arm about his brother. "Alberto, now that I have you all with me I won't be so lonely. This is Falcon Lair, the home of your family for as long as you want to live here.''

CHAPTER TWENTY-NINE

NINETEEN TWENTY-SIX! It was to be Rudolph Valentino's greatest year . . . and his last. Valentino's *Son of the Sheik* would become a classic example of the silent movie. The picture would be his crowning success, and yet he never liked the film. When it was first suggested, he felt he was again being taken advantage of by being given third-rate stories. He also felt that a second Sheik film would never meet with anywhere near the success of the first.

However, there was one great consolation. He finally had George Fitzmaurice as his director. Because Fitzmaurice spoke French, they carried on conversations in that language and became good friends.

There was another pleasant feature: Vilma Banky was his leading lady, as she had been in *The Eagle*. She was lovelier than ever, and was superb as Yasmin, the dancing girl whose "moving hips fill men with abandon." Her grace, her winsome beauty and charm were the wine of life to Valentino as well as to all the other members of the cast.

Some of the scenes were intensely romantic and Valentino lost himself in the emotional sweep of his portrayal. In *The Son of the Sheik* he attained a smoothness, a perfection of performance that could well serve as an authoritative example of interpretative pantomime. It was his own conception of an art form in which physical movement and emotional expression were employed with just the right degree of restraint. Fitzmaurice, the director, was so impressed he would stand and admire Valentino going through one scene after another, living them, not merely acting.

Although Valentino had a poor opinion of the story, the rides over the sand dunes, the physical action, the romantic interludes with the dancing girl, Yasmin (Vilma Banky), the skirmishes with Ghabah, the Moor (Montague Love), acted like an elixir to him. He threw himself into these scenes with great vigor.

For the sand storm sequences, the company went on location to the desert area outside of Yuma, Arizona. Giant wind machines were used to blow the desert sand into blizzardlike swirls and at times the velocity reached such a peak that no real-life storm could have been more devastating. The gritty sand particles cut the faces of some of the members of the company and frightened some of the actresses to such an extent that they tried to have their parts deleted from the storm scenes.

Only Valentino found the man-made storms exciting and stimulating. He rode into them with a fervor that startled his co-workers. When scenes had to be reshot in the desert, it created great consternation among every member in the cast except Valentino. He couldn't get enough of these storms.

During one of the storm sequences, he was engaged in chasing the fleeing Yasmin, when, without warning, the seizure came on him again. He doubled over on his horse as if he'd been shot. Karl Dane, one of the character actors, ran to his assistance and helped him off the horse. As before, the pain left him in a few minutes.

In the full-bosomed, tempestuous Pola Negri, meanwhile, Valentino had found a companion whose ardor exceeded even his own. Their excursions aboard his yacht became idylls of passionate love-making that left his body drained. Just as Valentino was more in love with the reluctant Natacha than she could ever be with him, so Pola felt a much deeper devotion for him than he could hope to return. Pola was jealous and hot-tempered, and whenever she found his thoughts drifting to his estranged wife she would become furious. After their sessions of love-making, she would con-

217

tinue to caress him, but he would simply curl up in the sun and absorb himself in writing poetry. He had promised his columnist friend O. O. McIntyre that he would put together another book of poetry, but these flights into the world of rhymes and stanzas annoyed his beautiful companion. She wanted Valentino's attention riveted completely on her as long as he was in her company.

His new poems concentrated on the highlights of his trips abroad and had memories of Natacha in them. However, to placate Pola he told her that his poems were dedicated to her. He would read them aloud while she held him in her arms, kissed and caressed his face, and nibbled fondly at his ears. One of his favorite poems was called "In an Art Museum." It recalled to him Natacha's expert knowledge of art and the many museums they had visited abroad. The poem follows:

There is a mysterious gloom where I stand,
But I hear the tinkle of a fountain,
The featherlike laughter of little waters, selfishly content.
And the frightened daylight
Is stumbling into the halls
Through stained-glass windows.
The purple curtains,
Like skies in the night lacking stars,
Breathe heavily, wearily.
Here all seems slumbering,
But in a dream of Eternity.
Time is but the fool
In this realm of the Infinite.
I hear the tapping of many feet
About me in the sacred silence—
'Tis the spirits of the artists
Wandering restlessly, and whispering little secrets to each
    other.
I hear the murmur
Of their sad, strange voices.
I am in a dream:
The marble statues live and move—
They pass me by, haughtily, without seeing me;

Proud and disdainful!
Beautiful women from the glorious ages of history
But for them I do not exist;
Glide about me in the shadows—
And I am perplexed, unable to understand their wondrous
    beauty,
Which is not of the Earth.
The Past becomes the Present;
Today is no more.
Art and Beauty pace the floor
In invisible splendor;
And for once I feel the heavenly intoxication
As I breathe the air of immortality.
Though I cannot understand,
I listen to the silent music
Flowing from the old, old founts of harmony.
In a cushioned chair
Sits a silver-haired woman,
Her eyes dreaming at a picture
On the shadowed wall.
Has she stepped out of a canvas?
Behind her, like broken rainbows,
Gleam the many-colored windows
And drench the room
In a shower of vari-tinted light.
Am I too much of the World
That I feel a stranger in this place?
I am soiled with the dust of Worldliness;
I have counted my worth in gold;
I have worshipped the gloss of vanity;
I have chosen the highroads of ease;
I have offered my soul to greed;
I have sacrificed beauty for coin;
I have laughed at the pleading of Art;
I have sinned; I repent; but is it in vain?
In this temple of Beauty
I realize the selfish pettiness,
The continuous vice
Of our impatient civilization . . .

I pass through an utter silence—
An hour might be a year;
Enchantment—
A divine spell;
And the daylight purples into night—
I am in darkness;
Darkness aflame with the colors of masterpieces,
Blinding in their majestic grandeur,
Too glorious in their eternal beauty
For my feeble soul.
Am I alone within this castle of Art?
No—the woman with the silver hair
Is in her place.
Why are the spirits of the masters
Laughing at me?
I am the subject of their jests;
They lean out of their paintings,
And grin at me in pitying scorn;
I am an exile in their midst,
And wretched and full of misery—
This is their stronghold,
And I am an humble captive,
Their slave forevermore.
There are sudden footfalls, and a light is flashed;
The guard has found me in tears
And expresses surprise.
This is the palace of the sublime;
I have come from the world—
To the World must I return.
But as the woman with the silver hair passes me,
She whispers with pride:
"You saw me looking at a picture—
I look at it many times;
My son painted it."
And then the silver of her hair
Became a halo of a saint.

Another, titled "The Spanish Dancer," recalled to him the unusually talented señorita whom he and Natacha had watched with great excitement in a cabaret in Seville. The poem follows:

> Gliding across the shining floor—
> Like a butterfly—
> Gleaming, glinting, flashing;
> Beads and jewels falling o'er all her dress!
> The gliding of little, shining feet—
> The tinkling of castanets;
> And dreamy magic of the music
> Floating in the air,
> Floating lazily—
> Lazily; then, with little starts
> And tremblings, and little frights and shivers,
> The tones rise
> In wondrous harmony—
> They float out wildly free,
> Happy with a dizzy emotion,
> Winding to their rhythm,
> And with them dancing,
> The bejeweled dancer;
> Her eyes flashing,
> Her eyes two jewels brighter than all the rest—
> About her swaying person;
> Also, the shining of pearly little teeth
> In a daring smile!
> A gliding across the hall—
> The smooth and polished floor,
> A little witch,
> And like a plant that sways itself
> In uncertain motion
> To the whispering breezes—
> Swaying, then dancing,
> Now smiling,
> Now sad of eye—
> Sometimes like a lone flower,
> Hurt by the cold

Of a sullen day
She drooped, drooped;
Her mass of raven-black hair,
Little billowy inky clouds
Fell about her lily-white face,
Draping it caressingly
Lovingly but wildly!
She rises, and energy returning,
She leaps up with a strange grace;
And swings with the music,
With the tripping tones,
The uncertain melody,
Now passionate, now calm,
Now trailing off into a plaintive sob—
Now laughing, now weeping
In wild voice!
The shadow followed her—
Imitating in mocking manner her gestures,
Her windings—
Trembling beneath her spell of enchantment,
In the center of the floor she is
Whirling, her light dress glowing—
Her red scarf flaming in the candlelight!
Flaming like a speeding comet,
Fantastic, unreal—a curious vision—
She is poised for a moment of time,
Poised, and then a rise,
A freeing of the music from confinement,
And the dancer has spun
On her little toes,
Her toes, gold-clad,
And has wavered uncertainly
With a sudden, weak fall to the floor—
The music has died—
And all is silent—not a sound—
On the floor, as motionless as in death—
Lies a gleaming heap of diamonds
And rubies, and a scarf
Of flaming crimson!

Since Pola was adept on the dance floor and particularly gifted in Latin dances, she told her companion, "What wonderful poems you write for Pola! I will always be Rudy's Spanish dancer. Tomorrow night, there is mask ball at Hotel Biltmore. You and I go? We dance Spanish numbers?"

"Wonderful, Pola. You are my Spanish dancer and I will wear the costume of Gallardo, the toreador I played in *Blood and Sand*."

Not only did they go to that ball, but they won a prize for their costumes and another for their tango. Pola was convinced that the poem Valentino had dedicated to her had brought them luck. He would, of course, gallantly refrain from ever telling her that she had never been the Spanish dancer of his memories or of his verse.

Valentino's most ambitious verse was called "The Inevitable," and he wanted this to be the title poem of his second book of poetry. It contains a deeply romantic, prophetic quality and displays his vivid imagination. Like his other later poems, it shows more depth of feeling and significance of thought than the verse in his first book, *Day Dreams*. This is the poem:

BABYHOOD

Birth!
My tiny soul
Laughed daintily in its glee,
My heart sang a sweet little tune—
Chanting Time's first measure,
Frightened so—
Perplexed.
My new, new being tiptoed into life with hesitating step—
Wondered at the kaleidoscope of life,
Turning, turning, changing, shifting
Into mystic prophecies
Of the future.
Fate
Stood waiting.
Hovering over my cradle and pointing ahead
To the future.

223

Time
Stood grinning—
Grinning merrily in the hour-glass of Eternity;
And my small, small heart beat a sweet and dainty song
To the tender rhythm of the cradle,
Cradle rocking softly, patiently,
And someone humming
Such a lovely lullaby—
Someone lulling me
To sleep,
Sleep.

CHILDHOOD

Kites!
With knotted tails
Swinging from the clouds,
Trimmed with gold
And kissed by breezes—
Breezes blowing on my kite!
Flying high—
Gliding along the smooth and measureless sky
Envied by the robins,
And the proud, beautiful bluebirds,
And the pondering crows;
And even the restless, fluttering colored butter-
*   flies.*
I loved to dream of heights—
Up above the pine-trees, up, up so high!
Where all the angel-children live—
Up there. Once I cried
Because I tried, and couldn't fly.
And often have I longed,
With racing heart,
To ride upon the moon right across the darkness
Touch the stars, and call them
All my jewels;
And bring the angel-children back with me
And keep them here
Forever.

BOYHOOD

Pirates!
I guess I'll run away and be a pirate—
Heavy and broad-shouldered,
Or long, lanky and lean,
Or short and rollicking fat—
But a grand, brave fighter of the sea!
And a ship
That proudly marches on the green, green waves
And rules the mighty ocean with its flag
Of the skull and cross-bones!
And treasures—
Heavy, massive chests of golden pieces, shining gold;
Chest of diamonds, pearls and blood-red rubies;
Chests of dazzling jewels from Queen and Princess;
Chests of priceless cloths and oriental silks;
And the pirates drinking rum,
Drinking rum—
And a bloody fight
With knives, the sport of men.
Hear it flapping in the salt-sea breeze—
'Tis the cross-bone flag
And it rules the seven seas,
On the reckless conqu'ring ship
Where the grand old pirates
Swear long oaths—
Long oaths—
Swear and fight!

YOUTH

Sweetheart,
I love you so;
My room is filled with many books of love,
Romance waits to meet me; but I want to dream—
Dreaming of a tropical sea,
And an isle of golden sands,
With a night
Clothed in stars,
With a moon
Casting silver

225

On the sea—
And a nightingale,
A nightingale singing, singing
While the warm, precious hours
Sleep through the night.
On the shore
You and I
Shall listen to the chorus of the many, many waves,
Watch them dancing in the silver
Of the moon.
In the West the proud star Mars
Shall watch us
And shine brightly, fiercely;
Because you are beautiful,
And you love me,
And he is so mad
And jealous.

MANHOOD

Humanity
Fights a constant battle
Of conscience against conscience,
Will against will,
Man against man,
For the joy of victory,
The spoils of conquest;
And the vanquished must suffer.
The law still holds:
Life to the fittest,
Death to the weak.
And a conflict rages
In each man's being.
Good against evil;
Virtue against sin—
The eternal struggle
In Man.
And I seek happiness everywhere, constantly;
I seek, seek, seek—
'Tis too elusive;

226

And, perhaps, has gone forever.
I seek beauty—
Have I seen it?
I seek—something—always—
Can it be that life is nothing but
A seeking?

OLD AGE

Life
Is so beautiful!
There is a gentle loveliness about it;
It breathes a divine spirit, and commands
My complete love.
A flower to me now
Is precious!
The song of birds, the blue of skies, the breath of winds
Are precious!
Life unreels again:
There is my old home; there are the pines;
There are the tears, the sorrows, the dreams;
The first flaming hopes and ambitions;
The sweetest of loves, the longings of youth;
There are the winnings and losings together,
Safe in the treasure-chest of the mind—
My memories.
I have journeyed through all, and Fate held my hand,
And Time gave me years for my journey.
Now the sands of Time are running low—
Running low—low . . .

CHAPTER THIRTY

DURING the first week of July *The Son of the Sheik* was completed. Private studio previews were held on several nights so that weak spots could be detected and remedied, and so that retakes could be made wherever necessary. The continuity was tightened up and polished, and the retakes were made. The film was edited and cut, with Valentino making numerous suggestions.

George Fitzmaurice, the picture's director, put his hand on Valentino's shoulder when it was all over. "Rudy, you did a splendid job—with the material you had. The next time I shall personally see to it that you don't waste your talents on inconsequential mediocrity. I sincerely hope this picture earns back at least what it cost—for the sake of United Artists."

The première of the picture was scheduled for Grauman's Million Dollar Theatre in Los Angeles. Valentino had arranged to escort Pola Negri. She wore a close-fitting silver sheath gown for the occasion, with a diamond tiara and a pearl necklace. Never before had she looked so regal and so radiant. At the theater, they were caught in the dazzling glare of klieg lights. The lobby was full of reporters, celebrities, and police to protect the celebrities, the floor a tangle of wires and cables that powered lights and microphones.

Valentino's doubts about the picture assailed him anew, though outwardly he appeared the calm, suave man-about-town. He bowed and nodded to the stars as they appeared and greeted him—Mary Pickford and Douglas Fairbanks, Mae Murray and her husband, Prince David Mdivani, Louella Parsons, Charles Chaplin, Marion Davies, and many others. Also, he saw in the lobby an arrangement of red roses eight feet high with his name in white roses upon it and he read on the attached card, "To Rudy, good luck, from Pola." He was pleased, and kissed and thanked Pola profusely as they took their seats.

The people finally settled in their places. The theater was packed.

Valentino remained tense. Next to him, the queenly Pola was waving and flashing a dazzling smile to her movie friends. He could hear the people buzzing about them. Would she be the next Mrs. Valentino, they wanted to know? They were also wondering about Valentino's performance in this film. They had all heard the whispers that he considered the scenario to be puerile.

He wanted to sneak out, run away from it all. He did not want to witness a debacle, to hear the ridicule of the cognoscenti. Pola's hand sought his, reassuring him.

"Rudy, like ice your hand is. My dearest, do not worry."

"I wish it were tomorrow."

The stage prologue was over. The lights went out. The projector started its low buzz. The beam of blue-white light issued forth from an aperture in the projection booth like an elongated cone and, to the accompaniment of the Grauman orchestra, the picture was on the screen.

THE CAST

Ahmed and the Sheik, Ahmed Ben Hassen	Rudolph Valentino (dual role)
Yasmin, Dancing Girl, daughter of André	Vilma Banky
André, father of Yasmin	George Fawcett
Diana, wife of the Sheik	Agnes Ayres
Ghabah, the Moor	Montague Love
Ramadan, Aide to Ahmed	Karl Dane

229

Mountebanks	.... Bull Montana and
	Binunsky Hyman

Locale: Desert in North Africa.

The first scene opens in a café in Touggert with a dance by Yasmin, daughter of André, head of a wandering theatrical group. Close-up of Yasmin dancing. Close-up of Ahmed, son of the Sheik, watching the dance. He falls in love with her—her grace and beauty are irresistible. Ahmed has a rendezvous with her at an old ruin in an oasis outside of Touggert. He sings to her the Kashmiri Song: "Pale hands I loved beside the Shalimar—"

While embracing and kissing her, he is suddenly ambushed and captured by Ghabah, the Moor, and his henchman. He is considered a threat to Ghabah's chief source of income—the silver coins that are cast at Yasmin's dainty feet by ogling admirers when she dances. Ahmed is strung up by the wrists against the wall of the old ruin and tortured. His retainer, Ramadan, rescues him. Believing that Yasmin used her charms to trick him into the ambush, Ahmed takes Yasmin captive, and accuses her of complicity. She tries to convince him of her innocence. Against her will, he brings her to his tent.

His father, the Sheik, Ahmed Ben Hassen, commands him to free her but the son refuses. His own will is as strong as his father's who, in his day, had himself brought a maiden—an English lady who was to become Ahmed's mother—to his own tent. Yasmin escapes, and Ramadan, Ahmed's aide, follows her to Touggert. Ramadan finds out she is not to blame for Ahmed's capture, and so informs his master. At once Ahmed rides through a raging sandstorm to Touggert. He enters the café, makes himself known to Yasmin as she dances her number while hooded desert chieftains and caravan merchants ogle her with lascivious eyes. He lets her know of his belief in her innocence. In attempting to take her away, a fight ensues with Ghabah and his cutthroats. The odds look bad for Ahmed when his father, the Sheik, arrives with Ramadan to help him. Together, father and son fight their way free. Ahmed mounts his horse and gives chase to

Ghabah who is trying to ride off with Yasmin. Ahmed overtakes Ghabah, leaps onto the latter's horse, overpowers Ghabah to the sand. Then Ahmed sweeps Yasmin up on his white charger, holds her close in front of him, and they ride off into the desert, and infinity. . . .

Pola leaned toward Valentino—her side close against his side—and flashed a brilliant smile. For a fleeting moment he remembered that first première—of *The Four Horsemen*—with Natacha sitting where Pola was now. He could imagine the derisive comments Natacha would have offered about this film.

The picture was nearing its end. The final desert scene was fading out. The decisive moment was at hand. Would they laugh? Scorn? Ridicule?

The lights were on, white and revealing. In stark relief, he saw all those faces, a sea of them. There was a silence, brief, bristling. He gripped the back of the chair in front of him, leaned over. Pola put her hand on his arm. The applause had broken out; it grew louder and louder. The noise became a roar—continuous, in a mighty crescendo.

Proudly, the manager of the theater appeared on the stage. He held up his hand, but the applause rolled over him. Valentino looked on in disbelief. The manager, at last, was able to make himself heard. He told them, "Thank you, thank you. We will now hear a few words from the star, Rudolph Valentino."

Valentino glanced about as though he had just emerged from a dream.

"Please, Rudy, go on the stage. You must say something. They are waiting," urged Pola.

From the audience came the calls: "Speech! Speech!" "Come on, Rudy!" "We want Valentino! We want Valentino!"

A dazed, bewildered "Son of the Sheik" went to the stage. He stood before the vast assemblage. He suddenly heard himself speaking.

"My friends, I thank you for your approval. I shall never forget this night. Your faith in me gives me confidence to try to improve. I want to thank Mr. Fitzmaurice, Vilma Banky,

231

Agnes Ayres and the entire cast—''

The next morning the reviews were laudatory. The first person to call Valentino was George Fitzmaurice. ''Rudy, this picture is going to sweep the country and knowing what both you and I thought about it, I don't know if we're crazy or if America is crazy. But whatever it is, you, my boy, are the biggest star in the country as of this minute, or at least you will be as soon as the picture makes the rounds. Don't fight it, Rudy. Laugh at it, if you will, but accept it and enjoy it!''

United Artists made plans immediately to cash in on the initial reaction to the picture by sending Valentino on a personal appearance tour across the country. His first stop would be San Francisco and Pola Negri accompanied him to the station. George Ullman was there, too, but he stood at a respectful distance away.

''Rudy, my darling, you come back soon?'' Pola asked him. ''I wait for you. You know what I feel for you.''

''Pola, you are the most ravishing creature in Hollywood. It thrills me that you care for me. But I—I am not worthy of you. I am moody . . . difficult . . . mixed-up. I can not make you happy. I will come back and we will see each other some more. But I want you to see other men, too. . . . So many men find you beautiful.''

Tears suddenly trickled down the face of the beautiful Polish actress. She brushed her cheeks angrily as if she were shamed by this show of weakness.

''It is still that woman, no? That cold woman who, who was so cruel to you . . . who made you so unhappy. Why you let her ruin your happiness? Put her out of your heart, Rudy, she is no good for you!''

Valentino's face reddened with embarrassment. He didn't know what to say. He didn't want to lie to Pola, but he didn't want to hurt her either. And he didn't want to argue about Natacha.

''I will write to you, dear Pola, a long letter too, as soon as I am able,'' he promised. He kissed her and patted her arms.

Then the train came and Pola threw her arms around

Valentino and kissed him passionately. "Rudy, come back soon to Pola," she said.

"Of course I will be back, Pola. . . . It will only be a few weeks."

It was a reverse scene from the one he had gone through a little over a year earlier. This time it was he who was standing on the step of the train coach. He was in Natacha's place and Pola was in his. As she waved to him, he could tell from the tears in her eyes that she realized she could never have his love.

What she didn't know was that she would never be able to have his companionship again either.

CHAPTER THIRTY-ONE

VALENTINO and Ullman stopped at the Blackstone Hotel in Chicago on the 19th of July, between trains on their way from San Francisco to New York.

The première in San Francisco had been, as in Los Angeles, a tremendous success. It was the same story repeated—huge crowds, dazzling lights, batteries of cameras trained on the bejewelled and glittering elite—the same ovation over again, with no abatement in the enthusiasm.

In that summer of 1926 a record-breaking heat wave hit the Midwest, with the thermometer leaping to the upper nineties. Valentino and Ullman tried to relax and cool off in the lobby until train time.

Valentino had a secret hope that Natacha would be in New York when he arrived there and that perhaps he could manage to meet her. He was anxious to communicate this plan to Ullman when he noticed his business manager reading a newspaper. Ullman looked up, caught Valentino's eye on him and hid the newspaper behind his back. Valentino murmured, "That paper, George—you were reading something."

"Oh, that was yesterday's—the Sunday *Tribune*. Nothing unusual."

"Nothing unusual? Then why that guilty look? Is it something you don't want me to see?"

"Rudy, why don't you sit down and take it easy?"

"Now George, answer me one thing—are you or are you not my friend?"

"You know the answer."

"Then why are you trying to hide the *Chicago Tribune* from me? Something in it about me—"

"Nothing of any importance, Rudy."

"Then I'm sure you won't mind if I read it myself."

Ullman sighed and handed over the paper. "The editorial page," said Ullman. "Something about powder puffs."

Valentino scanned the headings, came to the one titled "Pink Powder Puffs." He glanced at Ullman.

"How in the world does that apply to me?"

"Read it, if you still want to," said Ullman, "and be prepared to take it."

Valentino read the entire article, his eyes kindling into fire, his face livid.

PINK POWDER PUFFS

A new public ballroom was opened on the north side a few days ago, a truly handsome place and apparently well run. The pleasant impression lasts until one steps into the men's washroom and finds there on the wall a contraption of glass tubes and levers and a slot for the insertion of a coin. The glass tubes contain a fluffy pink solid, and beneath them one reads an amazing legend which runs something like this: "Insert coin. Hold personal puff beneath the tube. Then pull the lever."

A powder vending machine! In a men's washroom! *Homo Americanus!* Why didn't someone quietly drown Rudolph Guglielmo, alias Valentino, years ago?

And was the pink powder machine pulled from the wall or ignored? It was not. It was used. We personally saw two "men"—as young lady contributors to the Voice of the People are wont to describe the breed—step up, insert coin, hold kerchief beneath the spout, pull the lever, then take the pretty pink stuff and put it on their cheeks in front of the mirror.

Another member of this department, one of the most benevolent men on earth, burst raging into the office the other day because he had seen a young "man" combing his pomaded hair in the elevator. But we claim our pink powder story beats this all hollow.

It is time for a matriarchy if the male of the species allows such things to persist. Better a rule by masculine women than by effeminate men. Man began to slip, we are beginning to believe, when he discarded the straight razor for the safety pattern. We shall not be surprised when we hear that the safety razor has given way to the depilatory.

Who or what is to blame is what puzzles us. Is this degeneration into effeminacy a cognate reaction with pacificism to the virilities and realities of the war? Are pink powder and parlor pinks in any way related? How does one reconcile masculine cosmetics, sheiks, floppy pants, and slave bracelets with a disregard for law and an aptitude for crime more in keeping with the frontier of half a century ago than a twentieth-century metropolis?

Do women like the type of "man" who pats pink powder on his face in a public washroom and arranges his coiffure in a public elevator? Do women at heart belong to the Wilsonian era of "I Didn't Raise My Boy to Be a Soldier"? What has become of the old "caveman" line?

It is a strange social phenomenon and one that is running its course not only here in America but in Europe as well. Chicago may have its powder puffs; London has its dancing men and Paris its gigolos. Down with Decatur; up with Elinor Glyn. Hollywood is the national school of masculinity. Rudy, the beautiful gardener's boy, is the prototype of the American male.

Hell's bells. Oh, sugar.

Valentino finished reading. For a long moment he held the paper in his hands, staring at it as though it were part of a nightmare. Then suddenly he threw the newspaper down on the floor and his eyes blazed.

"Why do they do this to me? For years the newspapers have hounded me and heaped abuse on me. I've tried to take it in stride, realizing that many of the men who write about me are jealous of me. But this—this I cannot take. Ullman, the man who wrote this didn't sign his name, but that won't stop me—"

"Well," said Ullman, "what do you propose to do? Sue the newspaper?"

"No. I'll get his name from the *Tribune*. I'll challenge him to a fight in any way he wishes."

"I'm afraid the *Tribune* will never give you the name of the writer. They'll protect him."

"Then I will have my challenge published in a competing newspaper. There's the *Chicago Herald-Examiner*. I'll phone the *Examiner* for a reporter at once. When that 'he-man' of the *Tribune* reads my answer, he had better step forward or I'll tell the world that he's a no-good, yellow-bellied coward."

Ullman sank back in his chair. He knew that there was no stopping Valentino now. The man would not rest until satisfaction was his.

The heat wave seemed to be growing worse. Official temperature readings as reported on the radio indicated a range of 95 to 102 degrees, but to Ullman it felt like 120.

Valentino secreted himself in his room, asking Ullman to take care of any calls or interviews; he wanted no interruption while he was writing his challenge.

He composed the message, read and reread it to himself, and deemed it satisfactory:

July 19, 1926

TO THE MAN (?) WHO WROTE THE EDITORIAL HEADED "PINK POWDER PUFFS" IN SUNDAY'S *TRIBUNE*:

The above-mentioned editorial is at least the second

237

scurrilous personal attack you have made upon me, my race, and my father's name.

You slur my Italian ancestry; you cast ridicule upon my Italian name; you cast doubt upon my manhood.

I call you, in return, a contemptible coward, and to prove which of us is a better man I challenge you to a personal test. This is not a challenge to a duel in the generally accepted sense—that would be illegal. But in Illinois boxing is legal, so is wrestling. I, therefore, defy you to meet me in the boxing or wrestling arena to prove in typically American fashion (for I am an American citizen) which of us is more a man. I prefer this test of honor to be private, so I may give you the beating you deserve, and because I want to make it absolutely plain that this challenge is not for purposes of publicity. I am handing copies of this to the newspapers simply because I doubt that anyone so cowardly as to write about me as you have would respond to a defy unless forced by the press to do so. I do not know who you are or how big you are but this challenge stands if you are as big as Jack Dempsey.

I will meet you immediately or give you a reasonable time in which to prepare, for I assume that your muscles must be flabby and weak, judging by your cowardly mentality and that you will have to replace the vitriol in your veins for red blood—if there be a place in such a body as yours for red blood and manly muscle.

I want to make it plain that I hold no grievance against the *Chicago Tribune*, although it seems a mistake to let a cowardly writer use its valuable columns as this "man" does. My fight is personal—with the poison-pen writer of editorials that stoop to racial and personal prejudice. The *Tribune*, through Miss Mae Tinee, has treated me and my work kindly and at times very favorably. I welcome criticism of my work as an actor—but I will resent with every muscle of my body attacks upon my manhood and ancestry.

Hoping I will have an opportunity to demonstrate to

you that the wrist under a slave bracelet may snap a real fist into your sagging jaw and that I may teach you respect of a man even though he happens to prefer to keep his face clean, I remain with

> Utter contempt,
> Rudolph Valentino.

P.S.: I will return to Chicago within ten days. You may send your answer to me in New York, care of United Artists Corp., 729 7th Avenue.

He put it in an envelope and waited for the *Herald-Examiner's* representative. He was about to go down and speak to Ullman in the lobby, when a sudden, sharp stab of pain almost threw him to the floor. He tottered and leaned against the wall for support.

He raised his head in supplication. "Dear Lord," he prayed, "please—not now, not now. Please, Lord, make this pain go away."

But the pain did not go away directly. It lingered. It was a persistent ache attacking the lower part of his abdomen. He felt himself weakening.

He could hear Ullman at the door. The doorknob was turning. He must keep this from Ullman.

Then, as suddenly as it had come to him, the pain left him—and a sense of relief flowed through him. He sank into an easy chair, stretched out his legs, and breathed deeply. He was sure he would be all right now. Maybe this was the last one—the most cramping and torturous, but the last one.

Ullman came into the room, took one glance at Valentino, and said, "Rudy, you don't look well at all. That editorial sure is poison. Maybe we had better call off this tour and go back to Hollywood where you can rest."

"No, George. We must finish the tour. Also, I have a fight coming up with that cringing bully hiding behind the skirts of a newspaper. When do we take the train east?"

"In two hours." Ullman shook his head. "Rudy, you worry me. Look, whoever wrote that piece of venom would probably hang his own mother. If I were you, Rudy, I'd turn my back on the whole affair. It isn't worth your time and effort."

"I'm sorry, George, but I can't stand by and have anybody question my manhood and Italian ancestry. No, I'm going to hold him to it and as soon as he makes himself known—well, I'll show him who is a pink powder puff."

"Rudy, listen to an old friend. The newspapers have been panning you all along and you've managed to ignore them with no ill effects."

"George, you're not the one who's been called a pink powder puff. It's not a good feeling. Before I'm through, I'll make him eat those words."

Valentino sat for a few minutes in brooding silence. Then he said suddenly, "George, when we are in New York we'll try to locate Natacha. I must see her again."

"As you like." Ullman leaned forward. "Rudy, did you ever stop to think that Pola would be better for you?"

"Pola is a wonderful lady—warm, completely feminine— a fine artist . . ."

"But you want Natacha as your wife again. Is that it?"

"George, please be understanding. Love is a strange thing."

"Yes, Rudy, I guess that spells Natacha."

By train time, there was no answer from anybody on the *Chicago Tribune* and the two left for New York. Huge throngs of Valentino fans met them at the station and followed the star through the streets to his suite at the Ambassador Hotel. A swarm of reporters and photographers was waiting. For the first time in Valentino's career, sports writers formed part of the press contingent who wanted to interview him. They had heard the news about the star's challenge to the anonymous *Chicago Tribune* writer and they wanted to know if he was seriously willing to risk injury to his glorious profile in a fist fight.

"I will fight that man if he comes out of hiding, no matter whether he is seven feet tall and weighs three hundred pounds," Valentino said heatedly.

"What if your studio tells you they won't allow you to

240

expose yourself in a fight?'' one reporter wanted to know.

"The studio has nothing to say in this matter! It is I, Rudolph Valentino, who was insulted and maligned, not a motion picture company. I don't care what the studio thinks. Just let that coward come out from behind his editorial curtain and you will see if I mean business or not. If anyone wants to wager that I will back down from my challenge, I will cover his bet and give him ten to one odds besides.''

The reporters left, convinced of Valentino's sincerity. Their stories in the New York evening papers reflected this belief. The next morning, however, Ullman received a call from Frank "Buck" O'Neil, the boxing writer for the *New York Evening Journal*. O'Neil said that he had been told by Jack Dempsey that Valentino packed a he-man punch, but he was convinced that Dempsey was pulling his leg. "I don't believe Valentino can really fight and I'd like to take him on in a friendly bout myself to prove it," O'Neil said. "If Valentino is willing to meet me, I'll guarantee not to hurt him.''

When Valentino heard this, he insisted on fighting the boxing writer as soon as the match could be arranged. The roof garden of the Ambassador was selected as the site and the time was set for noon the following day. At the appointed hour, O'Neil appeared in his gym clothes. He weighed nearly two hundred pounds and was six feet one inch tall. Valentino weighed 165 and was one inch shy of six feet. Some of the newspapermen and cameramen who had turned out to cover the bout whispered to the star that O'Neil was taking unfair advantage of him. "I don't care if he outweighs me,'' Valentino insisted. "I'm going to teach this gentleman a few things.''

The two sparred lightly for most of the first round and then exchanged sharp blows to the chin. O'Neil followed this up by aiming a punch at the actor's jaw. He missed. Valentino countered with a blow to the side of the writer's head and O'Neil went sprawling to the floor. Valentino proved a gallant sportsman by rushing to help his adversary up.

The boxers went at it hot and heavy for another two rounds

before calling it quits. O'Neil shook the actor's hand and ruefully admitted, "I was wrong about you, Rudy, you're all man. That punch of yours that knocked me down had the power of a mule's kick! Next time Jack Dempsey tells me something I'm going to believe him."

The next day, *The Son of the Sheik* opened at the Mark Strand Theater. The reception it was accorded in the country's largest and most sophisticated city made everything that had gone before look pale. Crowds began to gather at the Mark Strand at eight in the morning and soon the lines stretched for blocks. The heat rose to 98 degrees, but the people just stood there and sweltered in the broiling sun. When the movie house finally opened, the crowd rushed in like a herd of elephants. Fans continued to mill about in the streets and it took a whole squad of police to get Valentino safely past them into the theater. The picture was treated to an ovation similar to what had been accorded it out west, and Valentino made an informal speech which charmed the standing-room-only audience.

By the time Valentino was ready to leave the theater, the streets outside had been turned into bedlam. Thousands of people were backed up from the theater entrance out into the street, effectively blocking traffic. When the star came out, his fans surged past police lines to seize him. They ripped off his tie, tore all the buttons from his coat, knocked off his hat, and snatched off his cuff links to carry away as souvenirs. Women fans by the hundreds screamed, "Rudy, Rudy, we love you," and tried to hug him. He was pummeled anew as the police strained to get him into his car, and he tumbled into the back seat with his clothes in tatters and his face a mass of scratches. He smiled and waved cheerfully to the crowd from his limousine seat, but as the car finally pulled away he exclaimed to Ullman, "Whew! These New Yorkers almost loved me to death!"

Despite all the hoopla and hullabaloo of his New York reception, Valentino left the big city in a downcast mood. Ullman had failed to find Natacha and though he said he would not give up the search, Valentino was convinced his former wife had not changed toward him and would remain inaccessible. In addition to his emotional miseries, his physical pain was becoming a chronic rather than a sometime thing. Before, it had come in sharp spurts, but it had also vanished quickly. Now it had reached the point where it was a gnawing, relentless hurt. He told himself doggedly that he could live with it . . . he would accept it like a nagging woman in the family—always chiding him, scolding him, annoying him, but not meaning any great harm.

He tried to evade Ullman's questioning glances. Had his business manager known of the extent of his pain, he would have taken positive action. No doubt he would have forced him to see a doctor. But the superstitious Valentino still clung to his ridiculous, old-country abhorrence of doctors. He was determined not to be treated by them.

Back in Chicago to attend still another successful opening of *The Son of the Sheik* at the Roosevelt Theater, Valentino called in reporters to learn if the "powder puff" editorialist had come out into the open. He was told that silence shrouded the Tribune Tower, which housed Chicago's largest newspaper. He therefore decided to put out another news story which he gave to all Chicago newspapers—with the exception of the *Tribune*—and to the national wire services.

The news release was printed as an open letter to the "Powder Puff Editorialist." It read:

It is evident you cannot make a coward fight any more than you can draw blood out of a turnip. The heroic silence of the writer who chose to attack me without any provocation in the *Chicago Tribune* leaves no doubt as to the total absence of manliness in his whole make-up.

I feel I have been vindicated because I consider his silence as a tacit retraction, and an admission which I am forced to accept even though it is not entirely to my liking.

The newspaper men and women whom it has been my privilege to know briefly are so loyal to their profession and their publications that I need hardly say how conspicuous is this exception to the newspaper profession.

From Chicago, it was back again to New York. A few days later the schedule called for an appearance at the Virginia Theater on the famed boardwalk at Atlantic City.

Valentino was taken by motorcar from New York, starting out at 12:30 P.M., on another 98 degree day. At five o'clock his automobile arrived at the entrance to Atlantic City. News of his visit had preceded him; he was met by a great cavalcade of motorcycle police and automobiles carrying the official welcoming party.

He was escorted in style to the boardwalk and the Ritz-Carlton Hotel. Thousands of spectators were waiting to catch a glimpse of him. His appearance that night at the Virginia Theater resulted in another by-now familiar mob scene.

After that, he visited the Steel Pier for a scheduled radio broadcast. The crowds there tore his shirt and ripped the buttons from his jacket for souvenirs. Ullman almost suffered physical injury in trying to protect his friend. The fans nearly broke down the glass enclosure of the broadcasting station.

When Valentino later visited the Gus Edwards show at the Ritz and danced the tango with some of Edwards' dancers, the crowds that had been following him broke into the theater and caused a near-riot.

On the following day, back to New York—and always the heat, stifling, burning, like the rising fever within him. He attended another opening of his film at the Strand Theater in Brooklyn, and again the inevitable throngs lined the streets waiting for him. None of these movie fans noticed that the face which had cast its magic on the theater screen was now drawn and pale. They were unaware of his suffering; they didn't realize that he had difficulty in getting around.

Valentino's hollow appearance disturbed Ullman, but since Valentino had been going to as many parties as openings, his manager concluded that lack of sleep and rest was responsible.

"You've got to get off the bicycle and stop running yourself ragged, Rudy,'' he warned his client. ''You can't burn the candle at both ends indefinitely.''

When he was by himself in his apartment at the Ambassador, Valentino sat down on the bed, leaned forward and placed both of his hands upon his abdomen. He could feel the pulsation of the blood stream against his fingers. And with every beat there was a pang.

He rose and paced the floor. He would make himself believe there was no pain. He would ignore it altogether.

But the pain was there. It gnawed and it grated. He looked up at the ceiling and he said in the quietness of the room, ''O Lord, not any more.'' The *Chicago Tribune* episode still bothered him. Undoubtedly, it added to his pain.

Perhaps, if a soft, cool hand—her hand—could just touch his fever-racked brow for a moment it would ease the hurt. But she would not be coming. Ullman had finally learned that she had gone back again to Europe.

He tried to follow Ullman's advice and sleep. But his nerves were too raw to permit easy slumber. He got out of bed, put on his tuxedo and stole out into the steaming city. Some of his theatrical friends were holding another party. Wine and liquor would be flowing. He would drink away his agony.

On Saturday, August 14, he attended another all-night party at the swank apartment of an acquaintance. The party began at six o'clock in the evening with sixteen merrymakers, including himself. It continued into the small hours of a new day and the champagne flowed freely. Gradually, with the approach of dawn, most of the revelers went home. Valentino and three others remained, celebrating through the dawn and into the morning.

At 10 o'clock Sunday morning, August 15, the effects of the wine and liquor wore off and his pain became unbearable. It began to ravage. It did not merely gnaw any more, it chopped its way into all parts of his body. He took a cab to his hotel and staggered into the lobby. He felt like something that had been put together imperfectly and was now beginning to fall apart.

He entered the elevator. The elevator operator inquired sympathetically, "Mr. Valentino, shall I call a doctor?"

Valentino shook his head, smiled feebly. The operator helped him to the door of his apartment. It took Herculean effort to reach his bed.

Then he fell across it and the world came crashing down about him. Tongues of fire seared his insides, blotted out his senses, came out of his very being and leaped about him in a *danse macabre*, pinning him to the bed. He could not move. A crimson sea of flame rose and fell toward him, overturned upon him. . . .

Two hours later an attendant found him sprawled across the bed, unconscious.

CHAPTER THIRTY-TWO

HEADLINES across the nation screamed the news that Valentino had collapsed. The newspapers told of how he was rushed to the Polyclinic Hospital, where he underwent an operation for gastric ulcers and appendicitis.

All over the world women prayed and cried and hoped and prayed. Each day . . . Monday . . . Tuesday . . . Wednesday . . . Thursday . . . the papers reported Valentino's condition. Fans flocked to the hospital to stand watch and to wait. Friends flocked to Valentino's room.

At first it appeared he was going to recover. He joked with the doctors, smiled at the nurses and talked to Ullman about fishing trips. Ullman spent hours at his bedside, angry at himself because he could do nothing.

Among Valentino's visitors were Joseph M. Schenck and his wife, Norma Talmadge; Frank Menillo; and Valentino's first wife, Jean Acker.

On Thursday, August 19, Valentino slept almost continuously. On Friday, he took a turn for the worse.

During his waking moments on Friday and Saturday, he kept his eyes toward the door as though he were expecting to see someone in particular enter.

When Ullman came to see him, again he implored him once more to try to find Natacha. She was the only person he asked for. Ullman called Natacha's mother in Nice to tell her about Valentino's condition. But Natacha was not there; she was drifting somewhere through Europe.

By Sunday, Valentino sank into a coma. He kept mumbling words—Italian, French, English. "*Mama mia*, I didn't mean it" . . . "Maria, your turn" . . . "Babykins" . . . "Mama, I'm coming home" . . . "George, last night, remember, we were lost in the woods" . . . "*Je t'aime*, Freckle-nose" . . . "Indian Chief Black Feather" . . . "I took all the bugs out of the rose bushes" . . . "Babykins" . . . "On the other hand, the other hand—I love you—you . . ."

On Monday, August 23rd, Rudolph Valentino opened his eyes once more and spoke his last words:

"Please raise the shade. I want to see the sunlight."

The shade had been up all the time and the sunlight had been flooding the room.

But for Valentino the twilight had already come and then the sudden fall of night.

A long and endless night, without pain, without loneliness.

On his deathbed and into his permanent tomb he wore the slave bracelet Natacha had given him. It was the emblem of the only true love of his life . . . and the tragic reminder that the man who was the symbol of love on the screen, who was worshipped by countless numbers of women throughout the world, had been unlucky enough to love a woman who could not return his love because she was a victim of her own ambition.

EPILOGUE

WHEN Rudolph Valentino died, with him died the glory of the silent motion picture era. He left a void which was never filled. At that time over 20,000,000 daily patrons were attending the movie houses in this country alone, and Valentino was riding the crest of the wave. (Today there are an average of 6,000,000 daily movie viewers in this country.)

Over 100,000 telegrams of condolence poured in from all parts of the world and a frenzied, hysterical mob of over 125,000 people lined ten city blocks in the funeral procession to pay their final respects to a movie star with a Golconda gift for projecting romance on a screen. This kind of public outpouring of grief over the passing of a motion picture personality had never been seen before and has never been equalled since.

Ever since Valentino was laid to rest in the white-marbled mausoleum in Hollywood's Memorial Cemetery, women mourners have come from all parts of the world to place fresh red roses and white chrysanthemums on his tomb.

For years, his best-known mourner was the so-called "Lady in Black." Wearing a black dress, black stockings, black shoes, black hat, and heavy black veil, she would appear at the crypt with thirteen roses—a dozen red, and one white. For the first three years, she came to the crypt every day. After that, and until 1955, she came once a year, on the anniversary of Valentino's death. For a long time, newspapermen regarded her pilgrimage as a publicity stunt. But then as it became evident that the "Lady in Black" was not using her visits to advance herself in any way, the newsmen decided she had another motive. Finally, she told this story: Her name was Ditra Flame; she was a violinist and a pianist. She had met Valentino in 1918 when he was working as a dancer. She was only fourteen years old at the time. Soon after, she became very ill and was taken to a hospital. Valentino visited her, and brought her red roses. She told him she was sure she was going to die. He assured her she wouldn't. She kept insisting that death was near and cried that nobody would remember her after she was gone. Valentino promised that if she were to die, he would bring roses to her grave every day.

"But you must remember that if I go first, I don't want to be lonely either," he added. And that, said Ditra Flame, was the reason she kept coming to Valentino's tomb; she didn't want him to be lonely.

Valentino is the only movie star about whom the present century has built a cult of the dead. Valentino's confrère, eighty-six-year-old former film star James Kirkwood, still recites his annual eulogy near the flower-adorned crypt which has probably seen more mourners than any other crypt in America.

For many years after the death of Valentino, members of the British Valentino Association provided a beautiful roof garden and a Valentino Ward for children of all nationalities, creeds and races in the Italian Hospital in London. In loving memory of the silent screen star, every August a group of underprivileged children were Valentino's guests for a happy week in the country. On the anniversary of his death these devoted members of the Association attended High Mass at Westminster Cathedral.

In DeLongpre Park, Hollywood, "Aspiration," the only monument ever dedicated to a film star, was unveiled several years after Valentino's death. This memorial was financed by donations from thousands of the actor's admirers from all over the world.

In the fall of 1961 a new monument to Valentino was dedicated in his home town of Castellaneta, Italy. It shows him as the Son of the Sheik with the inscription RODOLPHO VALENTINO: 1961. The town plans to convert his birthplace to a museum.

Although Valentino—as is the case with many public figures—was a victim of much bad publicity, the press was unanimous in trumpeting his artistic merits in their eulogies to his memory:

London Evening News: "Rudolph Valentino—there is a name to fill the swelling trump of fame! The greatest romanticist of the era."

London Daily Express: "Valentino was a great dedicated artist who mastered more than any of his contemporaries the genius that lies in simplicity and restraint."

Cleveland Plain Dealer: "Valentino's work in *The Sheik*, as in all the other pictures, was that of an able and conscientious artist. He made the most of his gifts; and, in the process, brought pleasure to the great American commonalty as well as to all the peoples of the world. He will long be remembered."

Newark News: "Rudolph Valentino made a sudden success as a motion-picture actor and tried earnestly to maintain a high standard. He was the victim of shoddy publicity and he tried his best to overcome its malign influence. He was a young Italian with a better educational background than most of his peers. He died without a relative at his bedside— perhaps without a single man or woman who loved him solely for himself."

Associated Press: "Rudolph Valentino, the greatest lover in the history of motion pictures and the greatest matinee idol the stage or screen has ever known, is with us no more but his romantic spirit will live forever. His death ended one of the most impressive careers in screen history. Valentino's popularity, from the time of his first appearance in a leading part in the *Four Horsemen of the Apocalypse*, was never dimmed. Statesmen and men of science, great teachers and men who have swayed the masses through the spoken and written word, have been stricken and died with far less public notice than was given Valentino who had a godlike appeal which eclipsed the greatest of men. A case in point: the newspaper

251

lineage accorded the demise of Valentino dwarfed a hundred-fold that of the country's greatest educator, Dr. Charles W. Eliot, president-emeritus of Harvard, who passed away within the same twenty-four hour period."

Heywood Broun in the *New York World*: "Valentino was to the millions the romance which they never knew. He was Prince Charming and he came from the other side of the moon. For those who have no access to music, Valentino was the violins of *Tannhäuser*. And many who have never read Shelley had seen *The Sheik*."

H. L. Mencken in the *Baltimore Sun*: "Valentino was a dedicated artist—inimitable and incomparable—whether it came to acting or writing fine sensitive poetry. A great loss to the world."

O. O. McIntyre, syndicated columnist: "His writing (of what little he created) as well as his acting contained the monumental stamp of immortality. Had he used his pen as an Alpine stock he would have scaled the Matterhorn."

F. G. Reiss, Germany's best-known theatrical photographer, in the *New York Sun*: "Rudolph Valentino, the world's most beautiful man, possessed a *film face*. On the screen Valentino possessed those rare physiognomical and photogenic qualities which transformed him into an Apollo Belvedere. The movies may wait long before another such striking case arises."

That final prophetic sentence can be repeated today, as we wonder whether tomorrow will bring another Valentino.